Game Character Modeling and Animation with 3ds Max

Game Character Modeling and Animation with 3ds Max

Yancey Clinton

Autodesk®

Media and Entertainment
Techniques

ELSEVIER

AMSTERDAM • BOSTON • HEIDELBERG • LONDON
NEW YORK • OXFORD • PARIS • SAN DIEGO
SAN FRANCISCO • SINGAPORE • SYDNEY • TOKYO

Focal Press is an imprint of Elsevier

Focal
Press

Senior Acquisitions Editor: Laura Lewin
Development Editor: Georgia Kennedy
Publishing Services Manager: George Morrison
Senior Project Manager: Paul Gottehrer
Assistant Editor: Chris Simpson
Marketing Manager: Marcel Koppes

Focal Press is an imprint of Elsevier
30 Corporate Drive, Suite 400, Burlington, MA 01803, USA
Linacre House, Jordan Hill, Oxford OX2 8DP, UK

∞ Recognizing the importance of preserving what has been written, Elsevier prints its books on acid-free paper whenever possible.

Library of Congress Cataloging-in-Publication Data
Application submitted.

British Library Cataloguing-in-Publication Data
A catalogue record for this book is available from the British Library.

ISBN: 978-0-240-80978-6
ISBN: 978-0-240-80978-8 (DVD)

For information on all Focal Press publications
visit our website at www.books.elsevier.com

07 08 09 10 11 5 4 3 2 1

Printed in the United States of America

Contents

Modeling a 3D Character ...53

The Unwrap 143

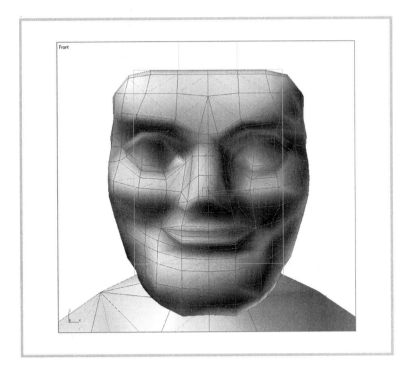

Figure I.1

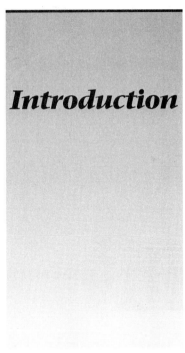

Welcome! You have just taken your first step into a larger world. The virtual world is an infinite space inside the box where you can create a world of your own—one in which you can have total control and manipulate all the rules of physics as you see fit. In this book, we will explore one aspect of that world: characters. As I lead you though the process, you will be introduced to the tools and methods of the video game artist. By the time you are finished with the book, I hope you will be excited enough to continue your exploration of this limitless world.

Who Is This Book For?

This is a book for the avid gamer who wants to take his or her real-time adventures to the next level: customization. This book is also for anyone interested in making a career in game production. Have you ever wanted to improve upon your existing games or perhaps even had an idea for a game you would like to play? You're in luck! The tools that are readily available and included with this book will

allow you to do almost anything you want to without having to learn any programming.

This, in effect, lets you focus on creating great art for your game. Unfortunately, nothing great comes easy. This book is the courseware developed from my 15-week class at Academy of Art University in San Francisco. That means this material requires quite a few hours of class time and many more between classes. So give yourself about a month or approximately 80–100 hours to work through the book.

It took about 2 years of development in order to refine a myriad of lectures into a cohesive workflow for 3D game character creation. The acid test was held in the summer of 2004 at the Digital Media Academy on the Stanford campus. I taught the material to groups of 20 people, ranging from teenage boys and girls to a fellow teacher who was in his 50s. Luckily for me, everyone had a great time making their own characters and playing them in Unreal Tournament 2004. Now you can, too.

How Is This Book Different?

This book is like no other, and I should know—I have read almost everything on this subject. In this book, I will show you the complete process to create a 3D character that can be played in most real-time 3D game engines and the Unreal Tournament 2004 game, specifically.

You will be learning not only a state-of-the-art 3D program, but also a production pipeline for modeling I have developed that can be used for the creation of assets for the next generation of video game engines.

In this pipeline, I use a method of modeling called spline modeling. It allows the artist to create a low-detail model that can be refined and given greater detail with ease. This is the new pipeline for real-time asset creation. All the next-generation game engines will need to have assets created in this fashion for the new rendering technique called normal bump mapping.

Most important is that I have designed this courseware so that anyone at any age will be able to understand and complete the project.

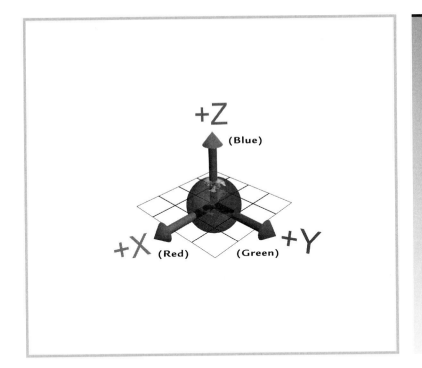

What It Takes to Make a 3D Character

Hardware Resources

There are two ways to look at the computers necessary to use 3ds Max and other programs: the minimum and the maximum configurations. The nice thing about creating real-time assets is that it doesn't take a supercomputer to do it. It can even be done on a sub-$1,000 laptop or desktop. 3ds Max 6 can be run on an Intel Pentium 3 running Windows 2000 or NT with a minimum of 512MB of RAM; to use 3ds Max 7 you will need a little more power. An Intel Pentium 4 running Windows XP SP 1a or better and at least 1GIG of RAM should work fine. The 3ds Max 8 and 9 work just fine on my Centrino Duo laptop with 1GIG of RAM; I suggest that you try 3ds Max 9 first.

The other hardware you will need is a current video card. In order to run the Unreal Tournament game you will need a video card that is DirectX 9+ compatible. While it is possible to use a video card that is DirectX 7 or DirectX 8 compatible, unfortunately, the game will hardly run and in some cases not at all. This, however, is not a deterrent to creating the assets, just to implementing them and seeing them in a game.

One other piece of equipment that is not absolutely necessary for using 3ds Max, but is extremely useful is a three-button mouse with a scroll wheel.

There is no maximum. 3ds Max and Unreal Tournament will use as much computer power as you can throw at them.

Software Resources

You're in luck; most of the software necessary for this course is free or can be used in demo mode. At this time a demo version of 3ds Max 9 that can be used for 30 days can be downloaded from the Autodesk website. The companion DVD with this book contains a demo version of the Unreal Tournament game but, unfortunately, not the Unreal editor (you have to buy the game to get that). So if you want to, you can do this project super cheap, just as long as you finish within 30 days. Fortunately, there are other options for owning 3ds Max. The cheapest is a 1-year student/educator license, which at this time is only $180. The second option is for an unlimited-time student/educator license for around $600 to $700, depending on options. The last licensing option is a commercial one that will run you around $3,600. This option is necessary only if you plan to sell or get paid for work generated using 3ds Max. I also suggest that you buy the Unreal Tournament 2004 DVD version, which at this time sells for around $30. The last piece of software that is not necessary but useful is Photoshop. At this time there is a downloadable demo version of Photoshop CS3 from Adobe's website, but again it is not necessary to complete the project. There are also a number of freeware and shareware image editors with similar functionality.

Time Resources

I am not going to kid you on this one. There is a steep learning curve, and it takes time to learn a 3D animation package like 3ds Max. Fortunately, one way to speed up the process is to play any real-time game. Yup, you heard me—for homework I want you to play games. I have found that my students who avidly played 3D real-time games had a greater advantage over the ones who had not. It turns out that the game will train your brain to think in the virtual world. The coordination involved in navigating a virtual three-dimensional world space mimics the navigation used in 3ds Max. A prime example is that it helps to use both hands when working with 3ds Max. One hand is for keyboard shortcuts; the other is for the mouse. This is the same for all video games, PC- or console-based; you have both hands on the controller, each button doing a different thing.

Once you have played enough, there is a point at which you no longer have to think about the controller and the things you want to happen. This will eventually happen with 3ds Max also. So here are the time frames I am talking about. For a professional modeler, it should take less than a week to create the model we will create, including the image used for the texture. I will introduce you to a technique that I use for creating textures, but to get into the details would require another book.

Because each student is starting this project with different experiences and backgrounds, it's difficult to pin down an exact time frame it will take to finish the project. What I can tell you is that the DMA summer class was a super-intensive 1-week class, where we worked 6–7 hours per day for 5 days straight to complete the project.

Depending on your experience, it may take you longer. That seems like a lot of time, but remember that you're still learning. The next time that you want to make a model it will take you about half as much time as it did for the first. The tutorial is a linear step-by-step process, so it can easily be broken up into sessions that are comfortable for you.

Of MODs, Maps, and Machinima

In the world of game modification, there are three different levels of application. A mod is a modification of an existing game. For example, adding a new character, weapon, or vehicle would be considered a mod. That's what we are going to do. There are tons of different mods you can download for most real-time 3D games. There are a couple of web sites that can help you start moding your games. The first is *www.gamespy.com,* which has everything you need to mod the most popular games. Another is *www.gamespot. com,* which has tons of good stuff for and about moding.

A map is the addition of a new level to an existing game. To create a map is to make a virtual world space and all that entails. The sky, the land, the water, and the physics are all things that can be created and modified in the games editor. Then, using 3ds Max, anyone can create objects to be placed in that environment. Maps can include characters, but it's usually a lot of extra work to add them. There are tons of maps available for popular 3D games.

Another kind of mod is called a Total Conversion mod (TCMod). This is a new game that uses an engine designed for a completely different type of game. One extreme example of a TCMod is something like the game Battlefield 1942. This is a WWII first-person shooter with planes and tanks from that era. Currently, there is a downloadable TCMod available for it called Galactic Conquest. It basically turns a WWII game into a Star Wars-style game, completely replacing the game's original WWII-era design. Most of the time, maps are not that extreme. They usually have the same kind of play as the original game. A prime example is Unreal Tournament 2003 and 2004. There are literally hundreds of different mods and maps that you can download and play, but they all basically have the goal to kill the monsters in their game play.

The level of difficulty in creating mods and maps for any particular game varies extremely. The support for most game editors is limited to the user base. This is one of the reasons I chose Unreal Tournament 2004. It has lots of documentation and a large user base for support. Even though it was easy for me to create a player mod, it was not very easy to create my own map. As it turns out, the game engines are very particular in the way they want you to make things.

There are literally hundreds of games that can be modified in one way or another as long as you use the same tools that produced the game in the first place. Those tools consist of the 3D modeling program and the real-time game engine's editor. As there are only a few real-time 3D game engines, most of the real-time 3D games are made with the same three or four engines. For the Unreal Tournament 2004 game, the Unreal Engine 2 is used to run the game and the Unreal Editor 3 is used to edit the game.

The Unreal Engine 2 is also used in 20 or so other games of the same style, like Splinter Cell and America's Army. For more details on the Unreal Engine, check out *www.unrealtechnology.com,* and while you're there check out the Unreal Engine 3 documentation.

This goes the same for id Software's engine. It's used for DOOM 2 and QUAKE; the most current game using their engine is DOOM 3. This is one of the top five technologically and visually stunning games on the market today.

The Unreal Engine 3 is the current top of the line real-time engine, that is changing the way games look for the better. It was late 2006 when the first games created using the Unreal Engine 3 were released. The look and level of detail are unparalleled; I can't wait until Unreal Tournament is released.

So, using 3ds Max to create your own assets, you can just replace or add to the existing game architecture. The big trick is how to do this. There are plenty of examples of games that were not intended to be modified that were hacked and the assets exchanged. This would be the hardest type of game to modify. The easiest would be ones that included an editor for the specific game. There are only a handful that do, and most of them I have just told you about. There are some third-party game editors, but they are not the easiest programs to learn and or use.

An interesting side effect of game moding is machinima. The word is a conjunction of the words "machine" and "cinema." Machinima is a new form of filmmaking. One little known aspect of the more common 3D games, like Unreal Tournament 2004, Half-Life 2, or even QUAKE, is the ability to animate and record free-floating cameras. This allows you to shoot a film in the real-time game. The tools you will learn in this book will allow you to make your own characters for your film. One of my favorite machinima serials is called Red VS Blue. It was made in Halo and does a whole lot with the simple environment of the Blood Gulch Map. For further information, check out *www.machinima.com*; it's a good place to further your education on all things machinima.

An Introduction to the 3D Environment

What is a 3D environment? Well, here's a hint: you live in one. While there are lots of similarities between the virtual 3D environment in the computer and the real world, there are several really big differences. The real world is limited by physics, and the virtual world is blissfully free of most rules of physics. Not only that, we are free to change any of them. Things like time, space, and size matter little in the virtual world. We have unlimited time both forward and backward, and we can work from the galactic scale all the way down to the microscopic without changing projects.

There will be two different 3D environments that I will introduce to you during this project. The first is that of 3ds Max. The other two are the Unreal Editor and the Unreal game itself. If you understand 3ds Max's environment, then the others should be easy for you to pick up. The best way to think about this is that you have an infinite, empty void. At an arbitrary point in this space is what we call the origin or center of the world. This point is our reference point, and the values are 0,0,0 on the X-, Y-, and Z-axes. To find any point in space, you need three values that reference the origin. The three values are labeled X, Y, and Z, and they define the offset for the origin. The letters have their origins in math and are used to plot three-dimensional points in space.

The part of coordinate systems that isn't usually talked about is orientation, or which way is up. In 3ds Max, Z is the up coordinate, but this is not true of all 3D applications. The other two axes, X and Y, create an infinite plane that goes on forever, as shown in Figure 1.01. This is what we call the world coordinate system.

In contrast, in the Unreal Editor, the Z coordinate is not up and down, but in and out. The reason is that the video game engines use a camera view for orientation reference. That is, the screen is the X–Y plane, and moving the camera forward and back is the Z coordinate, as shown in Figure 1.02. This is one of the reasons we have to use the Unreal Editor to interface with the game engine, to convert things like the coordinates.

In 3ds Max's virtual world there is no inherent gravity, and the objects in this world are not solid. Those effects have to be simulated using 3ds Max's integrated physics simulator, called Reactor. It does this in a way similar to that of the game engine when you're playing. In fact, the company that made the Reactor plug-in for 3ds Max, Havoc, is now being integrated into the next generation of game engines. This brings 3ds Max even closer to being a direct game-authoring tool.

Figure 1.01

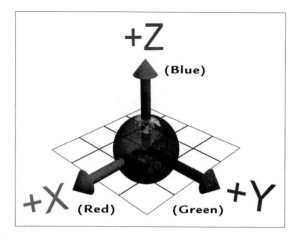

Figure 1.02

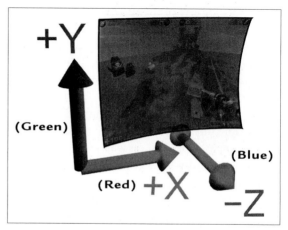

What Makes Up A 3d Character?

Mesh

The primary thing a 3D character is made of would have to be geometry. A broad definition of 3D geometry would be an object that can be edited and rendered. 3ds Max includes a few basic 3D geometric objects called primitives. One of the primary primitive objects we use is a box. As a primitive, the ways in which it can be edited are limited to things like the length, height, width, and the resolution of each dimension. If this were all we could change, it would be extremely difficult to create anything more complicated than box-shaped objects. Instead, we usually adjust the parameters of the primitive box and then convert it into an editable mesh, a much more editable form.

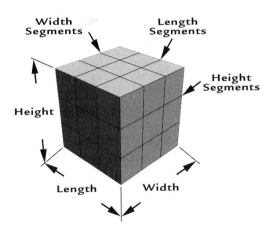

Figure 1.03

This opens up a whole other array of things we can play with. As an editable mesh we now have access to the sub-object parts of the box. These sub-object parts are the bits and pieces that give the box its shape and allow the program to render or draw the surface. The smallest bit is called a vertex. A vertex is a point in space de-noted by a plus symbol (+). Then, between the vertices of an object is what we call an edge. It looks simply like a straight line between two vertices, kind of like a three-dimensional connect-the-dots. Then, if we connect three vertices by three edges, we can create a renderable face, the third object. If you put a bunch of faces together, you get a larger shape that we call a mesh.

Figure 1.04

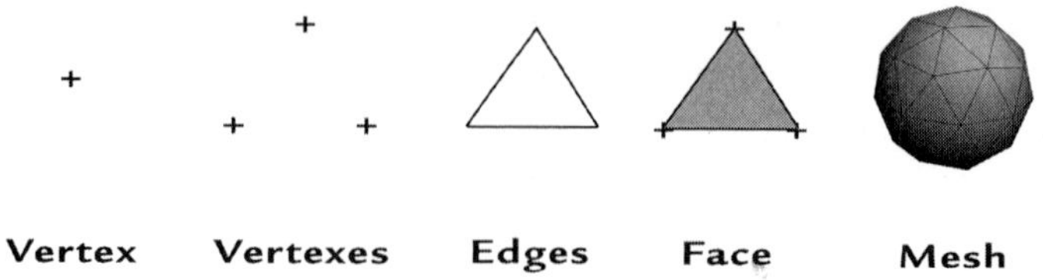

Vertex   Vertexes   Edges   Face   Mesh

There are several names for meshes; a mesh can be called a model or geometry. The density of the model or the number of faces in a model defines the smoothness of the rendered surface. For example, the digital dinosaurs used in *Jurassic Park* were made of several million triangles. That was in 1993. Now, the next generation of game engines will be able to handle characters of 5,000 triangles and will look like a model of a million or more. This will give us the ability to create film-quality models for real-time games.

Texture

The second most important part of a model is the texture. This is the image that will define what the rendered surface will look like. That's easy enough to say, but just a little harder to do. There are two big steps in creating a texture. The first part is called unwrapping. The problem is that an image is a two-dimensional thing, and we need to place it on a 3D object. In order to do that we need to separate the model into logical parts that can be flattened easily in order to place the image on it without distortion. Because the image is flat, it is much easier to place the map if the model is flat, too. Stretching is the bane of the texture artist.

There are two components that come into play when you're creating a texture map for a 3D model. The first component is the mesh. The second is the image. They both have limits on how much they can be modified in order to accommodate each other. Change one too much, and the whole process will fail. So let me break down the components a little more.

When you create a digital image it is made up of little squares called pixels. No matter how many pixels your image has, they remain square. The geometry is made up of triangles and unequal ones at that. The distortion in the shape of the geometry (triangles) causes the image placed on it to distort, and the pixels appear stretched out. This is because the image is trying to cover a nonsquare distorted surface. An easier way to imagine a texture is as a slide in a projector. If you project the slide on a flat screen, everything looks great. If you project it onto an uneven surface like a ball or a sheep or a ruffled curtain, the curves of the object distort the image. Texture maps work the same way. Fortunately, you can directly edit the way the map (projector) sees the surface of the object (screen) by editing the mapping coordinates. This is one of the trickier parts of the texturing process. I will show you the way.

Figure 1.05

Good   Stretched   Fixed

The second step is to create the image. Before we can do that we need to modify the mapping coordinates until all the geometry is laid out flat. We can take a picture of the flattened geometry and use Photoshop to paint directly on that image. When we apply the image to the geometry, everything should go where we painted it. What to paint and how to do it is a complicated process. There are many different styles and methods for creating images. For the painters out there, you can just paint what you want; for the rest of us, we can use pictures to cut and paste our way to a map.

Figure 1.06

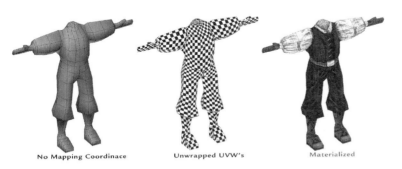

No Mapping Coordinace   Unwrapped UVW's   Materialized

Skeleton

The third ingredient is a skeleton. I am sure you're asking yourself, "What in the heck do you need a skeleton for?" Well, in the old days if you wanted your model to move around and bend like a human, you needed what was called an armature. When animation was done with Play-doh characters, there was a wire that ran inside

Figure 1.07

the "doh" to give it a substructure and support. We will revisit the subject of wire a little bit later. For now, think about your own skeleton. It's the same principle. We have bones to support the muscles that allow us to stand up and move around. They also constrain our movements. Basically, the skeleton acts like your bones, and the mesh simulates the flesh.

I wish I could tell you that this process is completely automated, but that would be a lie. The process of adding a skeleton to your model is called rigging, and it has two steps. The first step is to create a skeleton. This is a mostly automated procedure; for example, you just have to click and drag to create a biped humanoid. For creatures other than humanoids, there are easy ways of distorting the bones' shapes, even adding limbs or a tail. Once the skeleton is fitted inside the model we have to connect the two. This is the second step. What we have to do is turn the skeleton into a deformer of the mesh and tell the program what bones will control which vertices. This is also mostly an automated process. Unfortunately, we have to check the computer's work on a bone-by-bone basis. After all the obvious problems are fixed, we have to do animation tests to make sure the rig looks good when the model moves around. This leads us to the second-to-last procedure.

Animation

Animation for video games is a little different than you might imagine. Cyclical animations or actions are strung together to create the illusion of continuous movement from a limited library of motion. So when you press the Jump button, the game runs the jump animation, and when that's done, the game starts the run or stand animation. For every action you see in a game, there has to be an animation that can fit seamlessly with all the others.

Luckily for us, all the individual animations for the Unreal Tournament 2004 characters are included with the game. So we don't have to make all the animations from scratch. We will just cut and paste to add all the animations to your new character, unless you want to make a completely differently shaped character. For example, there is a raptor pack that you can download and play as a raptor. As you can imagine, the animations for a raptor would be quite different from those for a human. We will get into a little bit of that process in Chapter 7, but not into actually creating animation specifically. There are some great books on the topic of character animation; the one I suggest for my animation students is *The Animator's Survival Kit* by Richard Williams.

Compiling

The last step in the process is to compile all the different parts of your character into files that the game can use. This is another two-part process; one part will be done in 3ds Max and the other in the Unreal Editor.

After we have built our model, textured it, rigged it, and tested it with animation, it's ready to go. We will use a plug-in called Actor-X to export your models' information in a form that can be understood by the Unreal Editor. Then, from the Unreal Editor, there will be one more compilation into files that the game engine can understand. It sounds complicated, but this is one of the easiest parts of the whole process and should take about an hour. Then we can play our new character in the game.

The Process

Now that I have given you a brief overview of the entire process, let's do a short recap. First, we are going to make the model in two parts: the body and then the head. Next, we will unwrap the mapping coordinates of our models and apply the map. Then, we will add the skeleton and attach it to our models. Finally, we will export and compile our models in preparation for game play. By now you should have learned some new terms and, as we tour the interface, you will learn a whole lot more. In the next chapter we will take a look at the interface of 3ds Max before we start the project. For those of you who have experience with 3ds Max, I suggest that you scan over the next chapter, paying particular attention to the spline sections.

The Toolbox

Throughout most of this tutorial we will be using 3ds max. A simple way to think about it is that 3ds Max is a tool set, a whole big box of tools all arranged and laid out for you to use in the most marvelous erector set imaginable. You're limited only by your imagination and time. We are going to start by learning how to make geometry.

The 3ds Max Interface

The current version of the 3ds Max has an incredibly easy-to-use and easy-to-learn interface. Believe me, there are much harder 3D programs out there. Even 3ds Max has come a long way from its humble beginnings as a DOS program. The first class I taught was in the last DOS version of 3ds Max, Release 4, and 3ds Max 8 is infinitely better. It's this evolution that makes it possible to create such a complex project as this one in such a short time frame.

Primitive Creation

There are lots of different things that can be created with 3ds Max, but we are going to focus on just the parts we will be using for the project. When 3ds Max opens, on the right-hand side of the screen you will see a panel with six tabs on it. This area is called the command panel, where we will be creating and modifying things. The tabs open different panels. The first tab displays the Create panel. The buttons underneath the Create tab determine what kinds of things you can create. For the most part, we will be using the first two panels. The rows of seven buttons at the top of the Create panel are the object category buttons. The active object category on the Create panel is the yellow button; by default it's the geometry category. Under the object category buttons is a drop-down menu that contains many different kinds of geometrical objects that can be created. We will not be getting into all that 3ds Max can do, but I suggest that you play around with it as much possible.

Click the GeoSphere button in the center of the panel. In the window labeled "Top," click with the left mouse button and drag out a sphere.

You can use the left mouse button to change the active viewport, but it's a bad habit to get into. Instead, you should practice using the right mouse button to change the active viewport so that you will not deselect the currently selected object.

Take some time and try creating all the standard primitives. Some of the primitives take more than one click or drag to create. Don't fret, because we are working in a virtual space. You can't break anything, so it's okay to experiment. While there are other things we can create, like lights and cameras, we should stick with primitives for the time being. This will help you get used to the interface and become more proficient with the way that 3ds Max uses the mouse.

One thing I want you to take care to notice is what viewport or window I ask you to make an object or modify an object in. Most of the time I will ask you to make things in the Top or Front viewports. It is difficult to make objects in the Perspective viewport. We generally use the Perspective viewport to check the changes we make in the other ones.

Viewport Navigation

Now that you have some objects in your scene, you will want to take a look around to see them from all sides. If you take a look in the bottom right-hand corner of the interface, you will find the viewport control tools. Some of them you might recognize, like the Zoom tool. If you select it, you can go to any viewport and zoom in and out by clicking the left mouse button and dragging the mouse up and down. Go ahead and give it a try.

If you have a wheel mouse, I want you never to use that button again. The middle scrolling mouse button will act as an incremental zoom. If your mouse does not have one, I recommend that you get a mouse that does. It makes navigating in 3ds Max much easier.

So go ahead, click on any viewport and scroll away for a little while. If you hadn't noticed, you can also use the middle mouse button to change the active viewport. Doing so doesn't deselect the currently selected object.

The next button you might recognize is the Pan View tool. It's down and to the right, with the flat hand icon on it. Select it, and in any viewport click the left mouse button. You will be able to pan your view around. This is what we call a screen pan; no matter what viewport you're in, it will pan in the same way. Now that you know what this button does, I want you never to use it either. We actually use all four mouse buttons. Try depressing the scrolling mouse wheel. You should feel and hear a click, which is the fourth button. If you click

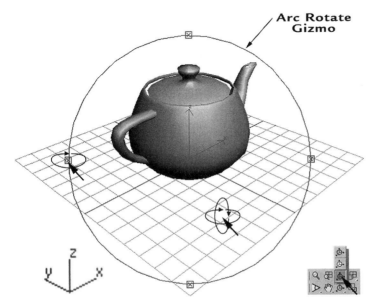

Arc Rotate Gizmo

Figure 1.08

the scroll wheel when you are in a viewport, it will change to the Pan View tool. This takes a little practice to get used to, so try it out.

The next tool we are going to look at is the one that allows you to rotate your view of the project. The use of this tool does not rotate the objects in your scene, just your view of those objects.

It's the Arc Rotate tool. It has a circle with three arrows pointing out of it. If you click and hold down the left mouse button, you will see a pop-up menu giving you three options. Select the icon with the yellow circle. This is the option for sub-object rotation. The other two options are for rotation around the center of the world and the selected object. Once you activate the tool, a yellow gizmo will appear overlaid on top of your active viewport. If you change the viewport, the gizmo will follow. Now put your cursor in the center of the gizmo, click the left mouse button, and move your mouse around. It's kind of fun to give a spin, but don't worry if you can't control it well. Try clicking and dragging one of the boxes on the gizmo; this way you can limit the axis of rotation. This is one of the hardest tools to become comfortable using. It is also one of the most important tools you have for working in the 3D world space.

It takes a fair amount of time truly to understand the 3D world space. That's why playing 3D games can help you train your brain to understand a virtual world. The problem is that we have a 2D interface into a 3D world. It would be like trying to view the real world out of a small window. It would be almost impossible to navigate the real world with such a small view. So we end up rotating our view to make sure we are working correctly. Of course, there is a mouse shortcut for the Arc Rotate tool. It's the middle scroll wheel button and the Alt button on the keyboard. So give it a try in any viewport. Hold down the Alt button, put your cursor in the middle of the viewport, and, with the middle mouse depressed, move the mouse around.

Having all the viewport navigation tools oriented around the cursor dramatically increases your working speed. Here's just a small plug for one of my favorite new toys, the 3D mouse. You can check them out online at *www.3dconnexion.com*. This device replaces the Pan View, Zoom, and Arc Rotate tools altogether and gives you the ability to do all three at the same time. This greatly improves the quality of your artwork while at the same time decreasing the time it takes to complete any kind of project. They have extremely good student pricing, as well as a 30-day trial program.

For now, I want you to practice all the things you just learned. The more time you spend on using the viewport tools, the faster, and easier the whole learning process will be.

Figure 1.09

There are a couple of viewport navigation buttons that are not self-explanatory. The first is in the very bottom right-hand corner of the interface. This button will make the active viewport expand and contract. The default keyboard shortcut for the same action is Alt-W.

The other buttons are right above it. The Zoom Extents All tool (the button with a small grid in the background) will zoom all the viewports to the extent of your project.

Just to the left of the Zoom Extents All tool is the Zoom Extents tool. This will zoom only the active viewport to the extent of your project, so if you ever get lost, click this button to reset your viewport.

Now you might ask why we have two buttons that do almost the same thing. Well, notice that in the bottom right-hand side of each button, the corner is knocked out. This means that there are other options for these buttons. Try holding the left mouse button down on one of them, and you will get a pop-up menu with two options. Select the one with the white box on it. This version of the button will zoom to the extent of the selected object.

Figure 1.10

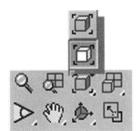

Making Selections

Most of the general working methods in 3ds Max are similar to the ones you are used to in Microsoft Windows. There are lots of drag-and-drop, click-and-drag, and right-click options. Let us not forget the ability to click and drag a rectangle to select multiple objects. As you might guess, if you click and drag out a rectangle in 3ds Max, the objects that are crossed or enclosed by that rectangle will be selected. It takes a little getting used to, so give it a try. Select individual objects by left-clicking on them. Try dragging out a rectangle and selecting multiple objects. Now that you have practiced that a little, let's add in another twist.

There are two keys on the keyboard that we use to augment our mouse clicks: the Ctrl key and the Alt key. The Ctrl key changes the selection tool to an additive selection tool. To the left edge of your cursor, a little plus symbol (+) appears. This also works with the drag window. If you hold down the Ctrl key before you drag out the window, it will be an additive window. The Alt key is for subtraction, so if you hold down the Alt key and select a selected object, it will be deselected. You should also be able to see a little minus symbol (−) next to your cursor.

The last method of selecting objects is by a list. In the main toolbar there is a button called Select by Name. If you click this button, a pop-up window will give you a list of all the objects in your project. The keyboard shortcut for the Select by Name window is "H." You can use the normal Windows selection keys, such as Ctrl and Alt, for adding and subtracting objects from the list. Then you can confirm your selection by clicking Select.

Figure 1.11

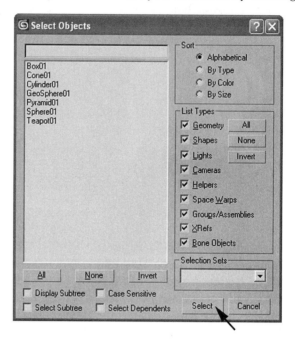

Primitive Editing

Transforms

The most primitive editing we can do is to change the position, rotation, and scale of the object, so that's where we will start. First, let's try moving things about. At the top of the interface, right in the center of the Main toolbar are three buttons. The Select and Move tool is the one that looks like a "+" with arrows on all four ends. If you click that button, it will turn yellow. Now select an object.

On top of that object will appear the Move gizmo. In the Front (f), Left (l), and Top (t) viewports you will only see two axes, X and Y. In the Perspective viewport you will see all three axes. The three axes are color coded red for X, green for Y, and blue for Z (remember, RGB = XYZ). This color coding is consistent throughout the program, so if you learn it now, when we get to more complicated things you will understand them more easily.

Let's start in the Top viewport. If you want to move the object around on the two axes, put your cursor on the red and green lines toward the center of the gizmo, and a yellow square will be shaded in if it isn't already. Now you can click with the left mouse button and drag the objects around. If you want to move an object on a single axis, all you have to do is put your cursor on either the green arrow or the red one and click with the left mouse button. Hold it down and drag. No matter how much you move the mouse in the other direction, it will not go. It gets a little bit more complicated when we try to move things around in the Perspective viewport. All you have to do is make sure that you have the right handle.

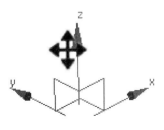

Try to put your cursor on the blue handle and move the object up and down. Take some time to practice moving objects around and up and down.

Let's take a short detour to a related subject. Now that you have had some time to practice moving objects around, this time try holding the Shift key down before you move your object. You will notice that instead of the original, now you are moving a copy of the object. As soon as you let the left mouse button up, a pop-up window will appear asking you if you want to make a copy, an instance, or a reference. For now, let's not get into the other options, so the default option of Copy is fine.

One more option that's fun to play with is the number of copies you want to make, so give it a shot and increase the number. After you confirm, you now should have a bunch of copies evenly spaced. Holding the Shift key while doing any of the transforms will create copies. So, as we take a look at the next two tools, remember to give the Shift key a try and see what happens.

The next button is the Select and Rotate tool. If you don't already have a teapot, go back to the Create panel and make one in the Top viewport. You must be asking yourself, "What in the heck, why a teapot?" Well, it's a kind of tradition dating back to the beginning of computer graphics. We will be using it because it's easer to see rotational effects on a teapot.

Before we get into the Select and Rotate tool, let's customize the interface a little bit. By default, the gizmo for rotation is called

Figure 1.12

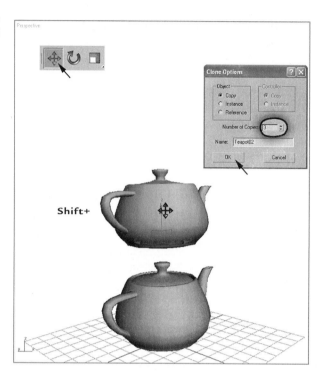

Figure 1.13

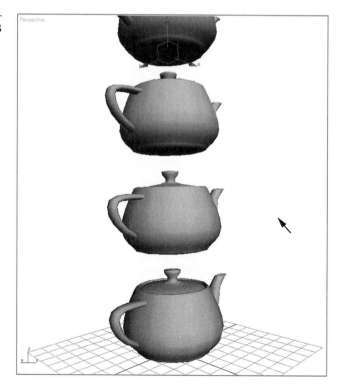

an orbital or spherical gizmo. Unfortunately, it is very hard to use for beginners, so we are going to change it to something a little bit easer to use. Choose the Customize>Preferences>Gizmos tab In the Rotate Gizmo area, click on the Rotation Method drop-down menu and choose Legacy R4. Click OK.

Figure 1.14

Figure 1.15

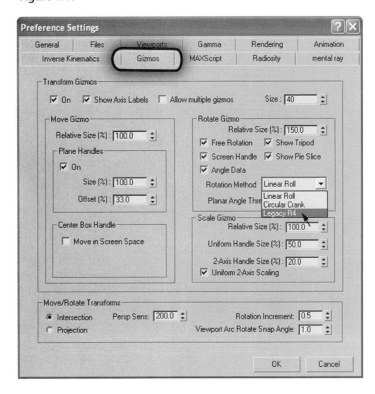

Instead of the Sphere gizmo, you now have one that looks like the Select and Move tool, but it controls only rotation.

With your teapot selected and the Perspective viewport active, remember to right-click to change the viewport.

Figure 1.16

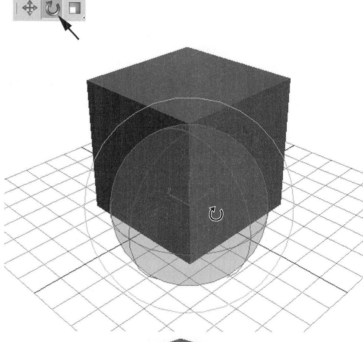

Figure 1.17

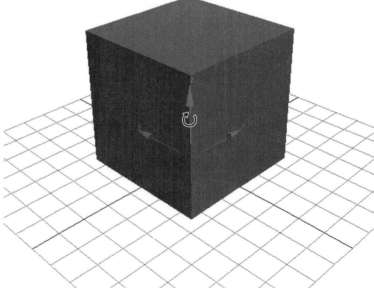

Then put your cursor on the blue handle, click, and drag left to right. The teapot should rotate only around the Z-axis, depending on which way you move the mouse.

How much you have rotated the object is shown at the bottom of the interface in the three little windows labeled X, Y, and Z. You can type values directly in these windows to rotate your object a specific amount.

The other important thing to notice is that the gizmo does not rotate with the teapot. So when you rotate on the Z-axis any amount and then try to rotate the teapot to pour the tea out, you can't. You would actually have to rotate it on both the X- and Y-axes in order to do the action. Even then it won't work quite right. In some cases, it's impossible to animate objects this way, so something has to change.

This leads us to another subject that I touched on earlier when I talked about the reference coordinate system back in the intro to the 3D environment section. Now we are going take a look at some of the other options we have for our coordinate system. In the Main toolbar, to the right of the Select and Uniform Scale tool, is a drop-down menu with the word "View" in it. The View option means that 3ds Max is using the active viewport as the reference for the coordinate system. The reference system is tool dependent, so you can have a different system for each tool. Make sure the Select and Rotate tool is active and change the reference coordinate

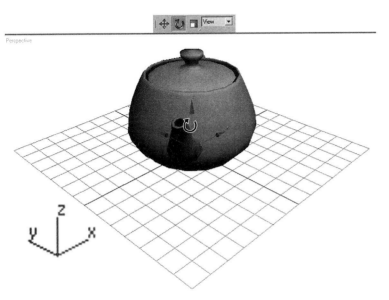

Figure 1.18

Figure 1.19

Figure 1.20

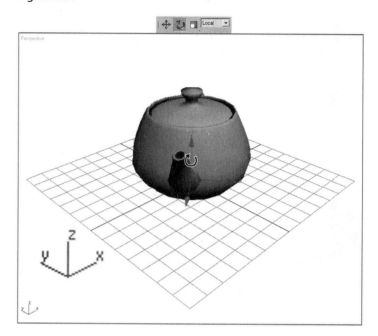

system to Local. The Local option means that 3ds Max is using the object's local coordinates as the reference system.

Now back to the teapot. Give it a spin on the Z-axis.

Notice that the gizmo rotates with the teapot and that at any Z angle you can pour out the tea by rotating on the Y-axis.

This may not seem like a big deal now, but later it will be necessary for the proper rotation of the skeleton's parts. If you want to know how much of an angle you have rotated, look for the three little windows at the bottom of the interface. They will show you the angle you rotated on all three axes.

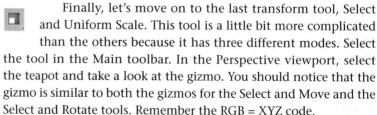

Finally, let's move on to the last transform tool, Select and Uniform Scale. This tool is a little bit more complicated than the others because it has three different modes. Select the tool in the Main toolbar. In the Perspective viewport, select the teapot and take a look at the gizmo. You should notice that the gizmo is similar to both the gizmos for the Select and Move and the Select and Rotate tools. Remember the RGB = XYZ code.

Drag the blue Z handle up and down. It will make the teapot taller and shorter. This is the first mode: scale on a single axis.

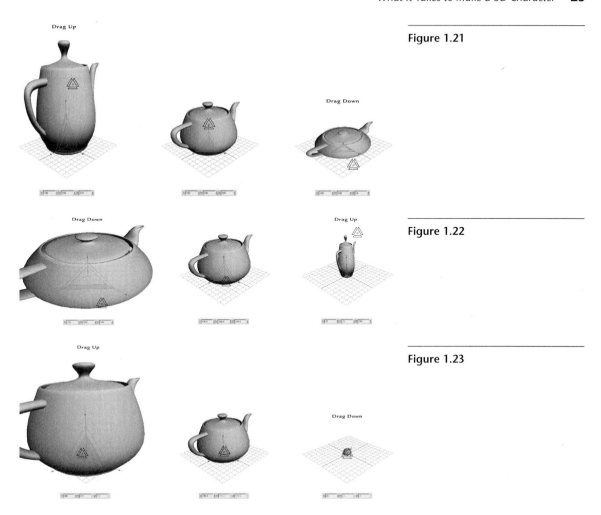

Figure 1.21

Figure 1.22

Figure 1.23

The second is scale on two axes. For this we will try scaling on the X- and Y-axes at the same time. Move the cursor over the bar between the red and green handles. When it lights up, drag it up and down. This will make the teapot get thinner and wider.

The third option is to scale on all three axes at the same time. Move the cursor over the center of the gizmo. When the triangle in the center lights up, drag it up and down. It will scale all three axes at the same time and by the same amount. Remember that, at the bottom center of the interface, there are the three little windows that have numbers in them. When you're using the Select and Uniform Scale tool, they will show you the percentage of scale you're making on each axis.

Figure 1.24

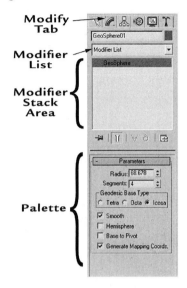

Figure 1.25

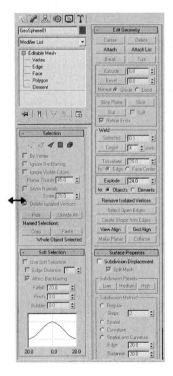

Parameters

Let's move into the other panel we will be using all the time, the Modify panel. As you might guess, this is the panel we will use when we want to modify things we have created. The Modify panel is separated into three different areas. The first area is the drop-down menu labeled Modifier List. This is a list of all the modifiers available for your selected object. The next area down is called the modifier stack area. If you select an object, you will see the type displayed in this window. The last area contains the rollouts. Within the rollouts are the object parameters that can be changed.

For simple primitives, there may be only one or two rollouts. For more complicated objects, there may be dozens. To help navigate so many rollouts, there are a couple of different things to help you.

The first is on the right-hand side of the rollouts. If the rollouts area can't fit in the available space, there is a scrollbar, a thin strip where you can click. The second is on the left-hand side. If you put your cursor on the edge of the window, the cursor will change to a left–right arrow. Then click and drag to the left. You can drag out the rollouts to occupy two or three columns.

The last tip and the one you will probably use most of the time is that if you click in a blank gray area of any rollout, it will turn into the Pan View tool. Then you can drag the rollouts up and down to view areas hidden from view.

If you don't already have a GeoSphere in your scene, change to the Create panel and make one in the Top viewport.

Then, back in the Modify panel, there will be only one rollout, called Parameters, because this is a simple object. In the Parameters rollout you will see the radius value of the GeoSphere. Right next to the value window you will see two arrows. They're what we call spinners. Spinners can be used to change a value incrementally, or if you drag up or down after clicking one, you can adjust the value up or down. Try it out; you should be able to get the hang of it quickly. One other trick with spinners is that if you right-click on one, it will set the value to the lowest value available. This is great for setting values to zero quickly. Also, any value that has a spinner can be animated. Most of the options that use a checkbox cannot be animated.

Make and select some of the other primitives, then check out what their individual parameters are. Play with the values so that you can understand what they control. If you want to, go back to the Create panel, click on the object category drop-down menu, and select Extended Primitives. Or you can choose Doors or Windows. Also check out the AEC Extended primitives. After creating some, go back to the Modify panel and tinker with the parameters.

One of the most important parameters you need to know is the segments. This is the way we can increase or decrease the detail of an object. On some objects, we can change the values on multiple dimensions. For example, with a box we can change the height, length, and width segments; however, for a Geo-Sphere there is only one—just the number of triangles. If you want to know the number of triangles in any object, press the number 7 key on the keyboard. In the top left-hand corner of the active viewport, a yellow number will appear giving you the total number of faces.

Figure 1.26

Figure 1.27

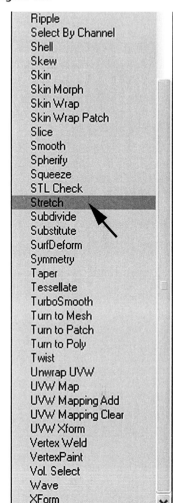

Modifiers

So far we have been using only a fraction of the power available to us in the Modify panel. Now we are ready to take the next step and start adding modifixers to our geometry.

First, make a GeoSphere and then in the Modify panel click on the Modifier List drop-down menu. You will see a huge list of modifiers that are available.

If you press the S key, it will take you to the first modifier starting with the letter "S". If you keep pressing S, it will keep going on down the list until you get to the one called Stretch. As soon as you can see it, select it with the left mouse button. Once you have added the modifier, you will see it in the modifier stack area on top of the word GeoSphere. Now, in the rollout area, you will see an entirely different set of values, so try to change the Stretch value by clicking and dragging on the spinner and see what happens to your GeoSphere.

Figure 1.28

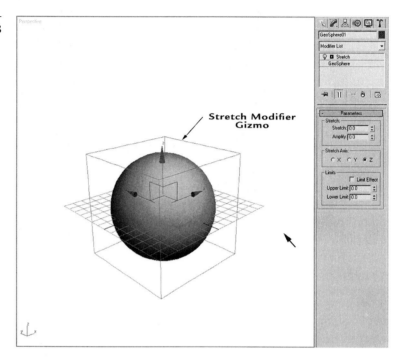

Wow! Isn't that cool? As with most modifiers, you can change the values to the negative, and the modifier will do the opposite. It means that the Stretch modifier is also a "squash" modifier. If you take a look at the modifier stack area, you will see that on top of your GeoSphere is the word "Stretch." Notice there is a plus symbol next to it. Click the symbol and see what happens. More options appear. This is consistent throughout the program. Wherever you see the plus symbol next to something, there is something hidden. Before we play with the gizmo, give the stretch a small positive value. Under the Stretch modifier there are two sub-object levels.

The first one is called Gizmo, which represents the modifier's relationship to the geometry. If you select the word Gizmo in the modifier stack area, the text will have a yellow highlight, which means it's active. In the Perspective viewport, try to move the modifier's gizmo on the Z- and X- or the Z- and Y- axes and see how it changes the effect of the modifier. To add another wrinkle, you can animate any transform made to the gizmo. This makes modifiers not only modeling tools but

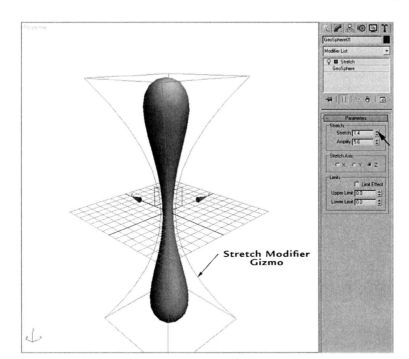

Figure 1.29

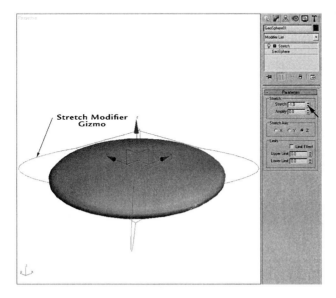

Figure 1.30

Figure 1.31

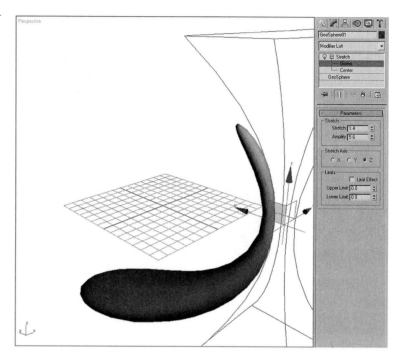

also animation tools. There is one more sub-object level, called Center, that controls the position of the center of the modifier's effect.

It also controls how the Limit Effect option in the Parameters rollout works. The Limit Effect option allows you to constrain what part of the modifier controls the mesh. To activate Limit Effect, first check the box in the Parameters rollout, then increase the upper limit and decrease the lower limit. You will notice that the stretch is affecting only the center part of the sphere. If you take a close look at the gizmo, you will see that upper and lower parts of the gizmo move away from the center part of the gizmo.

Another good example to use as a test is to put a Bend modifier on a cylinder, then test how moving the gizmo and center sub-objects affects the modifier performance. Note that modifiers are implemented from the bottom up. So it's very important what order your modifiers are in. By the end of this book, you will be an expert in modifier manipulation. Now give this a try. Right-click on the Stretch modifier and, from the pop-up menu, select copy; before you can select another object, you have to close the Bend modifier. Click on the word "Bend" in the modifier stack area and the highlight will change to gray. Then you can select another object, like the teapot. Right-click on the word "Teapot" in the modifier stack area and choose Paste.

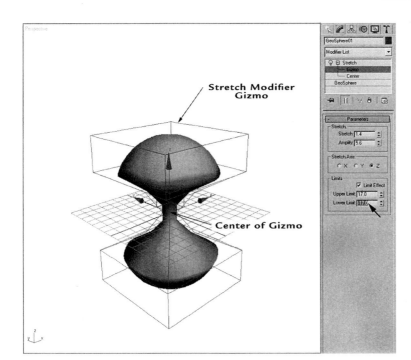

Figure 1.32

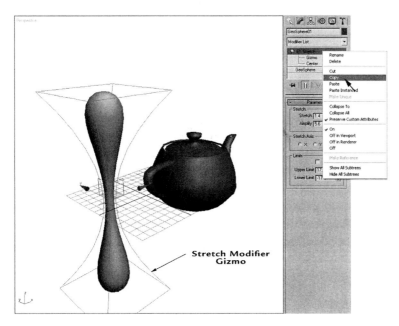

Figure 1.33

Figure 1.34

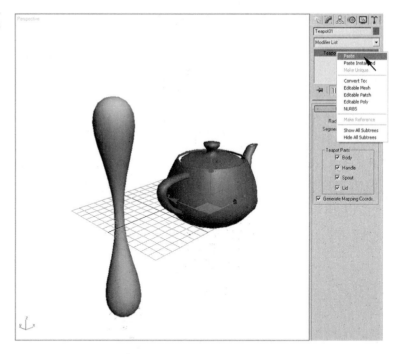

This will give you an exact copy of the modifier on your new object. This leads us to a new vocabulary word: "instance." There are several areas that use this term, and they all mean the same thing—a linked copy. Any change you make to the original will be passed on to the copies, and any change to the copy will be passed on to the original. This time, select another object and right-click. Instead of just pasting, choose Paste Instanced. Then change the Stretch value. Both objects will stretch at the same time. Cool, huh? This works for any modifier placed as an instance, not just Stretch. At this point, you're probably a little overwhelmed by all the possibilities of so many modifiers, but, before we move on, we have to go over one more subject: splines.

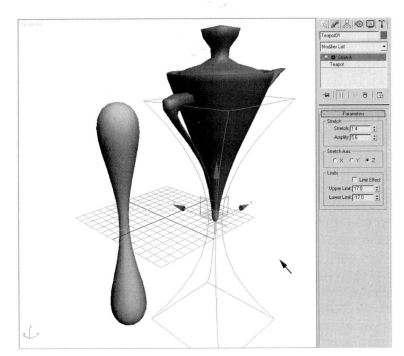

Figure 1.35

Spline Modeling

What Is Spline Modeling?

Spline modeling is a technique for creating 3D geometry using spines instead of mesh. Instead of creating a box and manipulating it, you create a spline cage and cover it with a surface. Even though the result is the same, the biggest difference is in the approach to creating the mesh. Modeling with splines is more akin to drawing than mesh modeling. The majority of my students find this method easer than mesh modeling. I have seen some of my students become highly prolific modelers after learning spline modeling. You still have to understand mesh modeling to work in the games industry. No matter what technique you use to create your model, eventually all models have to be converted to editable meshes before they can be used as assets in a real-time game.

Creation

There are two kinds of splines. The first, the primitives, should be familiar by now. Primitive splines are just basic shapes with some adjustable parameters. There are a couple of helpful primitive splines like circle and text. To find the splines, go to the Create panel and click the second button from the left, called Shapes. Click the Circle button and in the Top viewport, click and drag out a circle. That was easy enough. Try creating a text spline also; it's just a one-click creation. Then go to the Modify panel and check out the parameters for the text spline. You can change what the text says by clicking in the window that says "MAX Text" and edit it. Splines are nonrenderable by default. So, at this point, none of your splines have geometry and will not show up if you render the viewport. Not to worry—we will get into changing that soon enough.

Go back to the Create panel and click Line. This is not a primitive but what is called an editable spline, which is the most basic shape. It has no primitive parameters but has three sub-object levels. They are Vertex, Segment, and Spline. We will take a look at them in the next section.

Figure 1.36

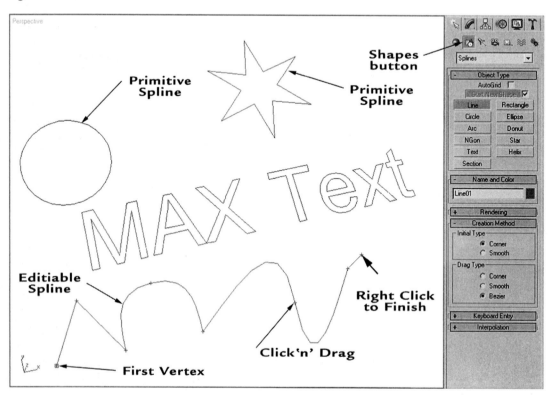

Let's now create a line. All you have to do is to click in the viewport where you want the vertex to go, and it will create a line between each new vertex.

If you click and drag, 3ds Max will add curvature to that vertex. We will explore the curvature when we look at editing splines next. To stop creating vertices, click the right mouse button. This will cancel most operations throughout the program.

Editing

With your line selected, go to the Modify tab. Click on the plus symbol in the modifier stack area and check out the sub-object levels of the line. It's actually simpler. There are only three, and for the most part we use only the first two, Vertex and Segment. The segment is easy—it's the line between two vertices. The vertex of a mesh is a little bit simpler than the one for splines. First click on the Vertex sub-object level in the modifier stack area. Then select all of the vertices on the line by using the rectangular selection method. Note that selected objects will turn red and that some of the vertices

Figure 1.37

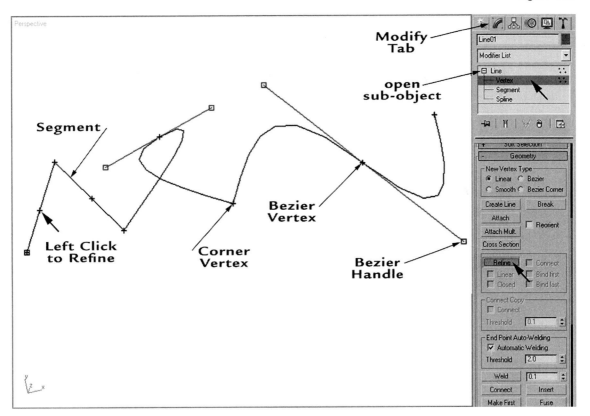

Figure 1.38

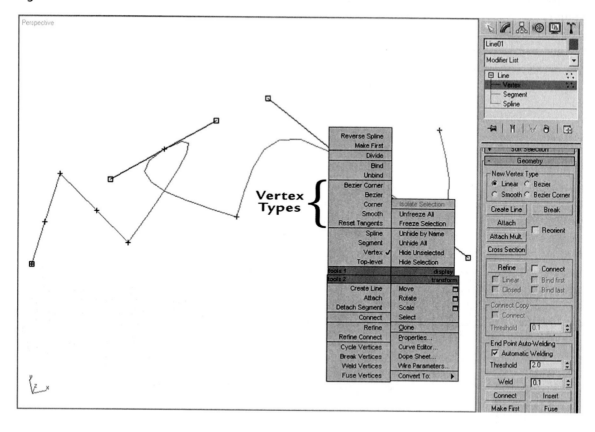

have yellow lines coming out of them with little green boxes on the tips. The green boxes are called Bezier handles. The handles change the way the line will curve into and out of the vertex. This can take a little getting used to, so select some vertices and practice moving them about. Adjust the handles and see how the curve changes as you move the handle closer to the vertex.

The next question you will have is: "How can I add some more vertices to my line?" Move the rollout area up until you can see the Geometry section. To add vertices to your line, click Refine, place your cursor on the line where you want the vertex to be, and click with the left mouse button. Because a line can be infinitely bisected, theoretically you can add as many vertices as you want.

A general axiom for working in 3D is, "Less is more." For the most part, you will want to use as few vertices as possible on your lines. If you want to remove vertices, all you have to do is select the offending vertex (or vertices) and press the Delete key. Away it goes, and it doesn't break the line.

To change the vertex type, we will access a new part of the program called the quad menu system. When you right-click in any viewport, the quad menu will pop up. There are four panels; each one has a different set of tools. In the lower right-hand panel, you can change the active transform tool and find out the properties of the selected object. It is a good habit to use the quad menu when you want to change your transform tool. The quad menu options will change with the type of object you have selected and the sub-object level that is currently active.

With your line selected and the vertex sub-object level active, select a vertex or several vertices and right-click in the active viewport. In the upper left-hand panel is a group of options that consists of Bezier Corner, Bezier, Corner, and Smooth. These are all the different vertex types available. Test them out and see how each one works.

Let's quickly go over each. The Bezier Corner vertex has handles that work independently from each other. The Bezier vertex has handles that are locked to each other so that they both move at the same time. You can also move them away from the vertex to create a rounded corner, or you can move them closer to create a sharp one. The Corner vertex has no handles and no curve into or out of it. The Smooth vertex type is a kind of automatic Bezier vertex that automatically adjusts to try to give you the smoothest curve into and out of the vertex.

There are lots of other tools for editing splines, and I will introduce them to you as we go along.

The Leaf Tutorial

Part One: Modeling

Before we start making a full 3D character, let's make a simple 2D model. It will also introduce you to the spline-modeling working methods and a couple of new areas inside 3ds Max.

In this tutorial we will be using an image as a template. When we work with images, it's easer if we use our thumbnail plug-in called the Asset Browser. The Asset Browser is extremely useful for many image-related manipulations. To access it we have to go to the Utilities panel. To get there, click the far-right tab, which has an icon of a hammer on it. Click the first button in the lower area of the panel, Asset Browser.

The Asset Browser acts like the Microsoft Windows explorer. On the left-hand side we can navigate our folders, and on the

Figure 1.39

Figure 1.40

right-hand side we have thumbnails of all the files in the selected folder. Navigate to the install directory of 3ds Max. Find the Maps folder, and inside that select the Organics folder, then LeafGreen. jpg. (If the maps are not installed on your system, all images related to the tutorial in the book are on the DVD.) A red highlight will appear around it.

Figure 1.41

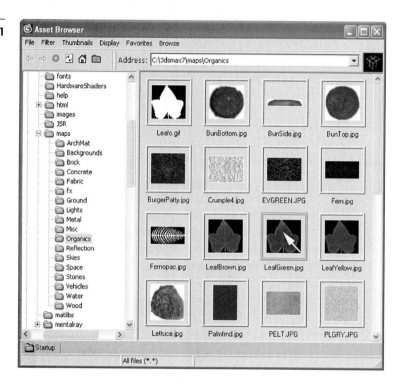

Drag it over onto the Top viewport and drop it. A box with two options will pop up. Uncheck the bottom option; we do not want to add this image as the environmental background of our project. All you really want to do is to see the image in the background of the viewport. That's the first option. Once you confirm, the image will show up in the background of the Top viewport, but notice that the image's aspect ratio is off. The image is squished down a little. You can now close the Asset Browser.

This is not what we want, so to correct the aspect ratio, first we need to activate the Top viewport. Then we are going to use a couple of keyboard shortcuts. The first one is G, which toggles the viewport grid on and off. For this tutorial we will not be using the grid, so turn it off. The second one is Alt-B, which opens the viewport

Figure 1.42

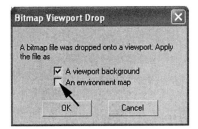

Figure 1.43

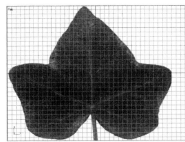

Figure 1.44

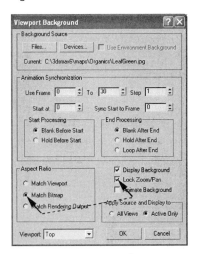

Background dialog box. In the bottom left-hand corner, click Match Bitmap. In the lower right-hand corner, check Lock Zoom/Pan. In the very bottom left-hand corner is the Viewport dropdown; make sure it's set to Top, then click OK.

The green leaf in the Top viewport should be the correct size and shape. The Lock Zoom/Pan option locks the image down to the X–Y plane. So, if we pan or zoom, the image stays in the center of the world. Don't zoom in too much or 3ds Max will give you a warning that you are using a lot of video RAM. That's okay; just confirm the warning and zoom back out. The third keyboard shortcut is Alt-W, which will maximize the Top viewport or any active viewport. This will make the leaf bigger and easier for us to see.

Now center the leaf in the viewport using your middle mouse button. Go back to the Create panel and click the Shapes object category button. Click the Line button. Starting from the top tip of the leaf, create vertices around the outside of the leaf as shown in Figure 1.45. For the last vertex, click on the first one and you will get a pop-up window asking if you want to close the spline. Click Yes.

Figure 1.45

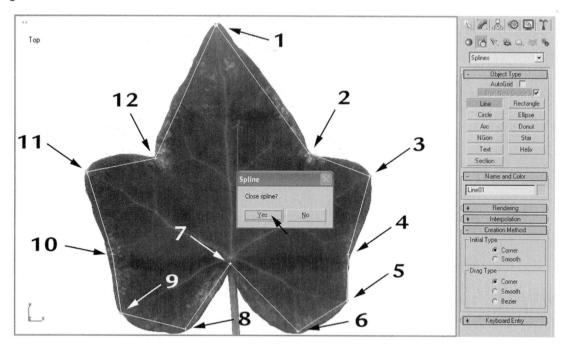

Figure 1.46

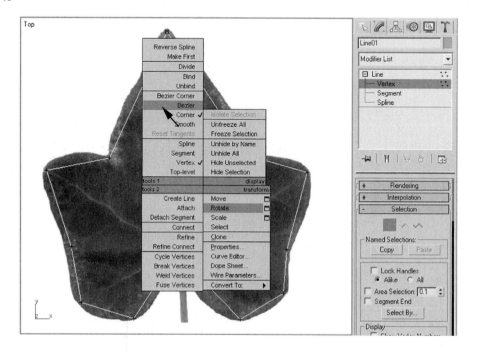

Change to the Modify panel and Click on the plus symbol next to the word Line in the Modifier stack area. Click on the Vertex sub-object level and select all the vertices of the leaf. Right-click in the active viewport, and from the upper left-hand panel, change the vertex type to Bezier. You will notice that all the handles have misshaped your line, but it will be good practice to fix them. Activate the Select and Move tool and move the handle that is easiest to select until it is parallel to the outside of the leaf as shown in Figure 1.48.

Figure 1.47

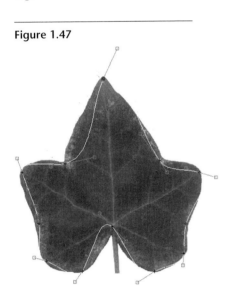

Figure 1.48

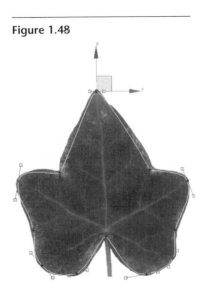

The next step is to create the inside of the leaf. In order for the modifier to generate a surface, we have to create three- or four-sided shapes with our spline. A small quirk of this technique is that the vertices of the cross-sections that will create our three- or four-sided shapes have to be right on top of each other. This is impossible to do by hand, so we need help. Let's activate the snap system. In the Main toolbar, toward the right middle, are four snaps toggles (see the top of Figure 1.49): Snaps Toggle, Angle Snap Toggle, Percent Snap Toggle, and Spinner Snap Toggle. Left-click Snaps Toggle to activate it, then right-click the same button. The Grid and Snap Settings dialog box will appear. Uncheck Grid Points and check Vertex. This will allow your cursor to snap to any vertex so that we can create a line between any two vertices.

To create a line, we would need to be in the Create panel, but to continue creating an existing line we have to be in the Modify panel. Let's give it a shot then. In the Modify panel, pan until you can see the Geometry rollout. One of the first buttons is Create

Figure 1.49

Line. Click it and put your cursor near the first vertex. A blue set of crosshairs will appear over it, which means the snap is working. Starting with the first vertex, click once and then go straight down to vertex #7, left-click, and then right-click to finish the line creation. It is not necessary to hold the left mouse button down as you move between vertices. In fact you don't want to for this example. Then do the same for all but the bottommost vertices as seen in Figure 1.50. Click the Created Line button again to turn it off.

Figure 1.50

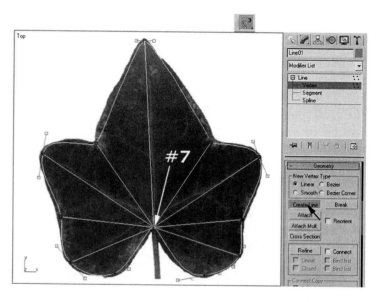

The last step is to create the mesh. This is the easy part. From the Modifier List drop-down menu, select and apply the Surface modifier. To see it better, let's use the Alt-W keyboard shortcut to minimize the Top viewport and check out what it looks like in the Perspective viewport. You should see the leaf area filled in with some color.

If not, then the first thing you should check is whether the viewport is in shaded mode or not, by right-clicking on the word "Perspective." If the Smooth + Highlights option is checked, all is good.

The next thing to check is to see whether flipping the normals will work. In the Modify panel with the Surface modifier selected, there is a checkbox for Flip Normals. Check it and see if that fixes it.

If not, then you may not have gotten all the vertices right on top of each other at that #7 vertex. In the Top viewport, zoom in on the #7 vertex and check it out. If they are not all together, return to the vertex sub-object level and then select them all. Then, in the

Geometry rollout, click on the Fuse button. Hopefully, this will fix any problems and you will have a whole leaf.

Now that you have the leaf geometry, the next thing we are going to do is to make and apply a material. Save your project, and turn off any active snap toggles; now you're ready to add a material.

To add the material and make our geometry look more like the leaf image, we will use the Material Editor. Before we get started, let's get an overview of the Material Editor.

The Material Editor

We use the Material Editor to change and preview a material's properties. A material is a set of parameters that define the surface properties of an object. The parameters are versatile enough to simulate any surface and substance. Again, to go into any great depth would necessitate writing another book, and there are already many on the subject.

Let's start by using the keyboard shortcut to open the Material Editor. It's the letter "M". There is also a button on the Main toolbar that has four colored spheres on it. As you might be able to tell, I want you to get used to using the M key to open the Material Editor.

The Material Editor can be broken up into two main areas: the material samples and, below that, the panel area similar to the Modify panel. Let's take a look at the material samples first. Each gray sphere is a different sample that can hold one material only.

Figure 1.51

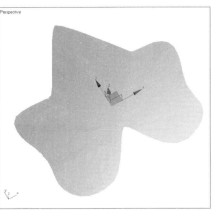

Figure 1.52

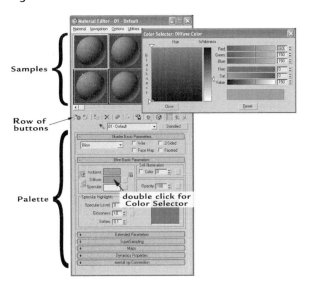

If you left-click on any sample, it will become the active material sample. If you need more samples, you can put your cursor between two of the samples. The cursor will turn into the Pan tool. Click and drag up and to the left, and you will see more samples. If you don't already have an object in your scene, it's time to make one. A box should be fine. Drag and drop one of the material samples onto your object, and it will turn gray. You should also notice that all four corners of that sample window are whitened out, which indicates that the material is being used in the scene. Once a material has been assigned to an object, it never needs to be reassigned; any changes you make to a material will be automatically updated.

We will not be getting very deeply into the Material Editor, but we do need to run through the basics. We will start by changing the color of your new material. In the left-hand side of the window, there are three color sample boxes. There should be two gray boxes and one white box. If you double-click on the Diffuse color, the Color Selector: Diffuse Color dialog box will pop up. To change the color, click in the rainbow box and then change the Whiteness slider that runs vertically on the right-hand side of the rainbow box. You can also enter values in the RGB fields.

Figure 1.53

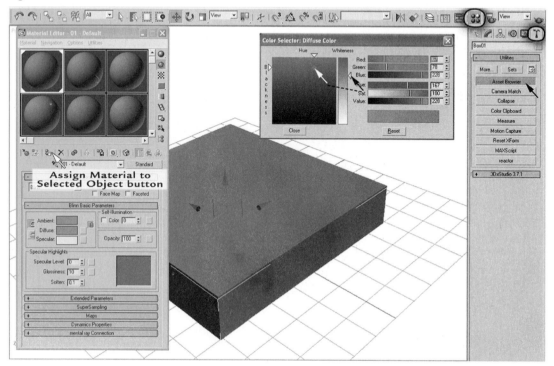

One of the ways 3ds Max is different from other graphic programs is in the way that it handles color. It does not use RGB values
to create color. It uses hue, saturation, and value, or HSV for short,
and they are right under the RGB values in the Color Selector. You
can always input RGB values, which 3ds Max will convert into HSV
values. This is not a bad thing—just something to keep in mind.
Notice that when you change colors in the dialog box, your object's
color is automatically updated.

The Diffuse color could be thought of as a base color. For the
most part, you will never use the Diffuse color as your material
color. If you do, it would be for a single-color plastic object, like a
transparent plastic or glass bottle. By changing the Diffuse color
you could easily make a green, red, or blue transparent material. So
what we usually do is replace the Diffuse color with an image. And
when we work with images what program do we use? That's right,
the Asset Browser.

Figure 1.54

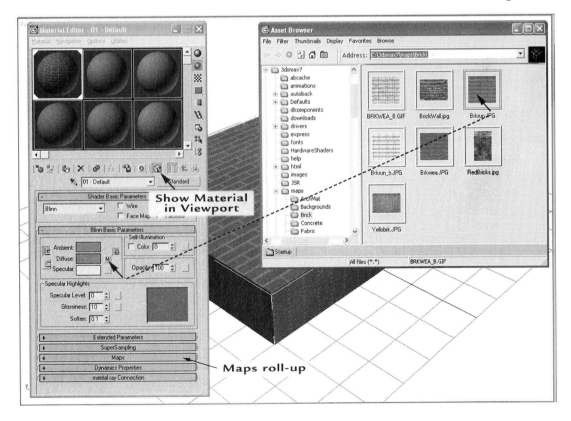

Go to the Utilities panel and activate the Asset Browser. Navigate to the 3dsmax/Maps/Brick folder and select Brkrun.jpg. Drag the brick image onto the little gray button just to the right of the Diffuse color sample. It can be a little hard to see the button, but it's there. When you get it right, the color will be replaced with the brick image and your sample will be a sphere of bricks.

What I want you to notice is what didn't happen: the image is not visible on your object. This is on purpose; back in the days when video cards had little RAM, it was not possible to show all the materials of all the objects in a scene. The original reason for video cards with a lot of RAM was to cache textures for video games, and now 3ds Max can take advantage of those cards. To see your material in the viewport, click the Show Map in Viewport button. It's a button that has a blue-and-white checkered box icon on it.

If you take a look back in the Material Editor, there will be an M in the little square next to the Diffuse color sample. Click on the M and notice the palette area change.

There are two areas in the panel that let you know what's happening. The first one is in the upper left-hand corner that says Diffuse Color. This area will change and let you know what map channel you're in. There are many aspects of materials where we can use a map to control it; we call them map channels. The other

Figure 1.55

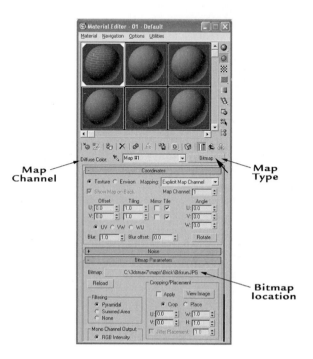

Map Channel

Map Type

Bitmap location

is in the upper right-hand corner of the panel where the button says Bitmap. This is the type of map that is in the Diffuse Color map channel.

There are two different types of maps that can be added to a channel. The first you already know: bitmaps, which are images. One kind of image you might not think about using is a movie. That's right, you can use movies as well as static images to control a channel. The other type is called a procedural material. Procedural materials are basically little programs that run in a map channel. Some, like Noise, create random black-and-white patches of color. Another good example is the Raytrace map. When used as part of a material it will automatically generate perfect reflections based on what's in your scene.

If you click on the Bitmap button, a pop-up window will appear called the Material/Map Browser.

In the list, only the first two are not procedural; the rest are. We will get to a couple of them, but most are not pertinent to our project. You can close the Material/Map Browser for now; we don't want to change our map. What we need to do now is to go back to the top of our material. We have a couple of buttons for doing that, and they are located in the row above the Bitmap button. The next-to-last button is the Go to Parent button and has a bent arrow pointing up; the last button is the Go Forward to Sibling button and has an arrow pointing right. Click on the Go to Parent button, which will take you up to the top of the Material Editor. You will be able to see the Basic Parameters again. The Go Forward to Sibling button will move you through the active map channels—that is, if you have more than one with something in it.

There is one button to the left of the Go to Parent button that looks like a blue-and-white cube. This is the Show Map in Viewport button. If you click it, the bricks will show up on your box in the Perspective viewport. One important note on rendering of the Perspective viewport: It is not totally accurate. The only real way to see what your scene will look like is actually to render it. With the Perspective viewport active, press F9 and you will get a rendering of your scene. It should look like a box of bricks—not real bricks, but maybe like a box wrapped in paper with bricks printed on it. So let's make it look a little bit better.

Let's add what is called a bump map, which is a kind of procedural effect. It creates the illusion of depth by taking a grayscale image and converting it into shadows. This happens at render time, so the only preview we get is in the Material Editor.

Figure 1.56

Figure 1.57

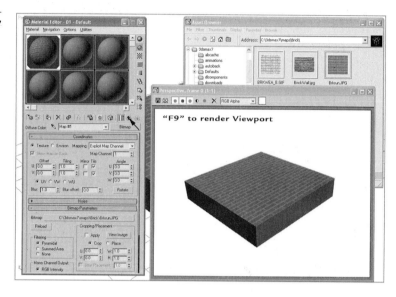

To add a bump map to the Bump channel we need first to open the Maps rollout, which is at the bottom of the Material Editor window. Once you open it, you should see a dozen or so channels. Towards the bottom is the Bump channel button labeled None. Remember that, when we need to work with images, it's best to use the Asset Browser. In the Asset Browser, if you are not already there, navigate to the 3dsmax/Maps/Bricks folder, and right next to the color image of bricks we used is a grayscale version called brk-run_b.jpg. Drag it onto the Bump channel button. You should see a big change in what your material sample looks like. It will look like a sphere of bricks with the grouted area lower than the top of the bricks. The illusion of depth is created by the generated shadows. Because a procedural map generates the illusion, it reacts appropriately to changes in lighting.

If you want to get a larger preview of a particular material, all you have to do is double-click it. The pop-up window is scalable if you put your cursor at the bottom right-hand corner and drag.

Press F9 to re-render your scene, which should look a lot more realistic. The Bump value is by default set at 30. If you increase this value, the bump will become more dramatic. If you reduce the value, it will go negative and invert the effect so that grout between bricks will look pushed out instead of recessed. So now you're asking, "How does that work?" The grayscale image creates the illusion of shadows. By converting the 256 levels of gray in the image into a depth map, it can create the illusion of shadows at render time.

To see the effect a little better, double-click on the material sample. Then you can scale it by dragging the lower-right corner. The Bump map is a great effect, but it does have limitations. It does not create any geometry. If you look at your box edge, the illusion of the bump map is broken.

The next generation of bump mapping, called normal bump mapping, will give the illusion of deformation on all three axes, but it still won't change the edge. The end result is that we can take the lighting information from a high-poly model and put it into the

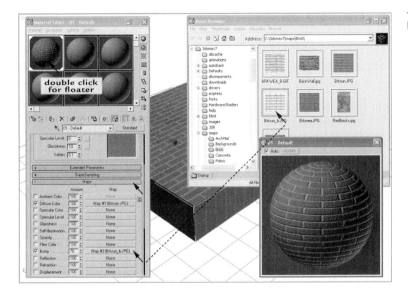

Figure 1.58

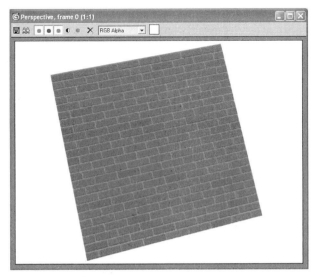

Figure 1.59

Bump channel of a low-poly model, giving it the look of the high-poly one. The high- and low-poly models must have the same general shape, but that is not too difficult to achieve using the spline-modeling technique. We will go a little more in depth on this subject later, but for now let's finish up our leaf by adding the material.

The Leaf Tutorial

Part Two: Texturing

Let's start by opening up your leaf project and opening the Material Editor and the Asset Browser. In the Asset Browser, navigate to the 3dsmax/Maps/Organics folder and select the same LeafGreen.jpg that we used for the background. This time, drag and drop it onto a material sample, right onto one of the gray spheres. This is a slightly different way of making a material, and it's a little dangerous. If you drop an image onto an existing material, the new one will replace it. Fortunately, this is an undoable action.

Now that we have our material made, let's assign it to our leaf geometry by dragging and dropping it from the material sample onto the object. Your leaf should turn gray, but why didn't the image show up on your geometry? Check to see that the Show Map

Figure 1.60

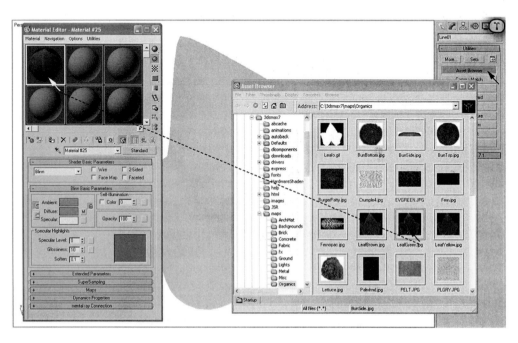

in Viewport button is active. But the image still will not show up on your geometry. This is because when you create geometry from scratch, 3ds Max does not know how to place your image on the geometry. So we have to apply a modifier called UVW Map. Let's do that now. Select the Modify tab, and from the Modifier List drop-down menu, select the UVW Map modifier. Now you should see the leaf image on your geometry, but it's not quite in the right place.

To change it so that the leaf image is in the right place, we need to modify the UVW Map modifier's gizmo. Click on the plus symbol next to the UVW Map modifier and select the Gizmo sub-object. You should notice that the gizmo has changed color from orange to yellow and green. The gizmo directly controls the placement of the image on the geometry. First, make sure that the Snap Toggle button is deactivated. Now activate the Select and Move tool so that you can change the placement of the image just by moving the gizmo around. You can also use the Select and Rotate tool and the Select and Uniform Scale tool on the gizmo to affect the orientation and tiling of the map.

The colors of the active gizmo will help you keep your orientation. The green edge of the gizmo indicates the right-hand side of the image you are trying to place, and the tail that sticks out of the top of the gizmo indicates the top of the image. Now you should be able to move and scale the gizmo until the image of the leaf is

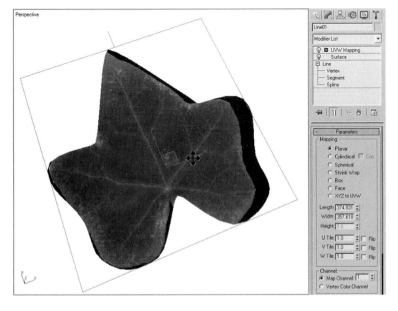

Figure 1.61

almost perfectly placed on the geometry. Unfortunately, you will not be able to get it perfectly placed, and you should see some black edges around the top of the leaf. The problem is that the image's size is greater than that of the geometry. So we will use an opacity map to solve the problem.

Figure 1.62

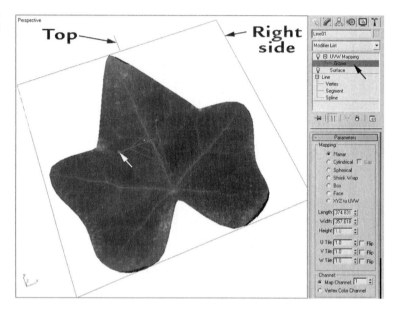

Open the Material Editor and the Asset Browser if you haven't already done so. In the Asset Browser, you should already be in the 3dsmax/Maps/Organics folder. The first thumbnail in that folder is of a white leaf on a black background. It's called Leaf0.gif or, from the DVD, GreenLeaf_A.jpg. Select it. In the Material Editor, with your leaf material selected, make sure you're at the top of the material so that you can see the Blinn Basic Parameters rollout. Expand the Maps rollout. What we are looking for is the Opacity map channel on the right-hand side of the panel. The total opacity of a material can be affected by changing the value, but what we want to do is to affect only the edge of our leaf. So we will use an image to control the opacity instead.

This is where the GreenLeaf_A image comes in. Drag and drop it onto the little gray button next to the Opacity values. All the black edges should have disappeared, leaving just the leaf. Using an image in the Opacity map channel is similar to that of the Bump map channel, except that the grayscale of the image's pixels are converted into levels of opacity. By using just total black and absolute white, we are effectively creating a mask. Anything in the white area will be visible; anything in the black area will be transparent. An easy example of modeling by opacity maps is the flags used in the Capture the Flag Games of Unreal Tournament. They are actually flat square pieces of geometry with an opacity material applied to them. The last thing is to render our leaf, select the Perspective viewport, and then press F9.

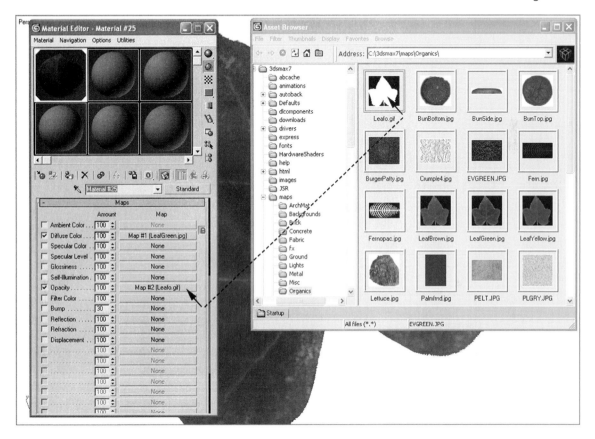

Figure 1.63

Now you have made your first photorealistic object. Congratulations! While there are more things we could do to make it more realistic, like adding a bump map, it's probably not necessary for this kind of object. What's more important is how many polygons we need to use for this object. For example, if there are a lot of leaves and they are far away from the camera, a low-poly leaf will look the same as a high-poly one and won't require the rendering overhead. On the other hand, if there is only one leaf and it is close to the camera, we would need a high-poly leaf to maintain the illusion.

This is another good thing about the spline-modeling technique. We can change the number of polygons easily. With your leaf

Figure 1.64

selected, go to the Modify panel. In the modifier stack area, select the Surface modifier. In the rollout area, look for the Patch Topology steps value. It should be set to 5. To see the current polygon count, press the number 7 key. In the upper left-hand corner of the active viewport, the number of polygons will be displayed. It should read 360. If you reduce the steps value to 0, it should read 10, which is the exact number of triangles we drew in the first part of the tutorial before we added the Surface modifier. You can see how easy it is to change the poly count of your model.

Figure 1.65

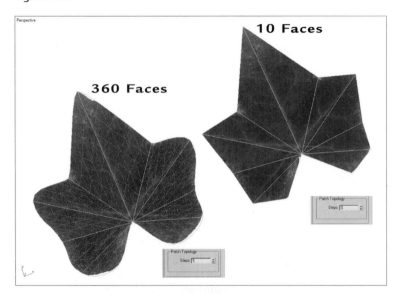

Conclusion

This all leads us back to the concept of creating a low-poly model that can be used to create a high-poly model. From that high-poly model, you could render the normal bump map so that it can be applied to the low-poly version, giving it the look of the high-poly version. In the next generation of both games and film, this technique will become the standard way things are done.

2

Modeling a 3D Character

Character Design

Now that you have completed the leaf tutorial, you have a good introduction to how we are going to start modeling our character. Like the leaf, our model will be based on an image. That image is called a model sheet. A model sheet is a design sketch used as reference when you are creating a character. Traditional model sheets might contain three to six full-body sketches in a relaxed pose, arm at the character's sides. While this is great for designing the character's costumes and attitudes, it is not very helpful when you have to build a model. Ours is not going to be a normal model sheet. What we need is a front and a side view, with the arms stretched straight out.

If you want to check out some traditional model sheets, do a search on the Web; you should find many different kinds of them.

In this tutorial we are going to build a male pirate named Jack. Don't worry; this tutorial can be used to create females or non-pirates as well. Actually, once you understand the principal of this tutorial you can make anything you want. All you have to do is make your own model sheet, and you're good to go.

Figure 2.01

Figure 2.02

Figure 2.03

Figure 2.04

One of the trickier aspects of making a good model sheet is to get the front and side views to be the same scale. In your image editor you can use the rulers to line up the two images as shown in Figure 2.03. After that, the setup is simple. If you want to know how to set up model sheets for anything, see Appendix A.

Building a Better Body

A body is a complex structure, and it is helpful to use a few tricks to reduce the complexity while you work. When I first started trying to build characters using the spline-modeling method, it was very difficult because I tried to make the whole model at once. So I figured that I needed to reduce the complexity of the whole thing. I cut it in half and tried working with that, but it was still too much. So I cut it in half again, and that did the trick. So we are going to create one quarter of our body and then mirror and copy it to the back to make a half and then one more time to make a full figure. When we are finished, we will have created one big spline far more complex than the parts that went into it.

We are almost ready to start, so put in the DVD included with this book. From the "Jack the P" folder, copy the Jack_max_PK folder to your 3dsMax/scenes folder. Open 3ds Max, and from the File menu choose Open. Navigate to the Jack_max_PK folder and open the Jack-start file. It should open up and look like Figure 2.04.

This file has more objects hidden in it, so when we get to the skeleton part of the tutorial you will be ready to set up the rig.

In a very similar method to that of the leaf tutorial, we will start by drawing a shape based on a template or reference image. One big difference is that we will not be going all the way around, but rather only halfway, then up the center. Before we start, I want to clue you in on a couple of things that will come in handy as you work through this tutorial. First, this quarter we are making needs to be all one shape. So if you stop line creation somewhere in the middle, do not start a new line. Instead, go to the Modify panel and click the Create Line button to continue expanding the existing line. Second, there is a keyboard shortcut that will allow you to pan your viewport and avoid stopping line creation. It is the letter "I," for interactive pan. When activated, the viewport will center wherever your cursor is in the viewport. Try this out. If you hold down the I key and move your mouse around, the viewport will pan in real time.

The last tip is to change the quality of the images displayed in the viewport. From the Customize pull down select the Preferences... option. In the Preferences Settings popup, select the Viewports tab and click on the Configure Driver button. From the popup, check the Match Bitmap Size as Closely as Possible options, as shown in Figure 2.06. Then click the OK buttons. Make sure you don't accidentally click on the Cancel button. Back in the viewport, you should notice that nothing has actually changed. That is because you have to close and restart 3ds Max for the preferences to be applied. Do it now and reload the Jack-Start file. Let's get it on.

Tracing the Outline

Change to the Front viewport and, in the Create panel, click on the Shapes object category button.

Click the Line button. Under Drag Type, click Corner.

We are going to start the front right-hand quadrant at the center of the neck as shown in Figure 2.07.

Click once to start the line.

Continue around the outline of the character as shown in Figure 2.09. Once you have made it all the way around, click for the last time on the first vertex. Click Yes to close the spline.

Remember that, if you stop drawing your spline for any reason, don't start drawing a new one. Just change to the Modify Panel and click on the Create Line button to continue. Now you might want to adjust some of your vertices around so that they match my outline better and are closer horizontally to their counterpartners.

Filling It In

The next step is to create the horizontal and vertical cross-sections by drawing them between the existing

Figure 2.05

Figure 2.06

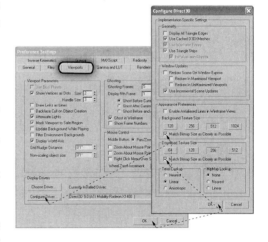

Figure 2.07

Figure 2.08

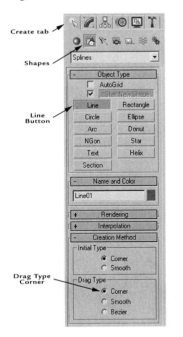

Figure 2.09

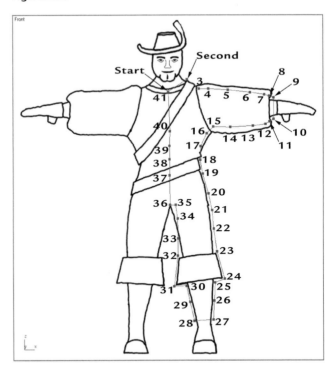

Figure 2.10

Figure 2.11

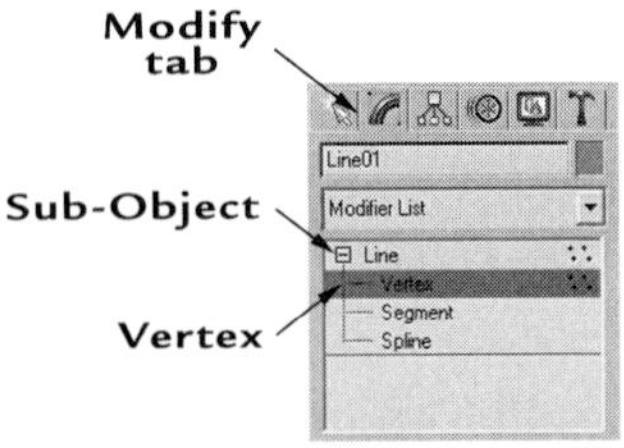

vertices, in effect creating a grid. But before we start drawing again, we need to activate the Snaps Toggle and set it to use only vertices.

Left-click Snaps Toggle to activate it, then right-click it to get the Grid and Snap Settings dialog box.

Uncheck Grid Points and check Vertex. It may already be set to Vertex, but it's always a good idea to double check. Click the Close Box button in the upper right-hand corner.

Now you should be able to draw the lines from one vertex to another, the same way you did in the leaf tutorial.

Change to the Modify panel, and in the modifier stack area, click on the plus symbol next to the word "Line." Activate the vertex sub-object level by clicking on the word "Vertex." Click the Create Line button.

In the Front viewport, put your cursor next to vertex #29. As you get close to it, you should see a small blue set of crosshairs appear over it. That's how you know the snap is working. If it doesn't appear, try deactivating Snaps Toggle and then reactivating it.

Once you're sure the snap is working, click on vertex #29, and then click on vertex #26. One thing to note is that it's not necessary to hold down the left mouse button when creating the line, just click once. This is all we need, so right-click to cancel line creation. Then, your next click will start a new line.

Proceed up the leg, connecting the cross-sections until you go from vertex #39 to vertex #17 cross-section, as shown in Figure 2.13. This will be the last horizontal cross-section.

Next will be the vertical cross-sections starting at the wrist between vertex #8 and vertex #11. These are made in the exact same manner as the horizontals.

Proceed up the arm until the last vertical cross-section of vertex #3 and vertex #16 as shown in Figure 2.13.

Before we proceed to the next step, deactivate Snaps Toggle and save your project.

Making the Grid

The next step will be to create the vertical cross-sections up the leg all the way to the top of the shoulder by using the Refine button with the Connect option checked. This creates a new vertex in the middle of an existing spline and allows you to continue on with the new line from there.

Hint: Turn on the Connect option before clicking the Refine button (Figure 2.14).

Click the Refine button. Starting towards the outside edge of the ankle, left-click on the horizontal cross-section to add a vertex as in Figure 2.15.

Figure 2.12

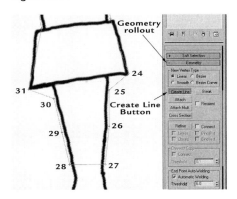

Figure 2.13

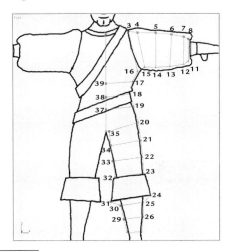

Figure 2.14

Figure 2.15

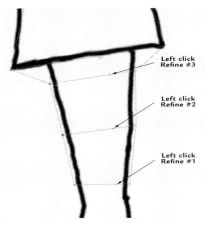

Figure 2.16

Making sure that you refine every horizontal cross-section, keep adding vertices all the way up to the shoulder vertex #2. When you click on vertex #2, the Refine & Connect dialog box will appear. In this case, click Connect Only because you don't want to add another vertex at the shoulder.

The last step is to right-click. This will end refinement and create a line all the way from the ankle to the shoulder. It's always a good idea to save your project with a new name after completing a major operation.

Next we will do the same for the horizontal cross-section of the arm.

Reactivate the Refine button. Starting at the wrist, refine all the way to the centerline as shown in Figure 2.18. Right-click to draw the line.

Repeat the process for another line of detail. Reactivate the Refine button. Starting at the wrist, refine all the vertical cross-sections all the way to vertex #40. Clicking on vertex #40 will bring up the Refine & Connect dialog box. Click Connect Only, then right-click to stop refining and draw the line.

Figure 2.17

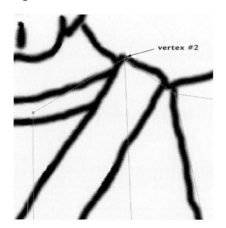

Figure 2.18

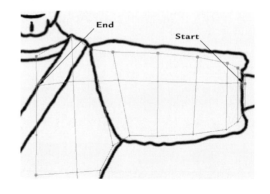

Figure 2.19

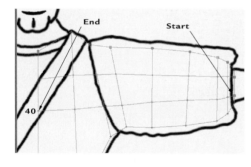

Figure 2.20

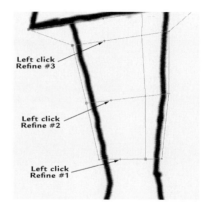

To complete the grid we need one more vertical cross-section starting at the ankle and ending at the collarbone, as shown in Figure 2.21. Remember to right-click to finish and create the line.

Check Your Work

Step back and take a look at your work.

Change to the Vertex sub-object level and select all the vertices of the shape.

You might notice that some of the vertices have handles or that some segments are curved. This happens sometimes when you are using the Refine button. It is very easy to drag just a little when you're clicking on the line. This will create a Bezier type of vertex.

To correct it, select all the vertices using the window select by left-clicking and dragging around all the vertices. Then right-click any place, and from the upper left-hand quad menu, click on the word "Corner." You will see that all the lines of your model will become straight.

This is a good time to save your work. The next step will be a big one, and you may want to give it a couple of tries.

Figure 2.21

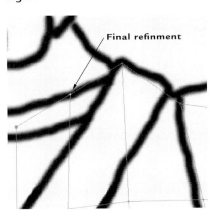

Figure 2.22

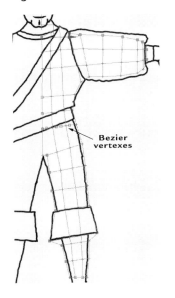

Figure 2.23

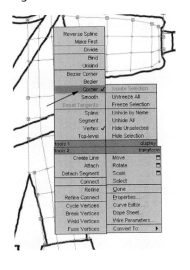

Figure 2.24

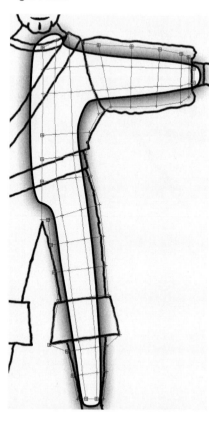

Going 3D

At this point your model is two dimensional—in other words, flat. We are now going to pull it into the third dimension. First, we are going to select all the vertices on the inside of the model and then move them out. It's very important that you get all the vertices selected because there are actually two vertices on top of each other where lines intersect.

Use the rectangular selection method to select the pairs of vertices circled in Figure 2.24.

Once we have selected the vertices, we should rotate our viewport so that we can see both front- and side-view images. Use the Alt-middle mouse button to rotate your viewport by dragging down and just a little to the left.

Before moving the vertices, we should make sure that the Automatic Welding option is unchecked. (It's in the Geometry rollout under End Point Auto-Welding.) Otherwise, a bunch of unrelated vertices will be connected based on proximity, and that's not exactly what we want right now.

Choose the Select and Move tool and move the selected vertices on the Y-axis out to the front of the body in the side view, as shown in Figure 2.26.

Figure 2.26

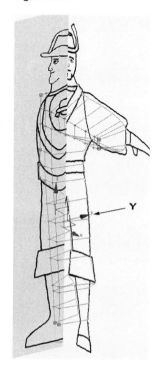

Figure 2.25

Uncheck

For the torso, not all of the vertices need to be aligned with the front outline of the body. Only the first two centerline rows of vertices need to be that far out.

Move the noncenter vertices toward the back on the Y-axis only.

Take a look at the ankles and wrists. You can see that they are way too thick and need to be moved back on the Y-axis.

Wow, this guy has amazingly large ankles! Take a look ahead to Figure 2.34 so that you can see where we are going.

Remember to move only on the Y-axis. It is good for your line to match the image as closely as possible, but don't worry too much about it now. The model will be modified and cleaned up several times before we are finished.

This looks much better. If you haven't caught on yet, we are literally drawing our polygons. Remember we need three- or four-sided shapes to create our surface. There are two spots in

Figure 2.27

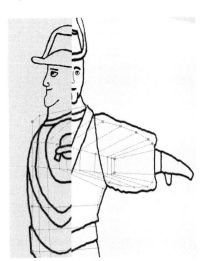

Figure 2.28

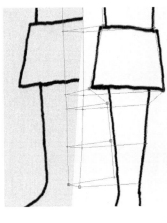

Figure 2.29

Figure 2.30

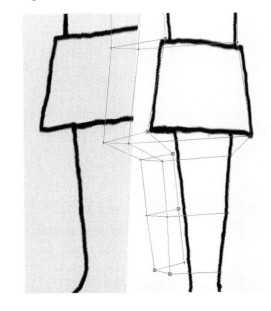

Figure 2.31

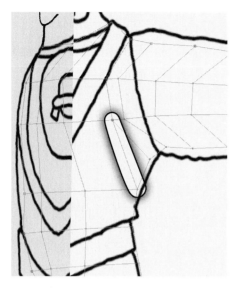

our spline that have five sides. Can you spot them? The first one we are going to fix is under the arm.

Remember to turn Snaps Toggle on. Then use the Create Line button to create the underarm line circled in Figure 2.31, turning a five-sided shape into a four-sided shape and a three-sided shape.

The second one is on the front of the pants.

First we have to refine the segment as shown in Figure 2.32 and then move the new vertex forward on the Y-axis only. Remember to turn off Snaps Toggle before you move the new vertex.

Click the Create Line button. Make sure Snaps Toggle is turned back on and create the new line circled in Figure 2.32.

We have checked our spline and closed all the five-sided shapes. Now it's time to look at our work.

Right-click on the active viewport label to bring up the display properties. In Figure 2.33 it's a User viewport, but it works in all of them. Make sure the Smooth + Highlights option is

Figure 2.32

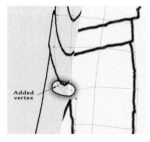

Figure 2.33

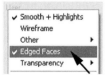

Figure 2.34

checked, and then check the Edged Faces option as well. The Edged Faces option allows you to see the wire frame and the shaded mesh at the same time.

From the Modifier List drop-down menu, select Surface to put a surface on the splines. If your mesh doesn't look like Figure 2.35, first check the Flip Normals box. Then set the Patch Topology steps to zero by right-clicking the values spinner.

Check your model and look for any holes in the mesh.

Fixing a Hole

If you find a hole, activate the Vertex sub-object level. When you do, your surface should disappear. Don't panic. When you pick a modifier below the top of the stack, you can't automatically see modifiers that are applied above it. To do that, you can toggle the Show End Result button as shown in Figure 2.36.

Look for any vertices that are close to each other but not on top of each other. They are usually in the center of an open area or around the edge of an open area.

Using a rectangular selection marquee, select the two vertices and click the Fuse button. This will place them directly on top of each other, and the mesh will be whole.

If that fails, it might be that, although it looks like there are two vertices, in fact there is only one. Sometimes two splines cross but only one of them has a vertex at the junction.

To find out how many vertices you have selected, look at the bottom of the Selection rollout. It should say "2 Vertices Selected." If it says something like "Spline 18/Vert 11 Selected," it means there is only one vertex at that junction.

To fix it, figure out which segment has the vertex by moving it up or down a little. Then add a vertex to the other line using the Refine button *without* the Connect option checked.

Figure 2.35

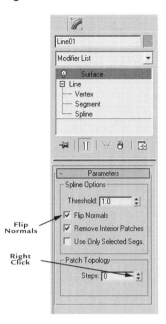

Figure 2.36

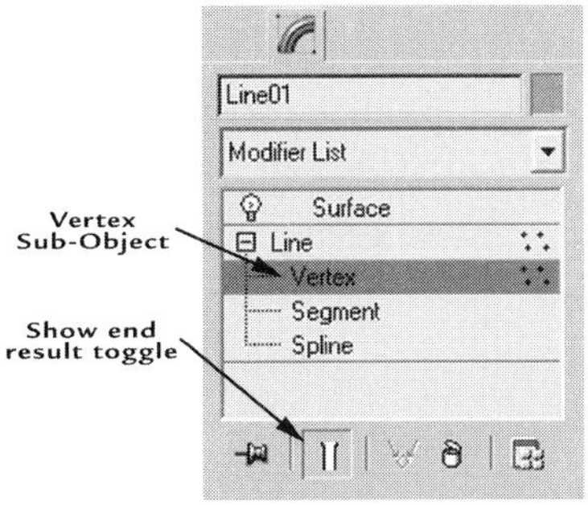

Figure 2.37

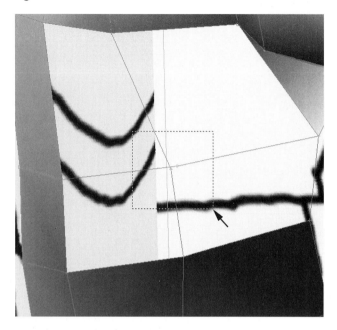

Select both vertices as shown in Figure 2.37 and click the Fuse button as shown in Figure 2.38.

This should fix any problems. If it doesn't, you should probably start again. Do not worry; practice makes perfect. Starting over is part of the learning process. It will become easier to use the tools, and you will make fewer mistakes the second time around.

Almost Halftime

Now we have one quarter of a pirate—isn't that amazing! We will be using the same technique for the head.

The next step will be to copy and mirror the front quarter panel to the back and hook the two together, but first we have a little cleaning up to do.

We have to remove the Surface modifier from our splines so that we can hook the front and back pieces together. Afterwards we can reapply it.

Figure 2.38

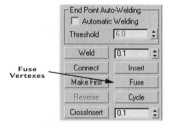

Figure 2.39

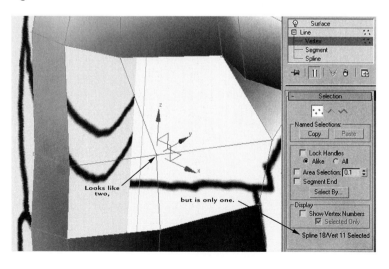

By right-clicking on the Surface modifier in the modifier stack area you will get a pop-up window with Cut, Copy, and Paste options. Select Cut.

Now we need to hide the front- and side-view planes. Currently, they are frozen and cannot be selected. So I want to show you a little shortcut that will both unfreeze and select the planes. It's no big secret; in fact, it's towards the right side of the Main toolbar, the Named Selection Sets pull-down menu. This is a menu that contains the selection sets that are associated with your project. It is blank until you choose a set.

If you click the arrow down button, you will see the selection sets that I have set up for you.

Select the Views set, and you will get a pop-up window asking if you want to unfreeze. Click Yes.

The planes will be unfrozen and selected. Right-click anywhere in the active viewport. In the upper right-hand corner of the quad menu, select Hide Selection as shown in Figure 2.43. Now is a good time to save your project with a new name.

Figure 2.40

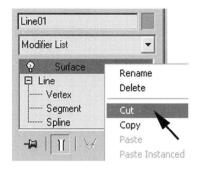

Figure 2.41

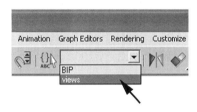

Figure 2.42

Figure 2.43

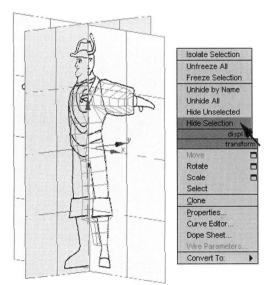

Figure 2.44

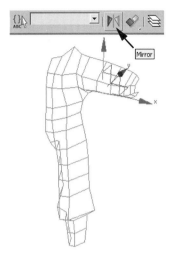

Figure 2.45

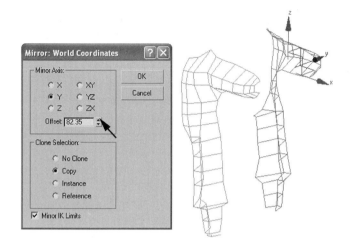

Figure 2.46

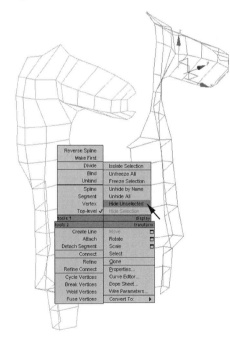

Mirror

The process of mirroring is done at the object level. When using the mirror tool, objects are transformed or copied along their pivot points on one or two axes.

From a User or Perspective viewport, select the spline. The button right next to the Named Selection Sets pull-down menu is the Mirror button. Click it, and the Mirror: Screen Coordinates dialog box will appear.

Change the Mirror Axis to Y and the Clone Selection to Copy. Increase the Offset value to around 70 so that the distance from the original to the copy is about that shown in Figure 2.45.

Before we can attach the two quarters into a single object, we have to do a little cleanup on the copy.

First, let's hide the front quarter spline so that we can work on the back quarter easily.

Figure 2.47

Figure 2.48

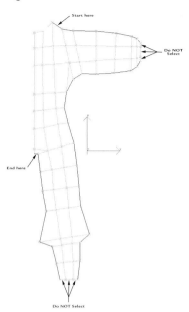

Figure 2.49

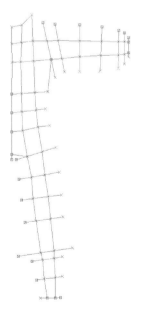

With the back quarter selected, right-click anywhere in the viewport and select Hide Unselected from the upper right-hand quad menu. That should leave only the back quarter visible.

Now change to the Front viewport by pressing the F key.

This copy of our original spline actually has more segments than we need. So the next step is to delete the redundant segments of the spline so that we can get a clean connection to the front quarter.

Change to the Select Object tool by right-clicking in the viewport and from the lower right-hand quad menu choosing Select.

Activate the Segment sub-object and select the segments around the outside as shown in Figure 2.48. Make sure you don't select the segments around the neck, wrist, and ankle, and along the centerline.

Press Delete and away they go! Figure 2.49 shows the spline with the segments removed.

Figure 2.50

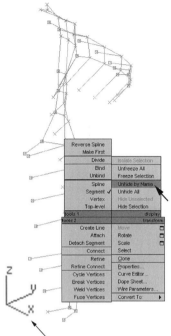

Viewport World-Space Tripod

Figure 2.51

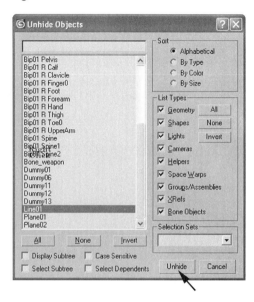

Rotate your viewport using the Alt-middle mouse button down and to the left until the world axis located at the bottom left-hand corner of the viewport looks like the one enlarged in Figure 2.50. This is a very important operation because it sets up our viewing angle to see both of the splines we are joining together. So spend a little time getting it just right.

Right-click anywhere, and from the upper right-hand quad menu, select Unhide by Name. In the Unhide Objects dialog box, scroll down until you see "Line01." Select it and click Unhide as shown in Figure 2.51.

Getting Attached

Now that both the front and back splines are visible, we need to make them one by using the Attach option.

The Attach button is active at any line sub-object level and is used to join two objects to create a single one. There is also an Attach Mult. button so that if you need to attach multiple objects, you can do it all at once.

With the back quarter still selected, click the Attach button at the top of the Geometry rollout, and in the viewport select the front quarter spline. The two are now joined into a single spline. Make sure to turn off the Attach tool by clicking on the button again.

Change to the Vertex sub-object level and select all the vertices on the back quarter.

Figure 2.52

Figure 2.53

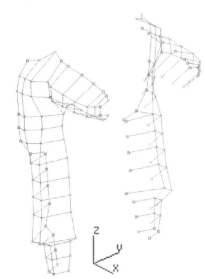

Activate the Select and Move tool and activate Snaps Toggle. Right-click on it to check and make sure that only the Vertex option is checked.

There is one more setting to adjust before we move the two quarters together. Remember the Automatic Welding option we turned off before? Well, now we are going to use it to weld the vertices automatically as we bring the two quarters together. We have to lower the Threshold value to 2.0 so that we don't weld everything together. Turn off the Snap toggle.

From the outside ankle vertex, click and drag the back quarter to the same vertex on the front quarter as shown in Figures 2.55, 2.56, and 2.57. Then a bunch of green Bezier handles will show up.

Select all the vertices, right-click, and, from the upper left-hand quad menu, select the Corner type.

That should make all the lines between vertices straight. If you ever start to see curved lines between vertices you can always repeat this process. Make sure to close your line by left-clicking on the word line in the Modify Stack area until it turns gray.

Figure 2.54

Check

Figure 2.55

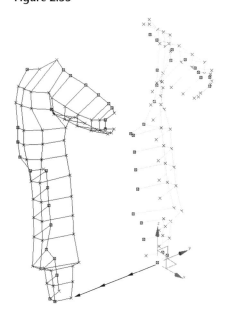

Figure 2.56

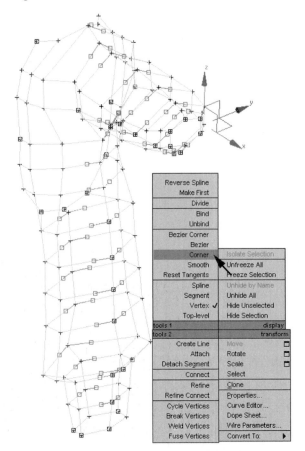

Figure 2.57

Figure 2.58

Figure 2.59

Figure 2.60

Figure 2.61

Smooth + Highlights
Wireframe
Other ▶
Edged Faces
Transparency ▶

Show Grid
Show Background
Show Safe Frame

Viewport Clipping
Texture Correction
Disable View

Views ▶   Perspective
                 User
Undo View Pan   Front
Redo   Back
                 Top
Configure...   Bottom
                 Left
                 Right
                 ActiveShade
                 Schematic ▶
                 Grid ▶
                 Extended ▶
                 Shape

Figure 2.62

Uncheck ⟶   End Point Auto-Welding
            ☐ Automatic Welding
            Threshold 2.0

Figure 2.63

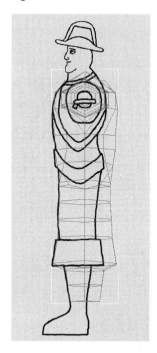

Figure 2.64

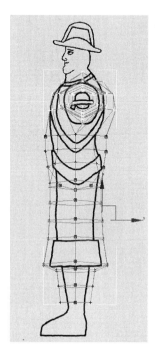

The Shape of Things

At the moment, the back of the model is an exact mirror of the front, which is not very realistic. We need to unhide the images we are using for reference and use them to customize this half of the model before we make a copy of it to complete the model.

From the Named Selection Sets menu, select Views. Click Yes, and your reference images will be visible and selected.

Right-click anywhere and, from the upper right-hand quad menu, select Freeze Selection. The plans are now frozen, and you will not be able to select or move them.

Change to the Right viewport by right-clicking on the viewport label and choosing Views>Right. There is no default keyboard shortcut for the Right viewport.

Before we start moving things around, make sure that the Automatic Welding option is unchecked and the Snaps toggle is off.

Looking at our model from this side, the first thing you will notice is that the centerline is not running down the center of the leg as it should be; select all the vertices from under the arm down to the ankle and move them as shown in Figure 2.63.

Use a rectangular selection marquee to select pairs of vertices and move them closer to the shape of the model sheet. Take your time and make your selections carefully until your model looks like Figure 2.64.

Figure 2.65

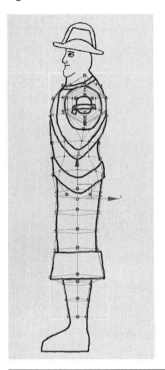

Figure 2.66

Figure 2.67

Front

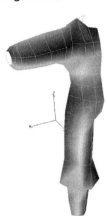

Back

Don't worry if your model is not exactly perfect; all that's necessary is a reasonable approximation.

Notice that I put a little curve in the vertices under the arm and in the low back. I moved the pairs of vertices back and forth until the curve looked good. At this time I don't want you to move them up or down on the Z-axis, just back and forth.

Also take a close look at the back of the neck and upper back. This area should have its own curve.

Check your work by adding the Surface modifier and hiding the reference images. Then save your project with a new name.

Going Poly

Figure 2.68

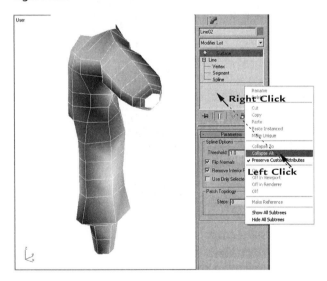

Now that the base of the character is made, it's time to convert the spline model into polygons. This is a fairly easy process, but there are a couple of things that are absolutely necessary to check before conversion. One thing to check before we go on is that there are no holes anywhere in your model. If there are, then they have to be closed before moving on. Also, in the Surface modifier make sure that, under Patch Topology, Steps is set to 0.

Then right-click in the modifier stack area and choose Collapse All.

Finally, right-click in the modifier stack area and choose Convert To: Editable Poly. Now that the model is polygonal, it's time to start working on the hand.

Figure 2.69

Figure 2.70

Figure 2.71

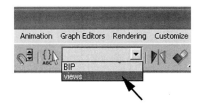

Figure 2.72

Lending a Hand

The technique that we are going to use for making the hand is a little bit different from the method we used for the body. We already have a base to work off: the wrist. So we are going to extrude the wrist edges out from there to create the extra geometry we need to shape a hand. We are going to start working on the left hand. Hands are very complex body parts, but for this video game all we need is a fairly simple object, so some corners will be cut. Fingers are not an integral part of the game play, so we will be making a simple hand with one big finger and a thumb, like a mitten.

We are going to start by unhiding the reference planes in the views selection set.

Click the Named Selection Set menu. Select the Views set, and you will get a pop-up window asking if you want to unfreeze. Click Yes.

The planes will be unhidden and selected. Right-click anywhere in the active viewport and, in the upper right-hand corner of the quad menu, select Freeze Selection, as shown in Figure 2.73.

Figure 2.73

Figure 2.74

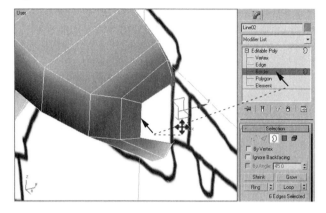

There are some similarities between spline manipulation and the way we can edit using the Editable Poly mode. An editable poly object has a unique sub-object level called Border. The Border sub-object allows you to select all the edges around the wrist with a single click. However, you have to make sure that the Edged Faces option is enabled so that you can see your selection.

Right-click on the viewport label and make sure the Edged Faces option is checked.

Select your model and in the Modifier Stack area click on the plus next to the word Editable Poly and activate the Border sub-object level and then select one of the edges around the wrist

Holding the Shift key, move the Border selection on the X-axis approximately five units out. Repeat two more times; this will create the wrist and thumb areas of the hand.

Holding the Shift key again, move the same selection on the X-axis approximately seven units out. Repeat two more times; this will create the "fingers" area of the hand.

Figure 2.75

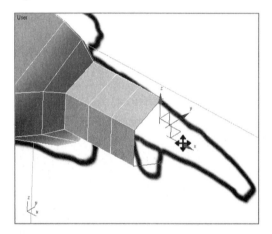

Figure 2.76

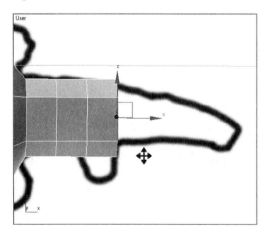

Figure 2.77

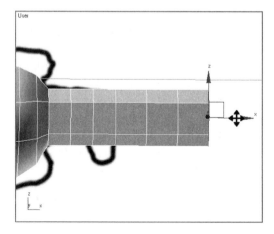

Figure 2.78

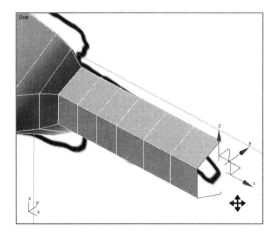

Another unique feature of the Border sub-object is the Cap function. Click the Cap button and the tip of the fingers will be closed up by polygons. This would be a good time to save your project with a new name.

Figure 2.79

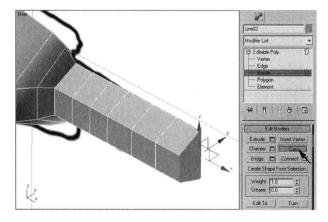

Now that we have the base geometry, we are going to start shaping the hand. First, in order to be able to work on the mesh and see the reference image, we need to make the mesh transparent. The hot key for that function is Alt-X, for what is called See-Through mode.

Start by pressing Alt-X, changing to the Front viewport, and activating the Vertex sub-object level.

Figure 2.80

From the Front viewport you will notice that the hand is a little bit too round, so let's fix that first. Be careful of your next couple of selections because you will be selecting vertices behind the image planes. Even though you can't see them, they will be selected. If you have problems, you can always hide the image planes and then unhide them at any time.

Using a rectangular selection marquee, select all the vertices on the top of the hand and move them down.

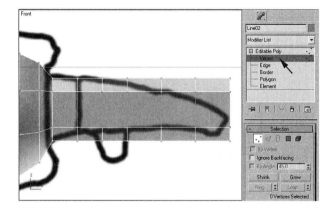

Figure 2.81

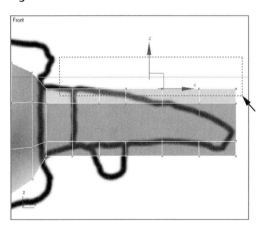

Then, pressing the Ctrl key while dragging, add the top-edge vertices to the selection, as shown in Figure 2.82. Move the bunch of them down.

Now we'll invert the process.

Select the vertices of the bottom of the hand and move them up. Then add the bottom edge vertices to the selection, as shown in Figure 2.84, and move the bunch of them up.

If necessary, you can move the whole hand up or down to center it on the arm. Just select all the vertices of the hand and move them.

Figure 2.82

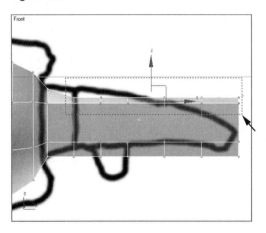

Figure 2.83

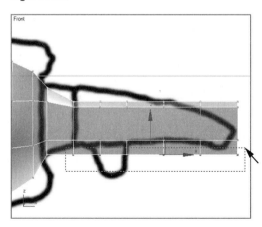

Figure 2.84

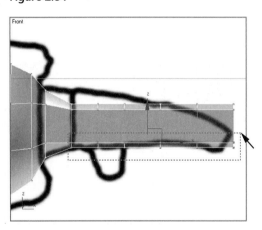

Figure 2.85

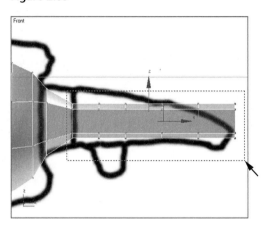

The last part of the hand we need to make is the thumb.

Change to the Polygon sub-object level and select the polygon shown in Figure 2.86.

Click on the settings button next to the Extrude button, and from the pop-up window change the Extrusion Height: value to 5. Then click on the Apply button once and then the OK button once. This will give you two extrusion segments and all the geometry you need to make the thumb.

So far we have shaped the hand from the side view; now it's time to shape it from the top view.

Change to the Top viewport. Change to the Vertex sub-object level and, using a rectangular selection marquee, select vertices and move them until the hand looks like that in Figure 2.89. This is a good time to save your project with a new name.

Figure 2.86

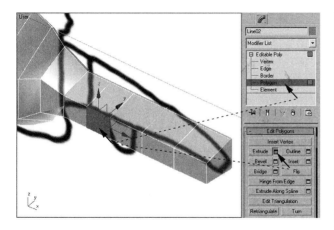

Figure 2.87

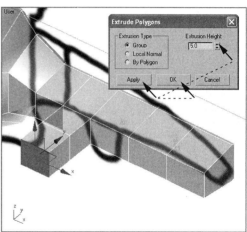

Figure 2.88

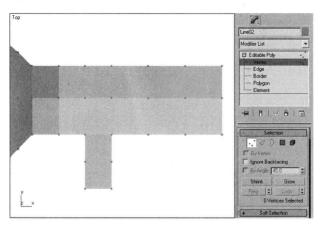

Figure 2.89

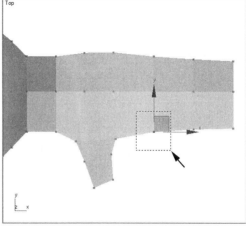

Figure 2.90

Figure 2.91

Figure 2.92

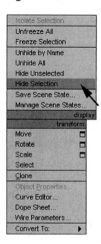

That should do it for the hand. If you want, you can hide the reference planes and check out your work.

To hide the reference planes, click the Named Selection Set menu. Select the Views set, and you will get a pop-up window asking if you want to select frozen. Click Yes.

The planes will be unfrozen and selected. Right-click anywhere in the active viewport and, in the upper right-hand corner of the quad menu, select Hide Selection, as shown in Figure 2.92.

Getting the Boot

We will create the boot using the same basic method that we used for the hand.

To begin creating the boot, we will need the reference images again.

From the Named Selection Sets menu, select Views and click Yes. Both planes should appear and be selected.

Figure 2.93

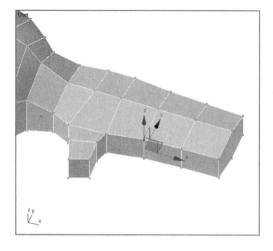

Figure 2.94

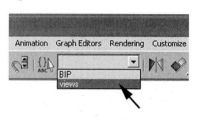

Figure 2.95

Figure 2.96

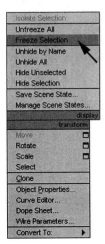

Figure 2.97

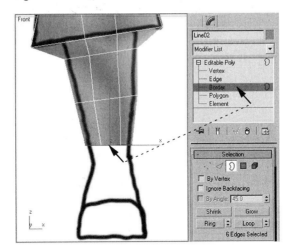

Right-click and, from the upper right-hand quad menu, select Freeze Selection. Now we cannot accidentally select them.

Change to the Front viewport. Select your model and change to the Border sub-object level and select one of the ankle edges. Activate the Move tool and, holding the Shift key, move and copy the edges down about five units as shown in Figure 2.98.

Repeat the process and copy the segments down two times, approximately 10 units each.

Just like we did with the hand, the last step is to cap the Border selection by clicking on the Cap button.

For the next step we are going to do something new. We are going to use the Select and Uniform Scale tool to move

Figure 2.98

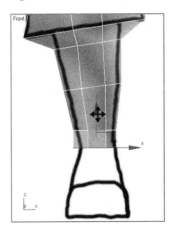

Figure 2.99

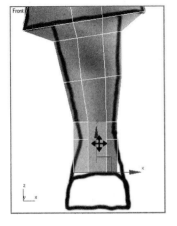

Figure 2.100

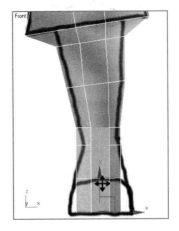

Figure 2.101

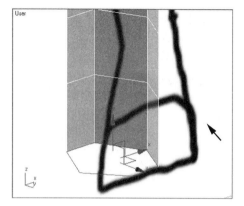

Figure 2.102

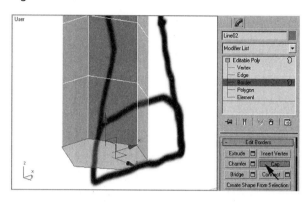

Figure 2.103

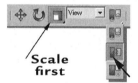

Figure 2.104

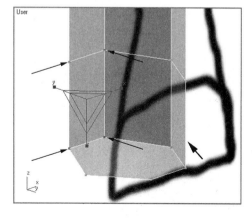

some vertices. That may seem a little strange, but it is useful. Change to the Select and Uniform Scale tool. To the right of the Reference Coordinate System drop-down menu is the Use Pivot Point button. This allows you to choose where the pivot of your group will be. The pivot is the origin point for transform operations like moving or scaling. Left-click and hold on the button. From the pop-up menu select the middle option, Use Selection Center. This option puts the group's pivot in the geometric center of the group. Now when we have two vertices selected, the Select and Uniform Scale tool will scale to and from the center point of them.

Change to the Vertex sub-object level and rotate your viewport so that you can see the front of the "leg."

Select the four vertices shown in Figure 2.104. Scale them on the X-axis only, until it looks like that in Figure 2.105.

Now we are going to make the geometry for the toe of the boot.

Rotate your viewport so that you can see the front of the leg. Change to the Polygon sub-object level and select the Polygon shown in Figure 2.106. Then click on the Settings button next to the Extrude button and, from the popup, change the Extrusion Height to 7. Finally, click on the Apply button two times and the OK button once. This should give you three total extrusions.

Finally, to finish off the boot, let's give it some shape. Change to the Right viewport. Change to the Vertex sub-object level and using a rectangular selection marquee select vertices and move them until your boot looks like that in Figure 2.110. Then rotate your

Figure 2.105

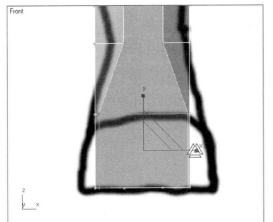

Figure 2.106

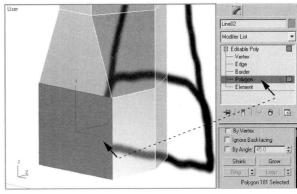

Figure 2.108

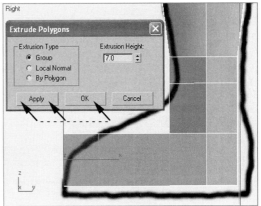

Figure 2.107

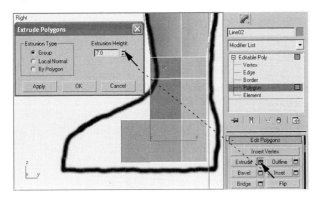

Figure 2.109

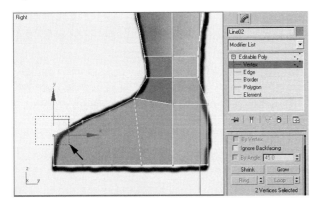

Figure 2.110

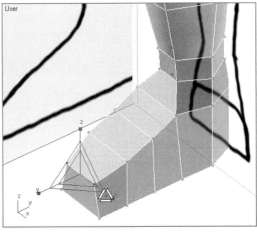

Figure 2.111

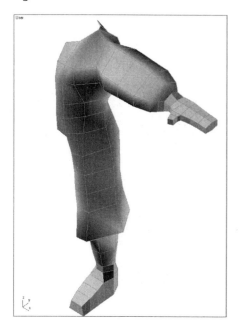

Figure 2.112

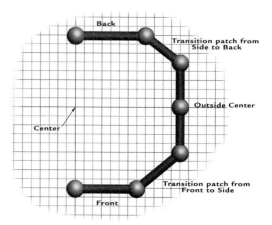

Figure 2.113

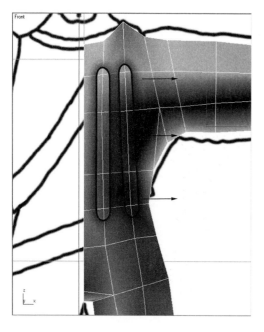

viewport and, using the scale tool, you can shape the toe a little on the X-axis.

That's it. The boot is modeled. Now you can zoom out, hit the Alt-X hotkey, and check your work. You now have half a body. However, this half of the body could still use some adjusting to better match our model sheet.

Getting in Shape

The curve around the waist needs some work. It is kind of difficult to see from a Perspective viewport, but from the top it should look like Figure 2.112. You can see that flat spots on the front and back of the body need to be relatively large compared to the transition patches.

To get our model's chest and waist rounder we are going to move the vertices around in the Front viewport. The edges circled in Figure 2.113 need to be moved toward the outside of the body. You might ask, "Why not just move the edges?" The answer is that you can, but it's not as easy as moving vertices around. And in this case you want to use the rectangular selection marquee to select both the front and back vertices.

Switch to the Front viewport. Activate the See-Through mode by the Alt-X hotkey so that you can see the reference image and change to the Vertex sub-object level. Use the rectangular selection marquee to select both the front and back vertices and move them at the same time until your chest and waist look like those in Figure 2.115.

Figure 2.114

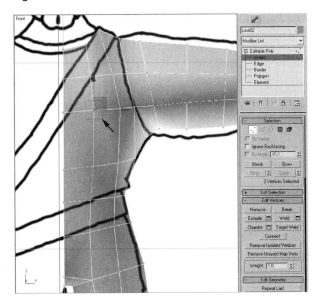

Figure 2.115

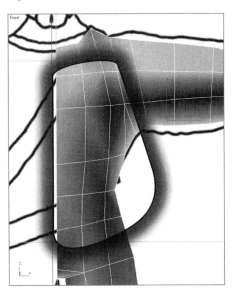

The next part that needs some rounding is the leg. Moving the center vertices toward the outside will round out the bottom of the pant leg.

Use the rectangular selection marquee to select both the front and back vertices and move them at the same time until your pant leg looks like that in Figure 2.117.

Figure 2.116

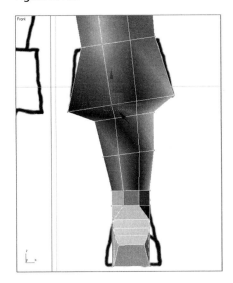

Figure 2.117

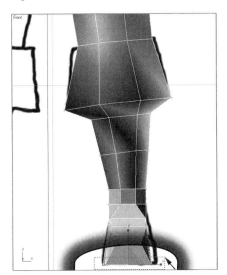

Figure 2.118

This is a good time to scale the bottom of the boot. Using the rectangular selection marquee, select all the vertices of the bottom of the boot and change to the Scale tool. Make sure the Pivot Point button is set to Use Selection Center and scale the selection out on the X-axis only.

The next area is the upper leg area. Use the rectangular selection marquee to select both the front and back vertices and move them out at the same time until your upper leg looks like that in Figure 2.121.

The last place that can use some rounding is in the arm area. Start with the Scale tool and straighten the vertical cross-sections if they are not already scaled.

By selecting all the vertices of the cross-section and using the Scale tool with the pivot button set to Use Selection center, scale down on the X-axis and the vertices will line up.

Now, to round out the arm, the two center horizontal cross-sections need to be moved out toward the top and bottom of the arm.

Remember to use the rectangular selection marquee to select the back-side vertex. Then move the pairs out so that the polygons are about the same size vertically.

Figure 2.119

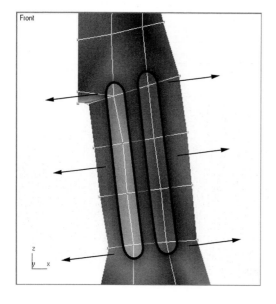

Figure 2.120

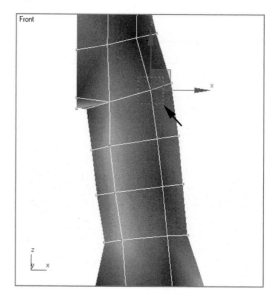

Figure 2.121

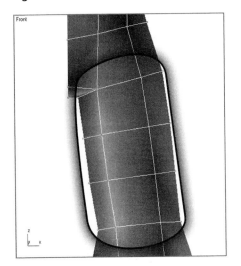

Figure 2.122

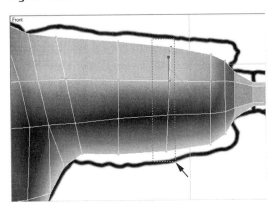

Figure 2.123

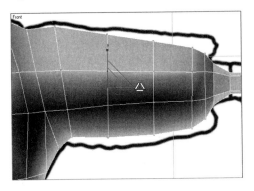

Figure 2.124

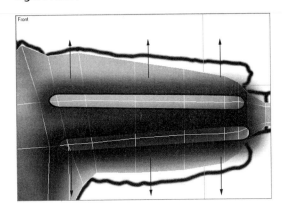

Figure 2.125

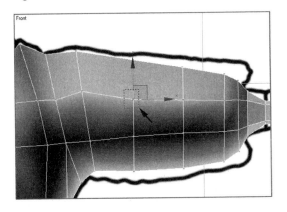

Figure 2.126

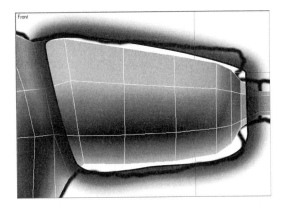

There is one more little edit to make. You need to close the neck hole and model a "neck" for the head to rest on. Start by rotating your viewport so that you can see the neck area clearly.

Change to the Edge sub-object level and select the two edges, as shown in Figure 2.127.

Click on the Settings button next to the Bridge button and, in the popup, change the Segments value to 3. This will connect the two edges with three polygons. The one in the middle will be the neck. Click OK.

To fill in the final hole, change to the Border sub-object level and select one of the edges around the hole. Then press the cap button.

You might be wondering why in this case a five-sided shape is OK. Well, the rules for meshes are different from those for splines and, actually, it's not a five-sided shape—it's just three triangles put together.

Figure 2.127

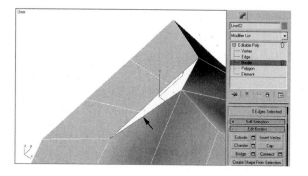

Figure 2.128

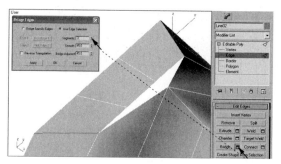

Figure 2.129

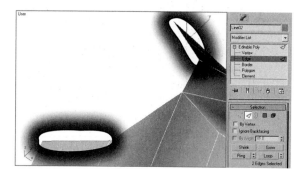

Figure 2.130

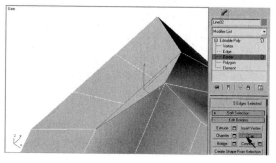

Now let's make the neck geometry.

Change to the Polygon sub-object level and select the polygon in the middle of the bridged edges. Change to the Front viewport and move it up about three units. Then click on the Settings button next to the Bevel Polygon button. In the pop-up window, first change the Height value to 6, then change the Outline Amount to a negative number. Your amount may be different from mine; just change the amount until the centerline edge is vertical. Then click OK.

This creates one extra polygon on the inside. Rotate your viewport and select the polygon shown in Figure 2.134 and delete it.

That's not it for the neck, however. It's a little on the skinny side, so let's make it thicker.

Figure 2.131

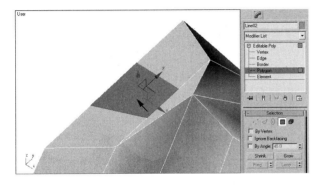

Figure 2.132

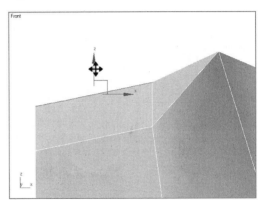

Figure 2.133

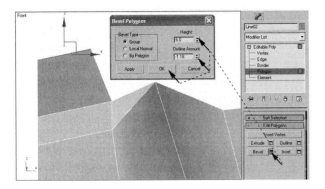

Figure 2.134

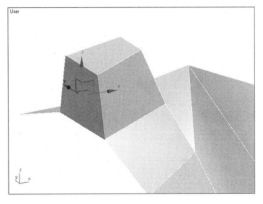

Figure 2.135

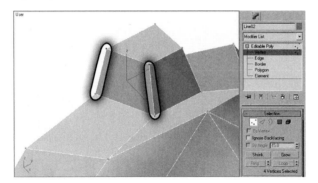

Figure 2.136

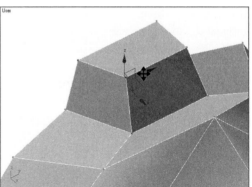

Figure 2.137

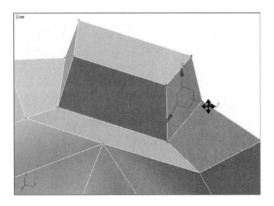

Figure 2.138

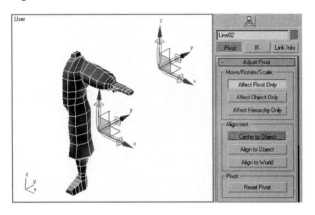

Change to the Vertex sub-object level and select the four vertices on the front of the neck and move them forward on the Y-axis three units or so.

Then, select the four vertices of the back of the neck and move them back on the Y-axis three units or so. Now is a good time to save your project with a new name.

Mirror, Mirror

That should be enough editing for now, so let's get to the mirror process and take a look at our work. This finishes the body geometry, but before we make it whole, there is one more little step.

Change to the Hierarchy panel and activate the Affect Pivot Only button and click on the Center to Object. This will put the pivot point of the body somewhere under the arm.

Change back to the Modify panel and add the Symmetry modifier.

You should get something like Figure 2.139, but don't worry; it's easy to fix.

Open the Symmetry modifier and change to the Mirror sub-object level. Then move the Mirror gizmo to the left on the X-axis only until you get a whole body.

A thing to note:

If you are using an editable mesh (which we are not doing here), the Symmetry modifier works a little bit differently with an editable mesh than with an editable poly object. The easiest solution is to convert your editable mesh into an editable poly before applying the symmetry modifier. If that is not possible for whatever reason, there is a solution.

After applying the Symmetry modifier and moving the mirror plane to the centerline, right-click anywhere in one of the viewports and, from the quad menu, select the Properties... option.

From the Object Properties popup, uncheck the Edges Only box and click the OK button.

Figure 2.139

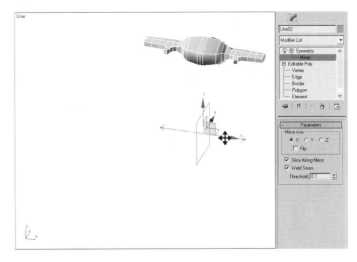

Figure 2.140

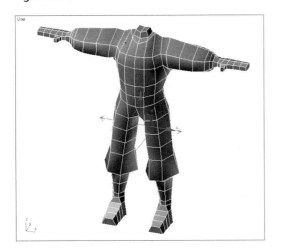

Figure 2.141

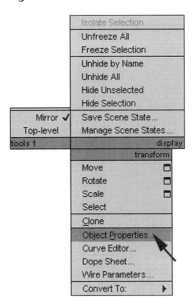

Figure 2.142

Figure 2.143

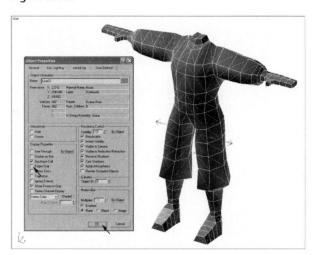

You should now see dotted edges all over your model. The problem we are trying to fix is how the Symmetry modifier welds the two halves together.

So zoom in and check the entire seam, from top to bottom. You may find extra polygons. If you find any bad welds (as shown in Figure 2.144), increase the weld Threshold value to 2 and it should weld them up.

In an editable poly object the Symmetry modifier will not create extra polygons around the seam.

Once the seam is good, you should turn off the hidden edges the same way you turned them on.

Figure 2.144

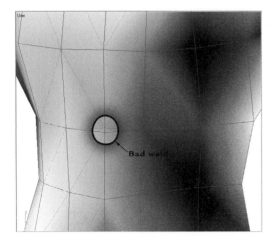

Figure 2.145

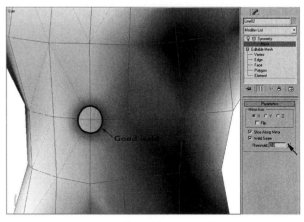

Figure 2.146

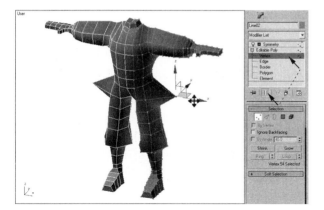

Figure 2.147

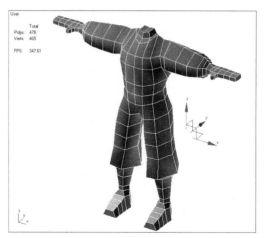

Now is the time to make any edits that your model might need. The nice thing about the Symmetry modifier is that if you make a change to one half, it is automatically applied to the mirror. This will help you trim the waistline or buff the chest out and keep your model symmetrical.

It is really hard to imagine what your model will look like until you get both halves together. So take a good look all around your model.

Change to the Vertex sub-object level and click the Show End Result button.

Now you can move the vertices around on your model. Keep in mind that the vertices around the centerline of the body should only be moved on the Z–Y axes.

Once you're done editing, press the number 7 on your keyboard. You should now see the total number of polygons displayed in the upper left-hand corner of the active viewport. Check to see if you have the same numbers that I do. You should have around 400; if you have a lot more, say 800 or more, then you have a big problem. More than likely when you collapsed your spline model the Patch Topology value was not set to 0. If you're off by ±100 or more, then you should check your model for any holes and close them up.

Figure 2.148

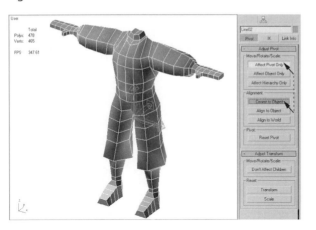

One more thing to do before we start on the head is to center the pivot point. Change to the Hierarchy tab and click on the Affect Pivot Only button and then the Center to Object button. Then save your project with a new name.

That's it for the body. Right-click in the viewport and hide the body.

Now we are going to build the head. First, we have to unhide the reference images again if they are not already visible. Once they are visible, remember to right-click and freeze them.

Figure 2.149

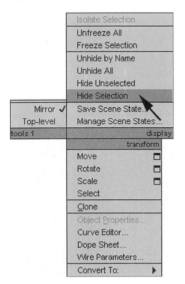

Figure 2.150

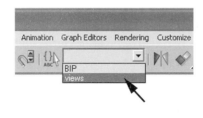

Figure 2.151

Figure 2.152

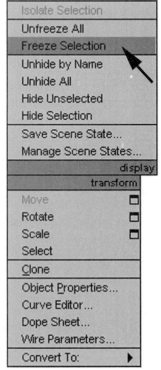

Building a Better Head

Now we are going to build a head using a similar method to the one we learned from building the body. However, this time we are going to work on separate areas of the face and bring them all together into a complete head. This way we can create a detailed face with relative ease.

In the brief history of 3D video games, characters have been very restricted in the number of polygons they could use. Even many of the games currently on the shelf are simplified to the point that the head is just an oblong sphere with a nice map to make it look like a more detailed object.

However, in the newest and future generations of games, heads will not be just mapped spheres. They will need details, even down to functional eyelids, so a sphere will just not cut it.

So we are going to make a fairly detailed face, what you might call a baseline face. It has all the major features that can be easily refined into high detail. With the addition of more splines and, of course, more time, this face can be used for high-poly applications.

Getting a Head

We will be creating a head with simplified eyes, mouth, and nose. We will not use splines to make an ear because ears can be easily extruded after the spline has been collapsed to an editable poly model.

Starting with just the reference images visible, we will be working on the eye area first. From there we'll work our way out.

Change to the Front viewport and zoom in on the head in the reference image.

We are going to start creating the eye area.

Create a new spline outlining the eye. Start in the corner of the left eye and create a six-sided shape, as shown in Figure 2.153.

Rotate your viewport and you will see that your new spline is too deep in the Y-axis and that you will need to move it forward. Rotate even more so that you have a mostly side view. Now, move the eye spline forward on the Y-axis only, until it is in the position shown in Figure 2.155.

Figure 2.153

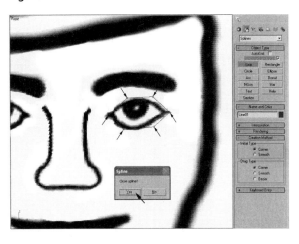

Change to the Vertex sub-object level. Select the two corner vertices of the eye and move them back on the Y-axis only, as shown in Figure 2.156.

Figure 2.154

Figure 2.155

Figure 2.156

Switch to the Front viewport.

Change to the Segment sub-object level and select the three segments on the top of the eye spline. We are going to copy them up three times.

In the Geometry rollout, make sure that, under Connect Copy, the Connect box is checked.

Holding down the Shift key, move and copy them up three times, as shown in Figure 2.157.

Select the bottom of the eye segments and copy them down three times, as shown in Figure 2.159.

Figure 2.157

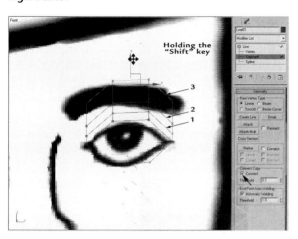

Figure 2.158

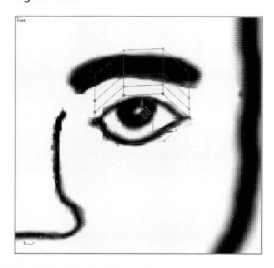

Figure 2.159

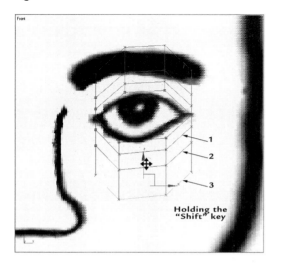

Figure 2.160

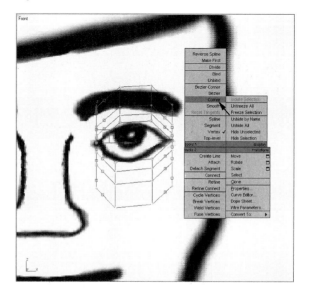

Eye Contact

Before we start to shape the eye patch a little, we should change to the Vertex sub-object level and select all the vertices of the eye patch. Right-click anywhere and change them all to the Corner type.

Now we are going to shape the inside corner of the eye.

Change to the Vertex sub-object level and make sure the Automatic Welding option is checked off.

Make sure to turn off Snaps Toggle before moving things around.

Remember that there are two vertices right on top of each other, so use a rectangular selection marquee to get both. Move the vertices around to match the spline in Figure 2.161.

For the outside of the eye, move the selected vertices to match Figure 2.162.

A Deep Stare

Our model's eye needs to have some depth as well. The inside corner of the eye needs to be farther forward than the outside of the eye.

We'll do this by selecting a group of vertices, moving them forward a tiny bit, and then deselecting some of them. Then we'll repeat with the new set of vertices. This way we will create depth, including the area from the corner of the eye to the bridge of the nose.

First select all the vertices on the left side of the patch, except for the very corner of the eye, as shown in Figure 2.163.

Figure 2.161

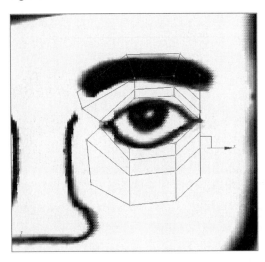

Figure 2.162

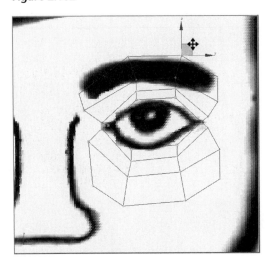

Figure 2.163

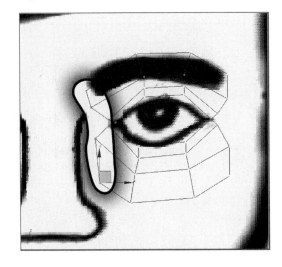

Rotate your viewport to the side and then move the vertices forward on the Y-axis only to about the middle of the patch, as shown in Figure 2.164.

Now deselect the two inner vertices using the Alt key with a rectangular selection, as shown in Figure 2.165.

Move the remaining vertices forward again until they are flush with the front of the patch, as shown in Figure 2.166.

One more time, deselect the inside pairs of vertices and move the remaining ones forward, as shown in Figure 2.167.

Figure 2.164

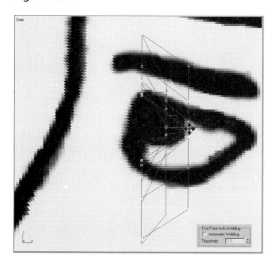

Figure 2.165

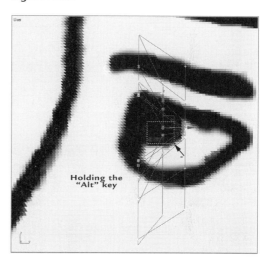

Figure 2.166

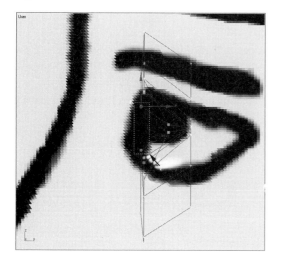

Figure 2.167

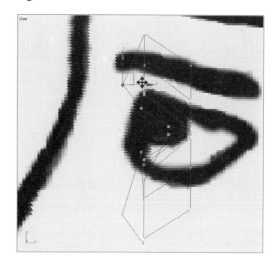

Figure 2.168

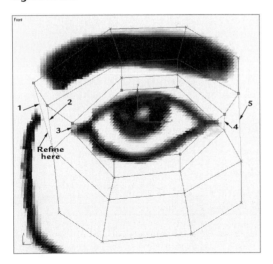

Figure 2.169

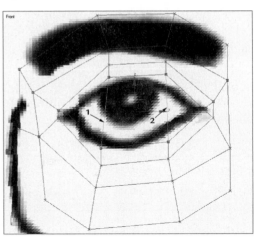

Figure 2.170

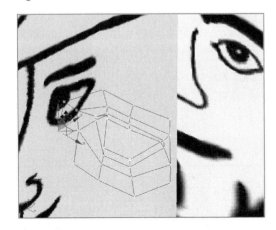

Activate the Front viewport. In the Geometry rollout, click the Create Line button, make sure Snaps Toggle is active, and create the five lines, as shown in Figure 2.168.

On the first segment in Figure 2.168, use the Refine button to add a vertex. Make sure the Snaps toggle is turned off, then move it on the X-axis so that it looks like Figure 2.169, then down and forward on the Y–Z axes, as shown in Figure 2.170.

This will eventually connect the eye patch to the bridge of the nose.

Don't worry too much if it's not exactly like the image. Once we finish the face, we will take some time to clean up.

One more little adjustment is necessary. Select the two pairs of vertices and move them forward on the Y-axis only, as shown in Figure 2.171.

Now let's close the eyeball patch before we move on to creating the mouth patch.

Change to the Front viewport.

In the Geometry rollout, click the Create Line button, make sure Snaps Toggle is active, and create the two lines shown in Figure 2.169.

Figure 2.171

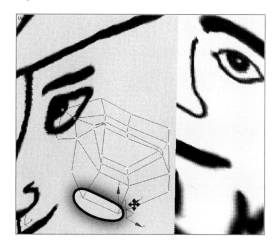

Figure 2.172

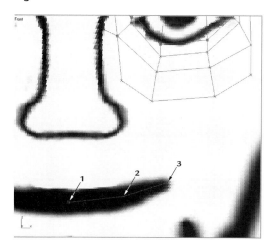

Mouthing Off

We are going to start the mouth patch by making a line from the center of the mouth to the corner of the mouth. Remember we only have to make half the face.

Make sure the Snaps toggle is turned off. With the Front viewport active, click the Create Line button. Click three times to make the mouth spline, as shown in Figure 2.172. Turn off the Create line tool.

Change to the Spline sub-object level and select the mouth spline. Rotate your viewport so that you can see the side as well as the front of the model. Notice that the mouth spline is way too far back. Move it forward on the Y-axis until it's in the right place, as in Figure 2.173.

Rotate your viewport some more, until you get a good side view. Change to the Vertex sub-object and move the corner of the mouth back on the Y-axis until it lines up with the corner of the mouth in the side-view reference image. Adjust the vertex in the middle of the mouth back on the Y-axis just a little.

Figure 2.173

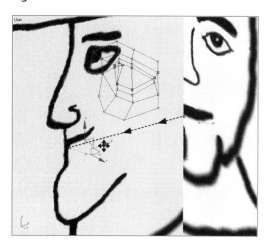

With the Front viewport active, change to the Segment sub-object level. Under Connect Copy, be sure that Connect is checked. Select the centermost lip segment and holding the Shift key; move and copy the segment up two times, as shown in Figure 2.175.

Reselect the original centermost lip segment. Holding the Shift key, move and copy the segment down three times to the top of the chin area, as shown in Figure 2.176. This gives us enough segments to create an upper and lower lip.

To actually make the lips, first rotate your viewport so that you can see the lip segments clearly. Now change to the Vertex sub-object, select the two pairs of vertices, and move them on the Y-axis, as shown in Figure 2.177.

Figure 2.174

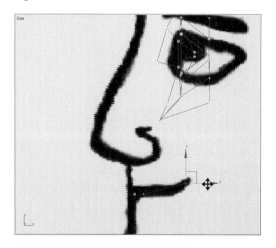

Figure 2.175

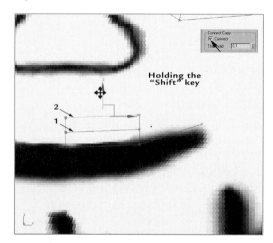

Figure 2.176

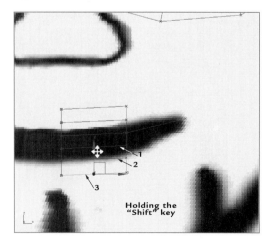

Figure 2.177

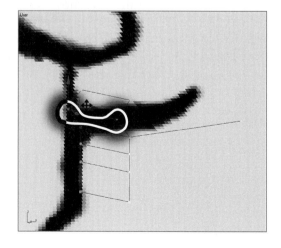

Figure 2.178

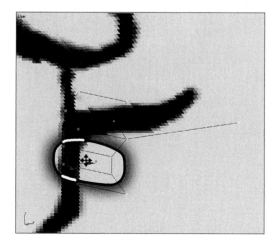

Figure 2.179

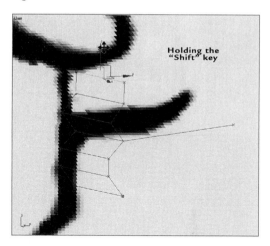

Select the four pairs of vertices that make up the bottom lip and move them forward on the Y-axis only, as shown in Figure 2.178.

Figure 2.180

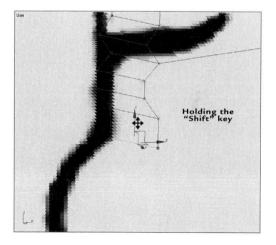

Change to the Segment sub-object and select the top lip segment. Holding the Shift key, move and copy this segment up to underneath the nose. This creates the little patch between the nose and lips. This would be a good time to save your project with a new name.

Take It on the Chin

We are now going to work on the chin.

Select the bottom segment of the bottom lip. While holding the Shift key, move and copy the segment down to the top of the chin area.

We have the start of the chin; now we are going to zoom out a little so that we can see the whole chin and neck area.

Figure 2.181

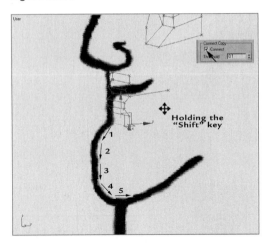

Figure 2.182

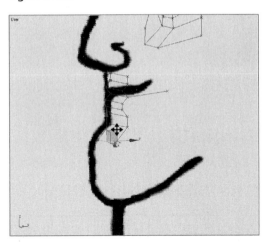

Figure 2.183

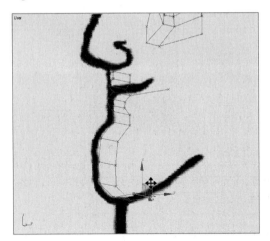

Figure 2.184

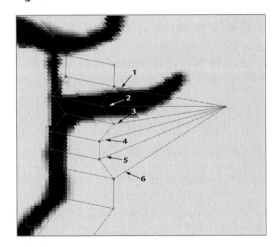

Leaving the same segment selected, hold the Shift key. Move and copy the same segment down and out on the Y–Z axes. Repeat, following the shape of the chin around, as shown in Figure 2.181 through 2.183. Note that the last two moves will be backward on the Y-axis.

Now that we have begun the chin, we can take a little step back and finish the lips.

Zoom in on the lip area, activate Snaps Toggle, click the Create Line button, and create the six lines, as shown in Figure 2.184.

Now back to the chin.

Figure 2.185

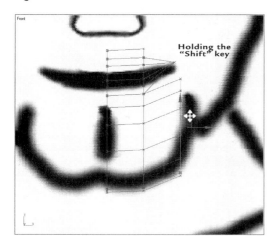

Figure 2.186

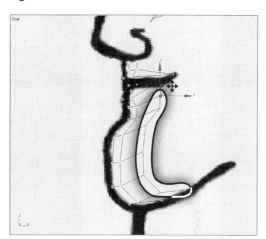

Figure 2.187

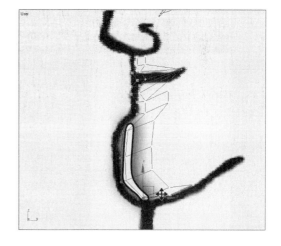

Deactivate Snaps Toggle and change to the Front viewport. In the Segment sub-object level, select the chin segments. Holding the Shift key, move and copy the segments up and to the right, as shown in Figure 2.185.

Change to the Vertex sub-object level and select the newly created vertices. Rotate your viewport for a good angle and move the vertices back on the Y-axis only, as shown in Figure 2.186.

Select the second row of vertices and move them forward on the Y-axis, closer to the front of the chin. This would be a good time to save your project with a new name.

Making a Face

Now we are going to use the Create Line button to connect the eye patch to the lips.

Rotate your viewport, select the bottom of the eye patch segments, and, holding the Shift key, move and copy them down and to the front, as shown in Figure 2.188.

Change to the Front viewport and move the vertices around the nostril area as shown in Figure

Figure 2.188

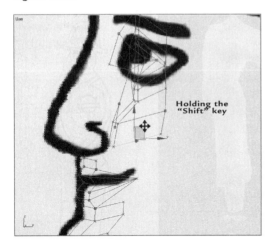

Figure 2.189

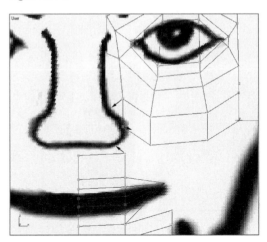

Figure 2.190

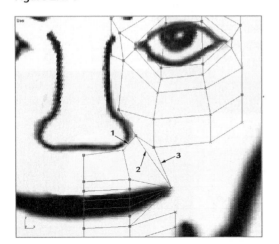

Figure 2.191

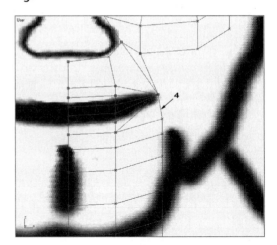

2.190. Then activate Snaps Toggle, click the Create Line button, and create the three lines, as shown in Figure 2.190.

Make one more line from the corner of the mouth to the chin patch, as shown in Figure 2.191.

Before we move on to another area of the head, let's shape these a little bit more.

Deactivate Snaps Toggle and move the vertices around to match Figure 2.192. If yours do not exactly match the image, that's fine as long as they are generally the same. Select all the vertices, right-click anywhere, and change them all to Corner.

Figure 2.192

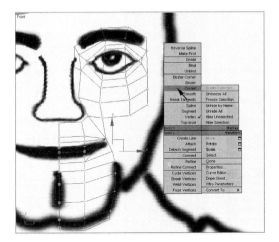

Figure 2.193

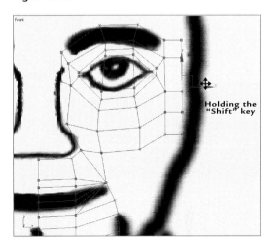

Figure 2.194

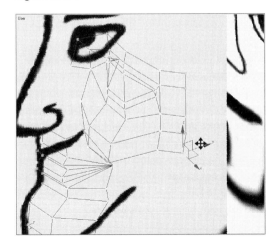

Figure 2.195

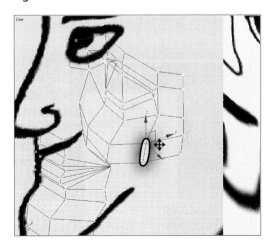

The Old Noggin

The next step is to expand our existing patch to create the connection to the side of the head, the forehead, and the nose. We are going to start by expanding the eye patch around the side of the head and up, creating the forehead.

In the Front viewport, change to the Segment sub-object level and select the segments on the side of the eye patch. Holding the Shift key, move and copy the segments out on the X-axis, as shown in Figure 2.193.

Change to the Vertex sub-object and select the newly created vertices. Rotate your viewport and move the vertices back on the Y-axis only.

Select the pair of vertices, as shown in Figure 2.195. Move them forward and out on the X–Y axes just a little bit.

Now let's make the forehead. It may seem like we are jumping around a bit, but sometimes it's better if we expand out our mesh a little bit at a time. Then the patches seem to connect all by themselves. You will see that the process speeds up a little at this point. Actually, we don't need as much detail for the rest of the head, so we will be creating larger patches without so much attention to the details.

Change to the Segment sub-object level and select the top three segments of the eye patch, as shown in Figure 2.196. Rotate your viewport for a good angle and then, holding the Shift key, move and copy the segments up and forward on the Y–Z axes, as shown in Figure 2.197.

One more shift move straight up (as shown in Figure 2.198) will create the brow ridge and nose bridge areas.

Change to the Vertex sub-object level. Now there should be two pairs of vertices outside the reference image, as in Figure 2.199.

Figure 2.196

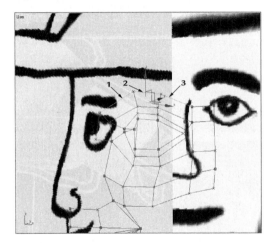

Figure 2.197

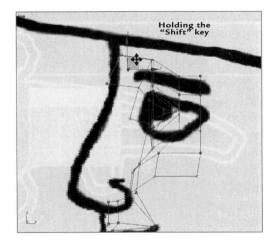

Figure 2.198

Figure 2.199

Figure 2.200

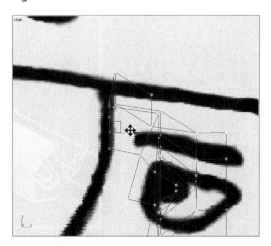

Figure 2.201

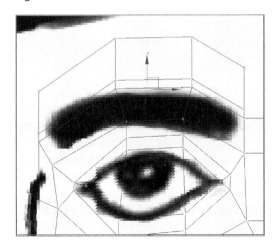

Figure 2.202

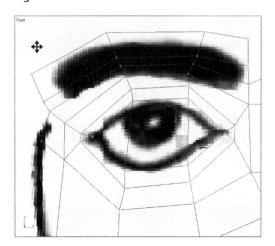

Window select them and move them back on the Y-axis in line with the brow ridge or even a little further back if you want. This will give him a dent in the bridge of his nose.

It's time to shape our eye a little. Change to the Front viewport and zoom in on the eye.

Select pairs of vertices and move them to match Figure 2.202.

Take a little time to get this right. The shape of the eye is complicated, and getting it to match your model sheet can take some time, but it's worth the effort. The eyes are the most expressive part of the face and will make your character seem more alive.

Right on the Nose

The next patch we are going to build is the nose.

Starting from the bridge of the nose and using the Connect Copy option, we will create a profile and then connect it to the cheek and upper lip.

With the Front viewport active, change to the Segment sub-object and move and copy the segment toward the center of the nose bridge.

Change to the Vertex sub-object and move the newly created vertices closer to vertical. Make sure that they are square, the same as in the Figure 2.204.

Change to the Segment sub-object and select the bottom segment of the new square. Rotate your viewport to match Figure 2.206.

Figure 2.203

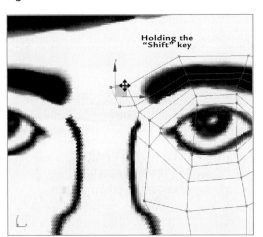

Figure 2.204

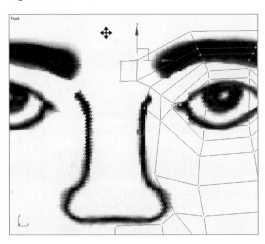

Figure 2.205

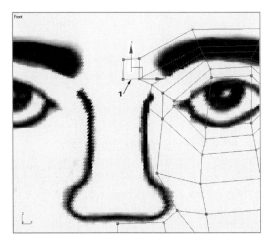

Holding down the Shift key, move and copy the segment on the Y–Z axes five times around the nose profile. Keep the last copy not quite all the way under the nose patch.

Before we create the nostril, we have to do a little patch-up work. The nose profile needs to connect to the upper lip area.

Delete the last copied segment. Activate Snaps Toggle and change to the Vertex sub-object level. Select the remaining vertices individually and move them to the corner of the upper lip quad patch, as shown in Figure 2.209.

Figure 2.206

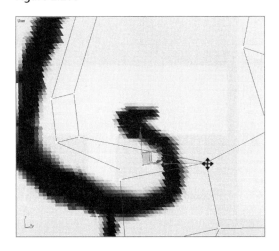

Figure 2.207

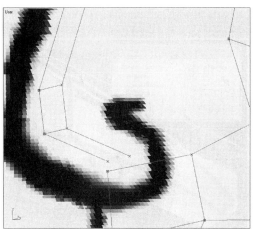

Figure 2.208

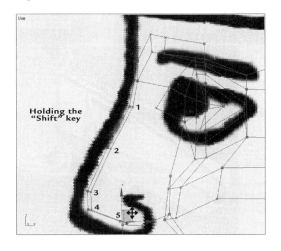

Figure 2.209

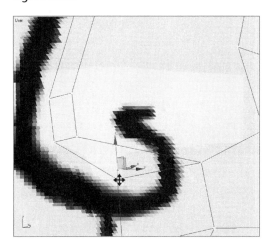

Click the Create Line button and create a new line across the nostril, as shown in Figure 2.210.

We need a vertex in the middle of the line you just created. Click the Refine button and click in the middle of the line. Once the new vertex is created, right-clicking in the viewport will deactivate the Refine button. Deactivate Snaps Toggle.

Move the new vertex up and forward on the Y–Z axes as shown in Figure 2.211.

Switch to the Front viewport and move the same vertex toward the center to a position similar to that shown in Figure 2.212.

If you look at the model from the Front viewport, you might notice that the nose vertices are not on the centerline. It's no problem to fix this by just selecting the vertices and moving them to the left.

Figure 2.210

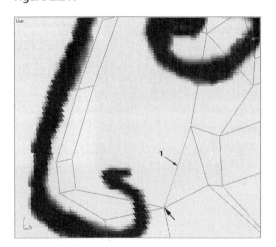

Figure 2.111

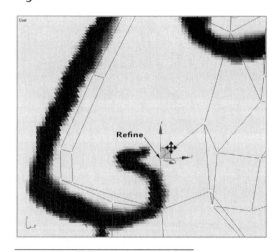

Figure 2.212

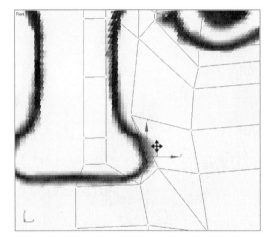

Figure 2.213

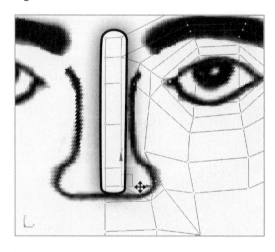

Let's get back to work on the nostril. Recreate the same line across the nostril that we made previously.

Activate Snaps Toggle, click the Create Line button, and create the line, as shown in Figure 2.214.

Now add a vertex in the center using the Refine button. Right-click to deactivate the Refine button, and deactivate Snaps Toggle.

Select and move the new vertex to a similar position as that in Figure 2.215.

Rotate your viewport and move it forward to a similar position as that shown in Figure 2.216.

Now that we have created all the cross-sections, let's connect them.

Activate Snaps Toggle, click the Create Line button, and make the line from the tip of the nose to the lower corner of the nostril as shown in Figure 2.217.

Figure 2.214

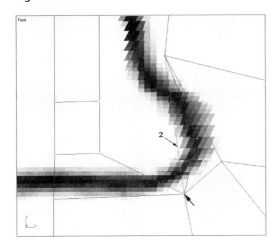

Figure 2.215

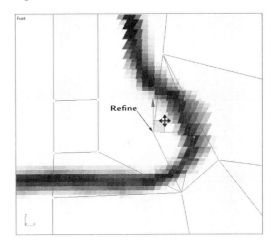

Figure 2.216

Figure 2.217

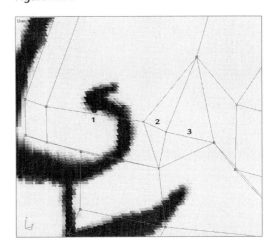

Then one more from the bridge of the nose and down to the inside corner of the nostril as shown in Figure 2.218. Turn off the Snaps toggle.

The final line runs over the center of the nose to the back corner of the nostril. To make it, we are going to use the Refine button with the Connect option checked.

Click once on the existing vertex to start the line.

In the dialog box, click Connect Only.

Refine the line you just made and then click the top corner vertex of the nostril. Click the Connect Only button again, and right-click to finish.

Figure 2.218

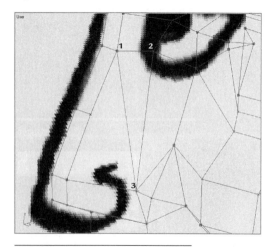

Figure 2.219

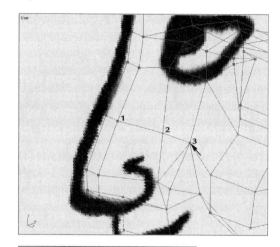

Figure 2.220

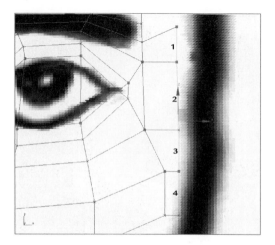

Figure 2.221

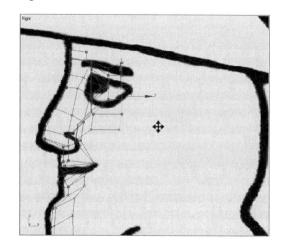

Forehead

That finishes the nose. Now we are going to create the temple area by selecting the segments on the outside of the eye patch and changing to the Right viewport.

Making sure that you check Connect under Connect Copy, hold the Shift key, and move and copy the segments back on the Y-axis only, to about the middle of the head.

Select the bottom segment you just created and change to the Front viewport. While holding the Shift key down, move and copy the segment down and to the left on the X–Z axes three times. The last

Figure 2.222

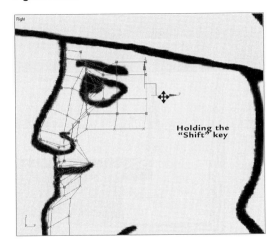

Figure 2.223

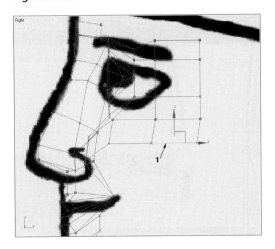

Figure 2.224

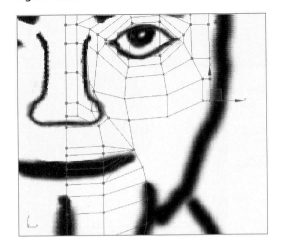

Figure 2.225

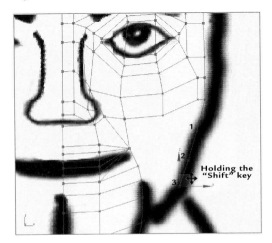

Figure 2.226

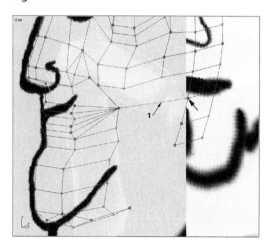

Figure 2.227

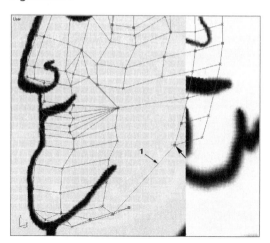

segment should be in front of the front reference plane. You should be able to see the edge of the front reference plane even in the side view.

Rotate your viewport down a little and to the left. We are going to connect the mouth and chin patch to the back of the jaw patch.

Activate Snaps Toggle, click the Create Line button, and create a line from the corner of the mouth to the first of the three new segments, as shown in Figure 2.226.

Create one more line from the bottom of the chin to the third segment.

Now that we have the horizontal cross-sections, let's make the vertical.

Figure 2.228

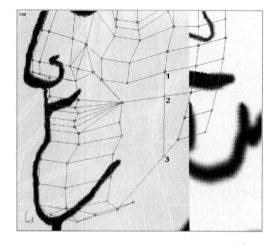

Figure 2.229

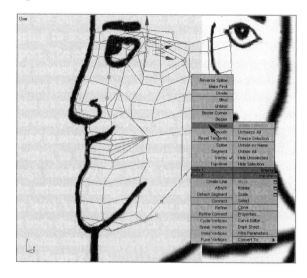

Turn off the Snaps toggle. Make sure that Connect option is checked and then click the Refine button.

Starting with the first vertex on the outside top of the cheek, click once to start refining. In the dialog box, select Connect Only.

Refine the horizontal lines all the way down to the jaw line and refine it. Lastly, right-click to create the line.

This might be a good point to change all the vertices to the Corner type.

Select the last pair of vertices you just made. Rotate your viewport and move them down and back on the Y–Z axes, as shown in Figure 2.230.

Getting Cheeky

Now we are going to fill in the cheek by creating a grid in the area.

Start by activating Snaps Toggle and click the Create Line button. Create the small line, as shown in Figure 2.231.

Next, let's create a vertical cross-section using the Refine tool with the Connect option checked.

Make sure the Snaps toggle is turned off. Click on the remaining unconnected cheek vertex and, in the dialog box, click Connect Only. Refine the horizontal cross-sections straight down to the jaw line and right-click to finish. This is the last vertical cross-section.

Figure 2.230

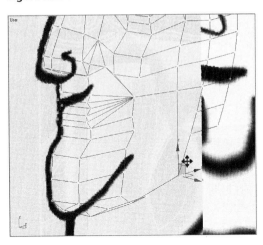

Figure 2.231

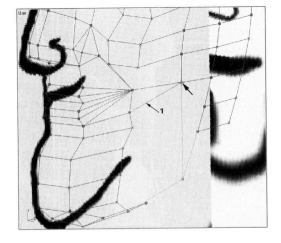

Figure 2.232

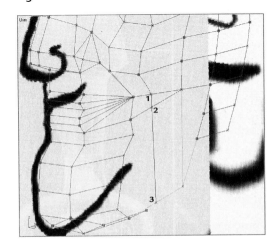

Now let's create the horizontal cross-sections and complete the patch.

Using the Refine button, create the next four cross-sections, as shown in Figure 2.233 through 2.236. Remember to choose Connect Only when clicking on existing vertices. Be careful to refine all the vertical cross-sections. If you don't, it may look correct, but in the next step it will not complete the mesh. Select all the vertices (Ctrl-A) and change them to the corner type. Now is a good time to save your project with a new name.

That's it; the face is now done.

Figure 2.233

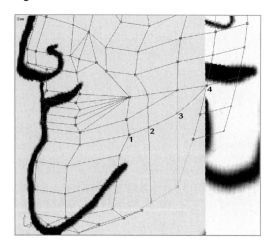

Figure 2.234

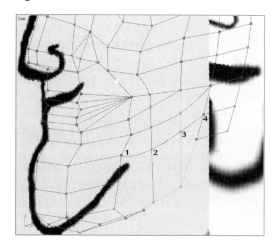

Figure 2.235

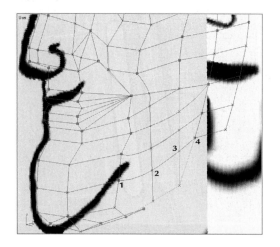

Figure 2.236

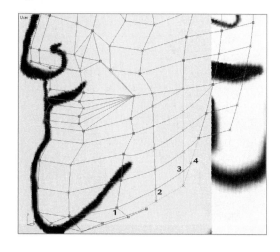

Face the Facts

Let's add the Surface modifier and check our work. At first it may not look quite like the example. It may even look pretty bad.

First, in the Surface modifier, under Patch Topology, set the Steps value to 0, and under Spline Options, set the Threshold value to 0.5. The Threshold value adjusts how close the vertices need to be in order to generate a patch. The more closely the vertices are packed, the smaller the Threshold needs to be in order to make the patches form correctly. You might notice that not all the patches in the eye area are visible. If you set the Threshold value to 0.3, you should see all the eye patches, though you might also need to check Flip Normals. If you added finer detail in the eye area, you might even need to set the threshold value even lower.

A Hole in the Head

If there are still holes in your mesh or if only half of the model shows up and, when you check Flip Normals, the other half shows up, then there are some problems with your spline cage. In Figure 2.239, I removed only one vertex. It looks like I have a big problem, but fortunately I don't. Changing the Threshold value to 0.3 shows that only one area is open.

Changing to the Vertex sub-object level shows you the entire spline and the vertices. It would be almost impossible to find the missing vertex with the object displayed like this. However, if you click the Show End Result button below the modifier stack area, you will see the effect of all the modifiers, and the surface will render under the spline.

It may appear that there is more than one vertex in the center of the open patch, but if you use a rectangular selection marquee, you will find that there is only one.

Make sure the Connect option is unchecked and click the Refine button. Add a vertex to the segment that's missing one, and then right-click to stop refining. Select both vertices and click the Fuse button. The vertices will be fused together. Remember to turn off Snaps Toggle when you're done using it.

Figure 2.237

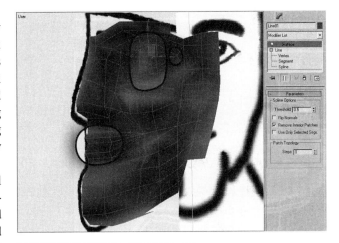

Figure 2.238

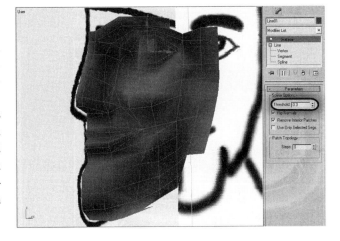

Figure 2.239

Figure 2.240

Figure 2.241

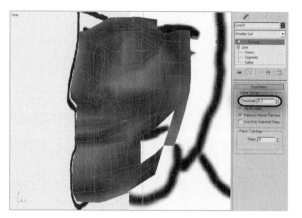

Figure 2.242

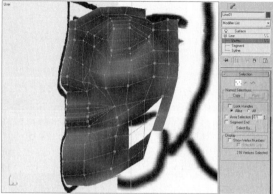

Figure 2.243

Looks good, but doesn't work

Figure 2.244

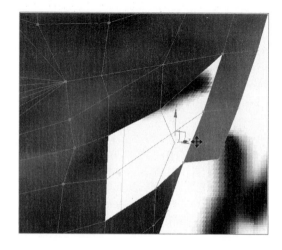

Figure 2.245

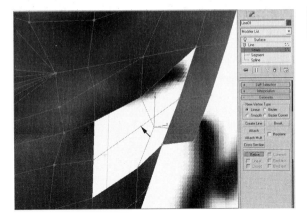

Figure 2.246

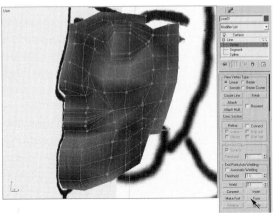

This is one of the most challenging tasks in spline modeling. If a patch is missing, there is an area that is bounded by more than four vertices. Sometimes you just need to look very carefully to find it. Just keep in mind that your model doesn't have to look exactly like mine, so long as all the patches are there.

Going Poly Again

Now that we have the hard part of the head done, let's convert the spline model into a poly object. Remember from the body conversion that one thing is absolutely necessary to check before conversion. In the Surface modifier, make sure that, under Patch Topology, Steps is set to 0. You should save your project with a new name.

Figure 2.247

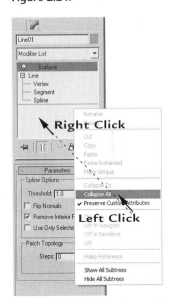

Figure 2.248

Figure 2.249

Figure 2.250

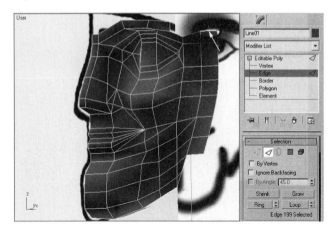

Right-click in a blank area of the modifier stack area and, from the popup, select the Collapse All option.

Then, right-click in the blank area of the modifier stack one more time and, this time, select the Convert to: Editable Poly from the popup.

We are going to start by making the temple area.

Change to the Edge sub-object level and select the one edge shown in Figure 2.250

Change to the Front viewport and, holding the Shift key, move and copy the edge around the top of the head, as shown in Figure 2.251.

As you move the segment around, make it as close as you can vertically to the existing brow line. This will make it easier to connect up later.

Next, we are going to make the forehead area.

Start by rotating your viewport and select the one edge shown in Figure 2.252. Change to the Right viewport and, holding the Shift key, move and copy the segment around the front of the head, as shown in Figure 2.253.

Having the forehead curve makes it easy to copy out a larger edge selection to create the forehead.

Rotate your viewport so that you can see both curves and then select the edges, as shown in Figure 2.254.

Holding the Shift key, move and copy the edges out three times on the Z–Y axes. Follow the forehead curve.

Figure 2.251

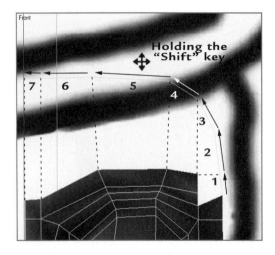

Figure 2.252

Figure 2.253

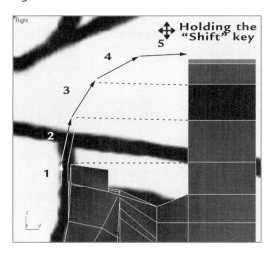

Figure 2.254

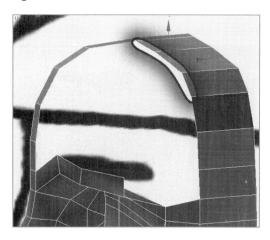

Figure 2.255

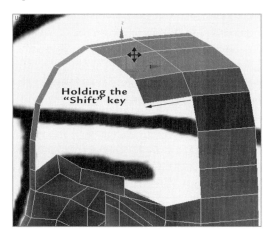

Figure 2.256

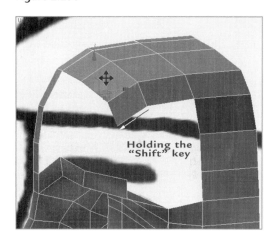

Figure 2.257

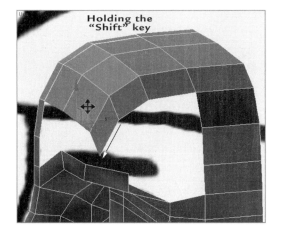

Figure 2.258

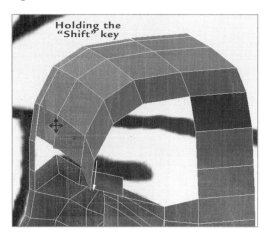

Figure 2.259

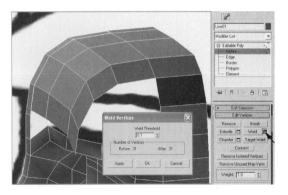

Figure 2.260

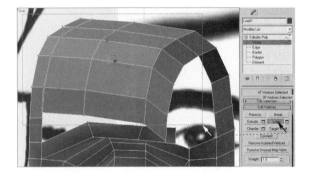

One of the drawbacks to this method of mesh creation is that some of the vertices are not welded. Fortunately, this is easily fixed by selecting all the vertices of the newly created mesh and welding them.

Change to the Vertex sub-object level and, using a rectangular selection marquee, select all the newly created vertices. Then press the Settings button next to the Weld button and, from the popup, increase the Weld Threshold until you start seeing them weld together. You may have to zoom in and check to see if everything got welded. You can always select pairs of vertices and weld them.

You should see a little change in the viewport and a reduction of the number of vertices.

Now it is time to connect the forehead polygons to the brow ridge ones using the Target Weld tool.

Activate the Target Weld tool and select the forehead vertices, one at a time. Then select the existing vertices of the brow ridge, as shown in Figure 2.261.

Figure 2.262

Figure 2.261

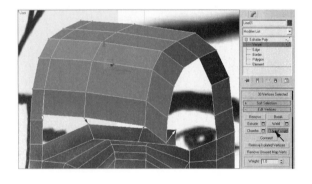

Now we are going to shape the temple area of the head.

Change to the Right viewport and move the vertices around so that it looks similar to the arrangement in Figure 2.264. This makes it easy to close up the temple.

Select the four edges shown in Figure 2.265 and click the settings button next to the Bridge. From the Bridge Edges popup, change the Segments value to 2 and click the OK button.

Now there is a hole in the forehead, so let's close it.

Change to the Border sub-object level, select one of the edges around the hole, and click on the Cap button.

We are going to fix the two remaining holes in a slightly different way to learn how to create polygons other than the cap tool.

Change to the Polygon sub-object level and click on the Create button.

Figure 2.263

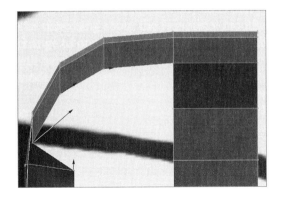

Figure 2.264

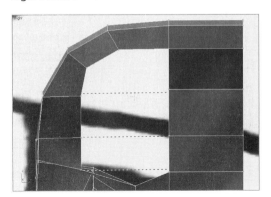

Figure 2.265

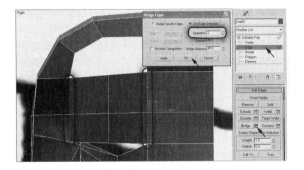

Figure 2.266

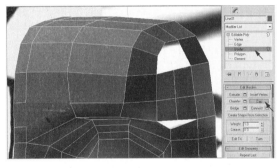

You should now see the vertices of the model appear. In order to create a polygon, you will need to select four vertices. The order in which you select them matters. Selecting the vertices in a counterclockwise direction means that the polygon will be created facing you. If you select the vertices in a clockwise direction, the polygon will be created facing the opposite direction. For the most part it doesn't matter which vertex you select first, but in this case I want you to start with a particular one.

Start with the vertex labeled in Figure 2.267 and select around the hole until a polygon is created. Repeat the process, creating the second polygon.

For the final hole I want you to create two triangles, one at a time. This time, select three vertices instead of four. Now would be a good time to save your project with a new name.

Now that the holes are closed, it's time to finish the jaw line.

Figure 2.267

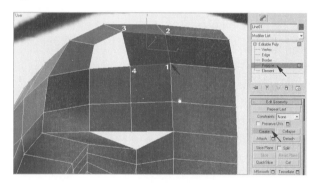

Figure 2.268

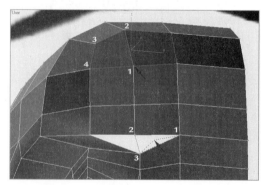

Figure 2.269

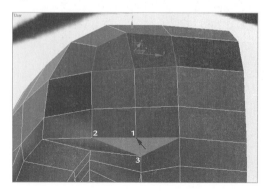

Figure 2.270

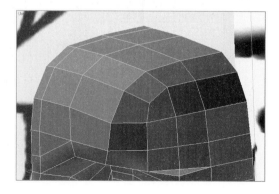

Start by changing to the Edge sub-object level and select the edge shown in Figure 2.271. Change to the Front viewport and, holding the Shift key, move and copy the segment six times around the jaw.

Now it is time to close up the hole.

Change to the Vertex sub-object level and select the four vertices shown in Figure 2.273. Click on the Settings button next to the Weld button; from the popup increase the Weld Threshold amount until the four become two. Then click the OK button.

Rotate your viewport so that you can see the bottom of the chin clearly. Next, change to the Edge sub-object level and select

Figure 2.271

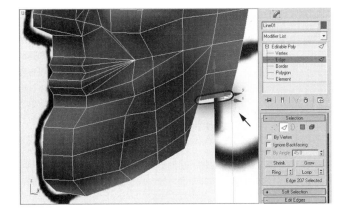

Figure 2.272

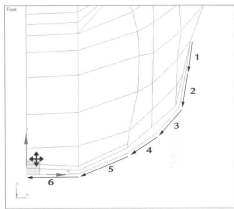

Figure 2.273

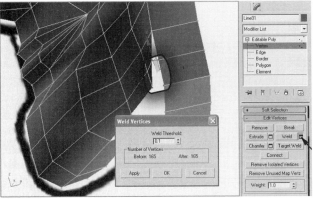

Figure 2.274

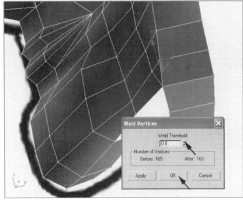

the four edges shown in Figure 2.275. Then, click on the Settings button next to the Bridge button. From the popup, change the Segments value to 1, if it's not already set at 1. Then click OK.

Change to the Polygon sub-object, click on the Create button and create the four triangles.

That should do it for the base geometry. Now we will shape the face before we start creating the back side of the head.

Figure 2.275

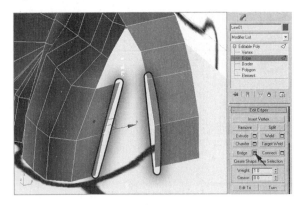

Figure 2.276

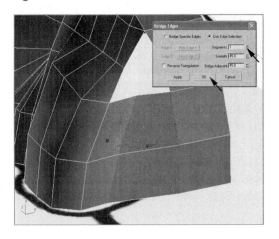

Figure 2.277

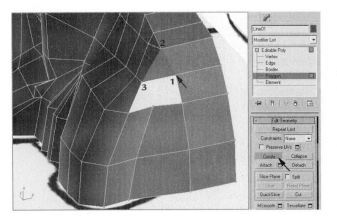

Figure 2.278

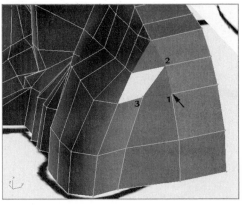

Figure 2.279

Figure 2.280

Smooth Sailing

At this point in the process, it's good to take some extra time to smooth out your model. Before you do, make sure you save your file. He may look like Frankenstein's monster right now, but 15 or 20 minutes of adjusting should shape him right up.

It's a little hard to explain the process exactly, but here goes. First, I look for any flat spots. There are only a couple of places on the human body that can be absolutely flat. All the others must have some kind of curve. The trick is to find the natural curve for each horizontal and vertical line. When you're working on the face, it is a good idea to look at your own face in a mirror and project the lines of your model onto it so that you can see how they could flow naturally. This doesn't mean that it has to be a big curve; slight curves work for most of the body. The face, however, has lots of sharp curves and indentations. This makes it hard to model with just a few polygons. Another thing to keep in mind is that the material will hide a lot of little mistakes. So don't worry that your model doesn't look exactly like mine. As long as it looks similar, the mapping will take care of the rest.

Starting in the Front viewport around the eye area I moved the vertices around so that the eyeball area is more rectangular than square. Then I moved up to work on the forehead area. By taking the vertices along the temple/forehead and spacing them out, I softened the curve along the side of the head. Finally, I moved down to the chin area; there I softened the curves along the bottom of the chin.

Figure 2.281

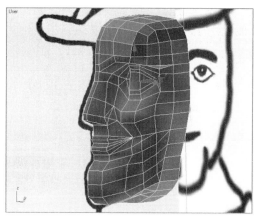

Figure 2.282

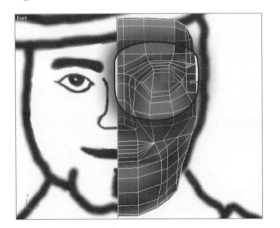

Figure 2.283

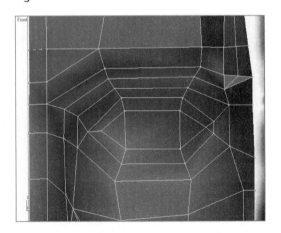

Figure 2.284

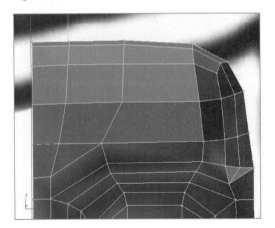

Figure 2.285

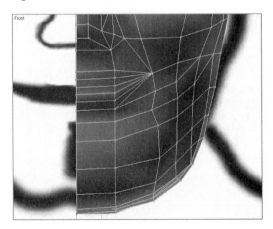

Figure 2.286

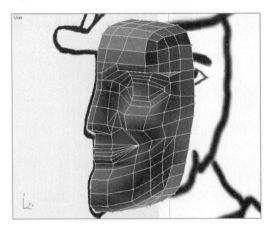

Then, from the side view, I went through the same process. In the Right viewport I zoomed in on the chin area. Again, I just spaced out the vertices under the chin so that it's not flat, but rather has a slight curve.

Moving up from the chin to the cheek area, the curve from the corner of the mouth out should be a slight upward curve that will eventually connect up with the bottom of the ear. I also did a little adjusting of the cheek and nostril vertices. Finally, I smoothed out the curves coming out the corner of the eye. I also pulled back the vertices at the very corner of the eye.

Figure 2.287

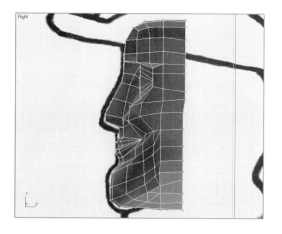

Figure 2.288

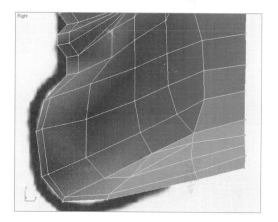

Figure 2.289

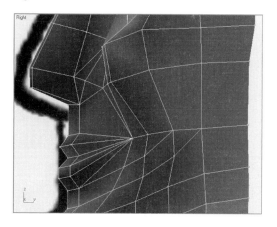

Figure 2.290

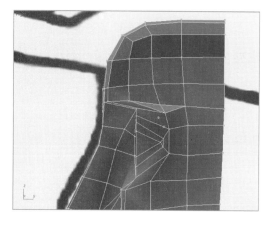

There's one more adjustment I made to the eye. This one was easier to see and make in a User viewport. I selected the four vertices shown in Figure 2.291 and moved them back on the Y-axis; this creates the "ball" of the eye area. Then I moved the vertices selected in Figure 2.292 and moved them back on the Y-axis. This will smooth the curves running through the eye.

I always pull back and check out my work just to make sure everything looks good.

Off the Top of Your Head

Now that the face is completed, we are going to make the side, back, and top of the head. This part of our character does not need a great amount of detail. All we have to do is fill in the area as simply as possible.

Figure 2.291

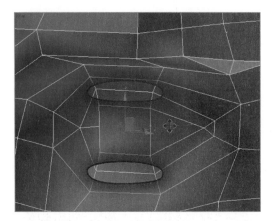

Figure 2.292

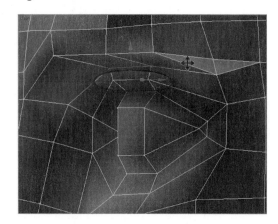

Figure 2.293

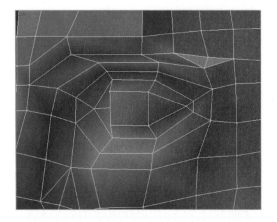

Figure 2.294

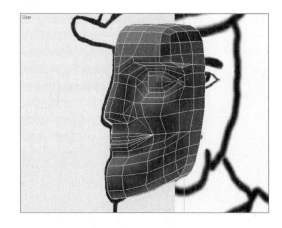

Start by changing to the Edge sub-object level and selecting only the vertical edges shown in Figure 2.295. Then, holding the Shift key, move and copy the edges up and out three times, similar to that shown in Figure 2.295.

Remember that it doesn't have to be exactly like mine, because we are going to remove some of it and move the remaining around. The smallest polygons in the middle are going to become the back of the jaw and the ear area, so place them approximately where the jaw should be.

Zoom in on the top of the head, change to the Vertex sub-object level, and activate the Target Weld tool. Click and weld the top three vertices to their lower counterparts.

The next couple of Target Welds are hard to describe, so take a look at Figure 2.298. This will reduce the number of polygons and give us a start on the top of the ear area.

Another method of reducing the polygon count is to use the settings button for the Weld tool.

Move the vertices shown in Figure 2.299 together, select them all, and click on the Weld settings button. From the popup, change the Weld Threshold value until the selected vertices weld together.

To create the geometry for the ear, all we have to do is to move around the existing vertices until they look like Figure 2.301.

To create the back of the jaw line, select the vertices shown in Figure 2.302. Then rotate your viewport so that you see the bottom of the head and move the

Figure 2.295

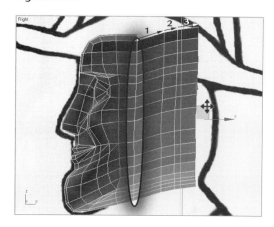

Figure 2.296

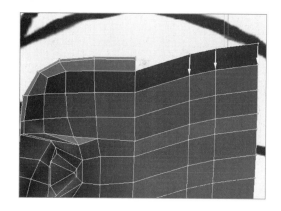

Figure 2.297

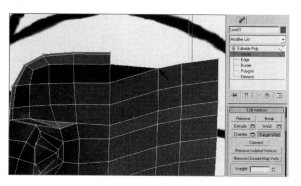

Figure 2.298

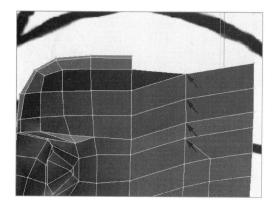

vertices in on the Y-axis only, as shown in Figure 2.303. A little curve smoothing can be done at this point. Bringing the vertices of the jaw line together a little will increase the edginess of the jaw line.

Figure 2.299

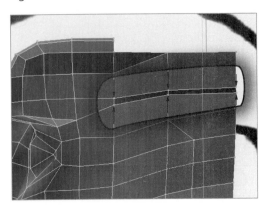

Figure 2.300

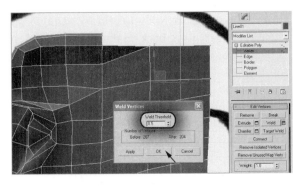

Figure 2.301

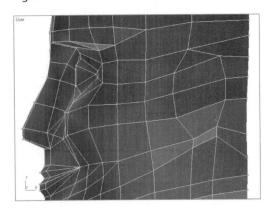

Figure 2.302

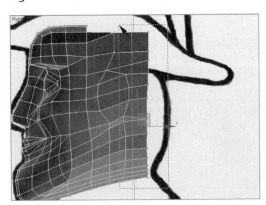

Figure 2.303

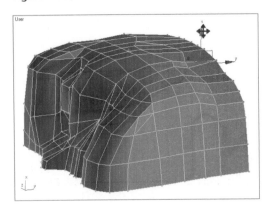

Figure 2.304

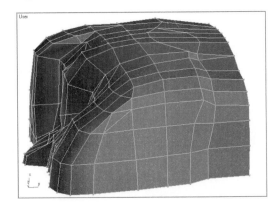

To make the back of the head, change to the Edge sub-object level and select the edges shown in Figure 2.305. Rotate your viewport so that you can see the bottom of the neck. Then, holding the Shift key, move and copy the edges in and back on the X–Y axes at approximately 30 degrees. Now change to the Rotate tool and rotate the edges approximately 45 degrees on the Z-axis.

Change to the Move tool and, holding the Shift key, move and copy the edges in and back on the X–Y axes so that the leading vertex is about the same depth as the first vertex in the existing neck area,

Figure 2.305

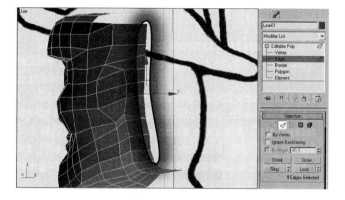

Figure 2.306

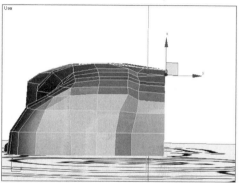

Figure 2.307

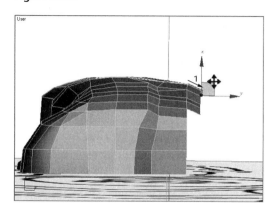

Figure 2.308

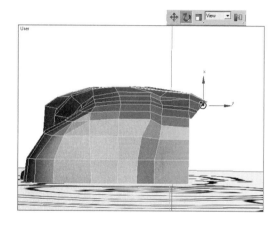

as shown in Figure 2.309. Change to the Rotate tool and rotate the edges approximately 45 degrees or until it looks like Figure 2.310. Change to the Move tool and, holding the Shift key, move and copy the edges three times on the X–Y axes towards the center.

Change to the Vertex sub-object level and, using the Target Weld tool, weld the vertex at the outer corner of the neck to its neighbor.

Then change to the Edge sub-object level, select the open edges, and use the settings button for Bridge tool to fill in the hole.

That's it for the bottom of the neck, so on to the top of the head.

Figure 2.309

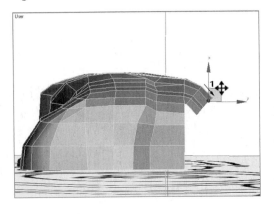

Figure 2.310

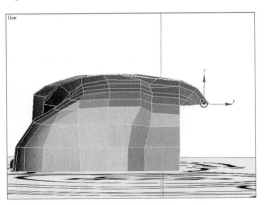

Figure 2.311

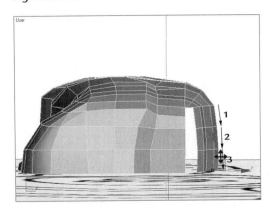

Figure 2.312

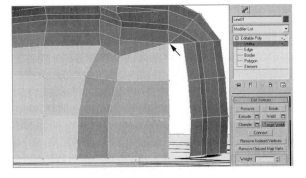

Figure 2.313

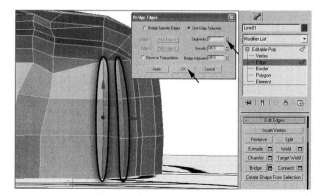

Figure 2.314

Rotate your viewport so that you can see the top and back of the head. Select the three edges shown in Figure 2.314. Then, holding the Shift key, move and copy the segments four times on the X–Z axes. To close the back of the head, select the three edges shown in Figure 2.316 and, holding the Shift key, move and copy the edges down and back on the Z–Y axes one time.

Rotate your viewport around and change to the Vertex sub-object level. You might notice that the vertices of the top of the head are in a little disarray. Move them around so that the edges are a bit straighter. Then, using the Target Weld tool, weld the vertices from the top of the head to the corresponding back of the head vertices. Finally, change to the Border sub-object and cap the final hole in the head.

Some vertices are not welded, so, to weld all the vertices, select the vertices shown in Figure 2.320. Click on the settings button for the Weld tool and change the Weld Threshold value to 0.5. You should notice that there should be a decrease in the number of vertices. I also noticed on my model that the neck line is a little strange, so I smoothed it out a little.

Finally, to make the ear, change to the Polygon sub-object level and select the ear polygons. Click on the settings button for the Bevel tool and increase the Height value to something small like 0.7 or less.

Figure 2.315

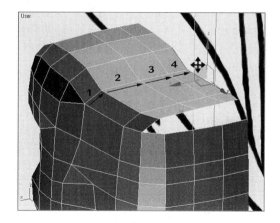

Figure 2.316

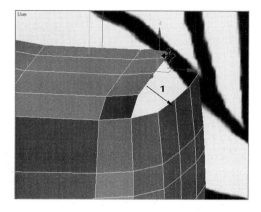

Figure 2.317

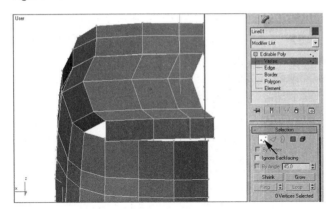

Figure 2.318

Figure 2.319

Figure 2.320

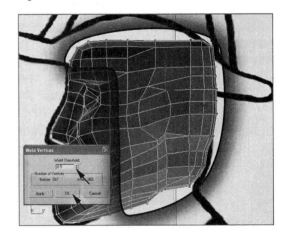

Figure 2.321

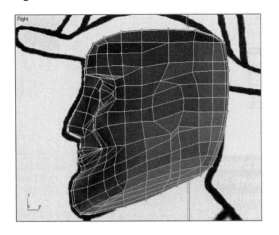

Figure 2.322

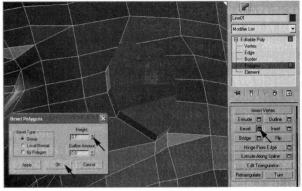

Then change to the Vertex sub-object level and, using the Target Weld tool, close up the front of the ear edge, leaving only the back of the ear raised.

Now that we are all done with the half, let's make it whole. First, make sure you have no sub-object level open and then add the Symmetry modifier from the Modifier list. You might get a Cyclops, but in any case you need to open the Symmetry modifier and click on the mirror sub-object and move the gizmo to the left on the X-axis until you get a whole head.

That's it; the head is done. One more little thing to note for those using 3ds Max 8 or lower: You have to check the seam the same way that we did for the body.

The last thing to do is unhide the body because the head might be a little small for the body.

Right-click in the viewport and, in the upper right-hand quad menu, select the Unhide by Name option; from the list, select your body mesh to unhide it.

You can see that the head of my figure is a little small for its body in Figure 2.328.

Select your figure's head and scale it to fit; then, change to the Front viewport and move it so that it's centered on the body.

Now is the last time to make any geometric changes to your model. One way of manipulating your model in a general fashion is to use the Loop and Ring selection tools.

If you change to the Edge sub-object level and select one vertical edge, click on the Loop button. Now all the edges in a loop are selected.

Now select one horizontal edge and click the Ring button. Now all the horizontal edges around the arm are selected. This selection style works with the Connect tool. Click on the Settings button next to the Connect button and you can see that

Figure 2.323

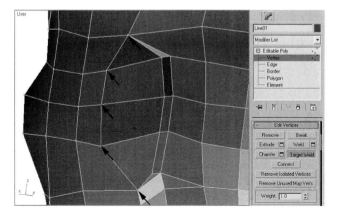

Figure 2.324

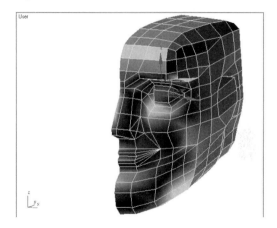

Figure 2.325

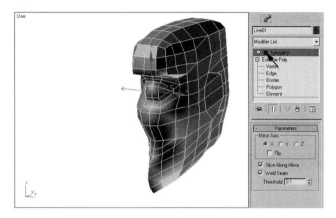

Figure 2.326

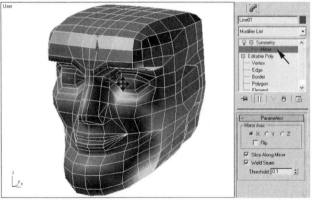

Figure 2.327

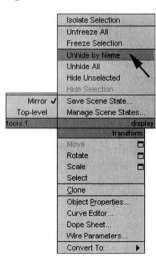

Figure 2.328

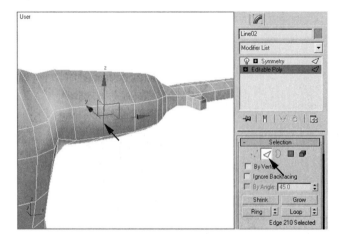

Figure 2.329

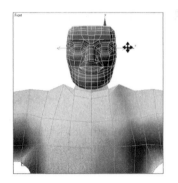

Figure 2.330

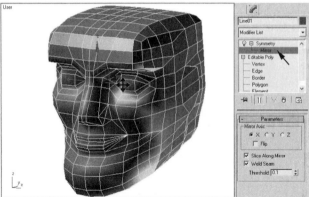

it will change your selection into loop edges. This is an easy way to create extra cross-sections; however, you want to keep things simple, so just press the Cancel button on the popup and the change will not be applied.

Both models need a little treatment before we start the next process. You might notice that some of the polygons are a solid color and some have a shadow or highlight on them. The solid color polygons are not included in what we call Smoothing groups. Smoothing groups are the way 3ds Max controls what areas of the mesh are smoothed together and where corners can be defined.

Figure 2.331

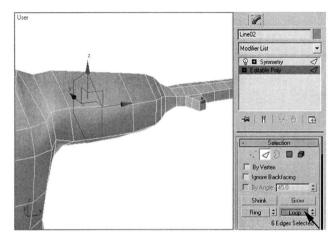

Figure 2.332

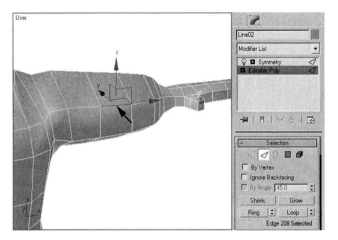

Figure 2.333

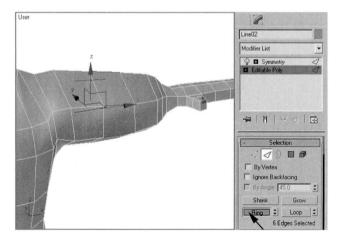

Figure 2.334

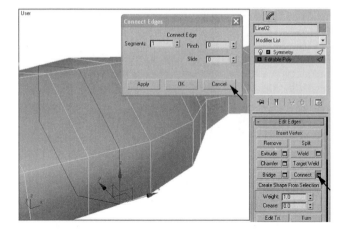

To add all polygons to the same smoothing group, select all the polygons (Ctrl-A), and in the Polygon Properties rollout, change the Auto Smooth value to 60 and click on the Auto Smooth button. Make sure that you close the sub-object and select the Symmetry modifier to finish.

You should notice a change in the surface. Now we have to give the body the same treatment.

Select the body; select all the vertices and this time just click on the Auto Smooth button. The default settings are fine for the body.

That's it for the models. We're all done, so on to the next process.

Figure 2.335

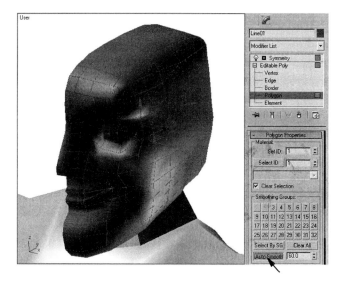

Figure 2.336

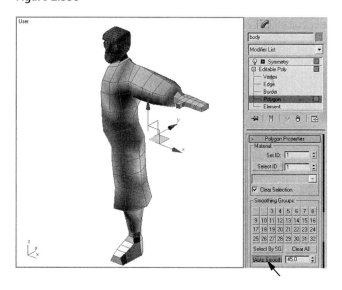

Figure 2.337

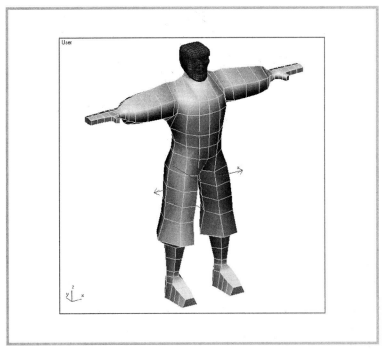

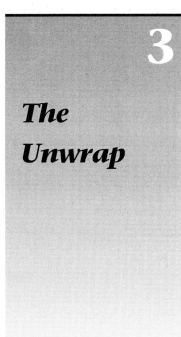

The Unwrap

3

In this chapter I am going to show you how to unwrap a character. During this process we will always have to keep in mind what we are trying to achieve: to lay out our geometry in a way that maximizes the available pixels and makes it easy for the texture artist to create a good map. To make it a little easier on you, we are not going to try to maximize the available pixels as much as possible, but we will focus on making it easy for the texture artist to make a map.

To reiterate a little, the process of unwrapping a model is to take your 3D model and flatten it out so that a 2D image can be placed on it without distortion. That may sound easy, but it's quite an interesting puzzle. The problem is that all the polygons have to be proportional to each other so that the proportions of the image can remain consistent. The next question I am sure you're thinking is, "How can I tell if the polygons are proportional?" Well, if you put a square map with black and white squares in it onto your model, you would see the squares on the disproportionate polygons as distorted or stretched. Using the UVW Unwrap modifier, we can change the geometry virtually and fix any distortions. This will make the texture map maker's job easier.

Figure 3.01

Figure 3.02

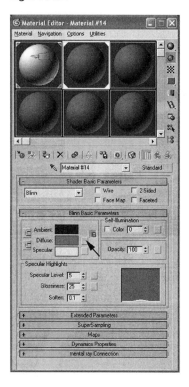

Figure 3.03

Body Unwrap

We'll begin with unwrapping the body. The process has many steps and takes a little longer than unwrapping the head, but it gives a good introduction to the tools and processes. The experience will be valuable when we get to the head.

Luckily for us, there is the Checker procedural map, which allows us to change the size of the checkers. This is the main reason we use the Checker map instead of a bitmap. Procedural maps are based on global coordinates, so they wrap around objects automatically.

In order to flatten out our geometry in such a way to make it easy to create a map, we use a modifier called Unwrap UVW. Don't let the "UVW" confuse you; the letters describe the local coordinates of the objects' polygons in the same way that the X, Y, and Z coordinates are used to describe the world.

So it's not until we add UVW mapping coordinates that we start to see our checkers stretch. Using the Unwrap UVW modifier, we can edit the UVW coordinates of our geometry and correct the nonproportional polygons. So that's what we are going to do now.

Checkers

Open your final model project. Open the Material Editor by pressing M, and assign a blank material to the body.

Click on the little gray button next to Diffuse color box and, from the Material/Map Browser, double-click on the Checker map.

In the Material Editor, you will be in the Diffuse Color channel. Change the U and V Tiling settings both to 10. This will give us a smaller checker pattern so that we can see any stretching. The smaller the detail in your object is, the smaller you want the checker pattern to be. Therefore, on an object like the head, you want even higher numbers for the tiling value because of the detail of the object.

Click the Show Map in Viewport button, and your body turns … white?

Remember that your model has no mapping coordinates at the moment, so even a procedural map like checker will not show up on the surface. You will see the checker material appear as we apply the mapping coordinates.

Figure 3.04

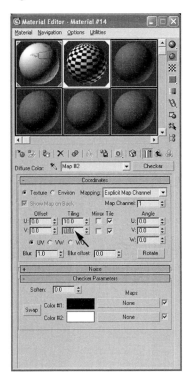

Figure 3.05

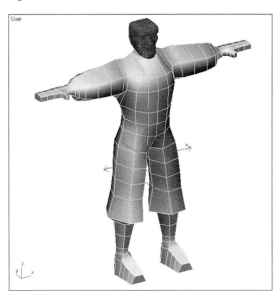

Mapping

We will start the mapping process with the chest area. In the first part of this process, we will lay out all the different parts of the body. Then we will fix the distortions.

At this point we will not need the head, so right-click in the viewport and select Hide Unselected. The head should disappear.

From the modifier list, select and add the UVW unwrap modifier. You should now see checkers on your model. Open the UVW Unwrap modifier and change to the Face sub-object level.

Notice that by default the Ignore Backfacing option is checked. This means that the selection tools will only select faces that are facing you, rather than the ones on the back side.

Figure 3.06

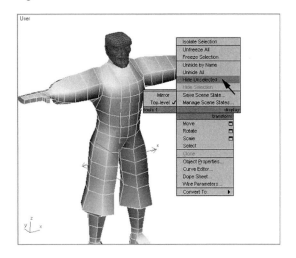

Figure 3.07

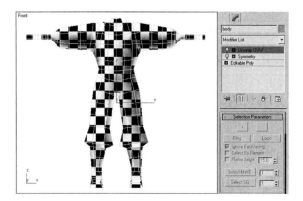

Figure 3.08

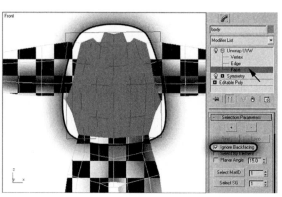

Figure 3.09

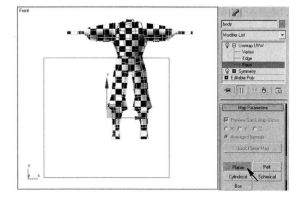

Select the faces of the chest, as shown in Figure 3.08. Make sure you get the little polygon under the arm. Then scroll the Modify panel up and, in the Map Parameters rollout, click on the Planar button.

You should see a large yellow box somewhere around your model.

Getting Things Square

Now you should be able to see the checkers on the chest of the model again. If you take a close look, you see that they are not exactly square. We know that the checkers in the material are square, so the distortion is in the mapping coordinates. Since the pixels of our map will be square as well, we need to fix this distortion.

Click on the Fit button; now it should be around the selected faces. Change to the Select and Uniform Scale tool and scale the gizmo on one axis only, until the checkers are all square.

If you rotate your viewport, you will notice that the checkers that looked fine in the Front viewport now look stretched out under the arm and at the shoulder. After we finish laying out the rest of the body, we will go back and fix this.

Now click on the big Edit button and the Edit UVWs window will pop up with the front polygons selected. This is where we can

Figure 3.10

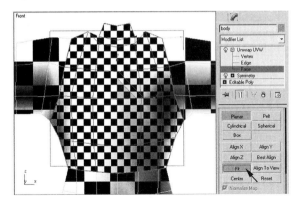

Figure 3.11

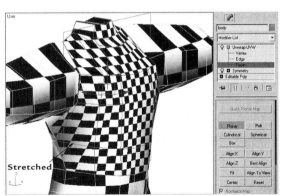

edit the mapping coordinates without changing the mesh. At this point we cannot edit in the Edit UVWs window, but we can check our selection.

If your face selection is not the same as mine, now is the time to add or subtract polygons from the selection. It's a little tricky; first deactivate the Planar button and then, in the 3ds Max viewport, add or subtract polygons. Click on the Planar button again and the Fit button again. Rescale the Planar gizmo until the checkers are square.

Figure 3.12

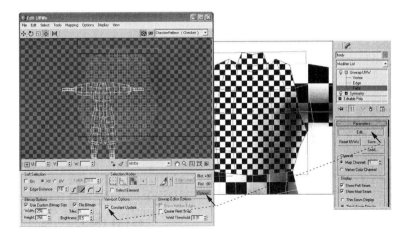

If your selection is good, then we are going to move the selected polygons away from the others.

First click on the Options button in the lower right-hand corner of the Edit UVWs window. From the Viewport Options area, check the Constant Update option. In order to move the faces in the Edit UVWs window, first deactivate the Planar button. Then move the faces up, as shown in Figure 3.13.

That's all the editing of the front polygons we are going to do at this point. Now is a good time to save your project with a new name.

Figure 3.13

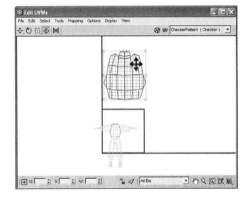

Figure 3.14

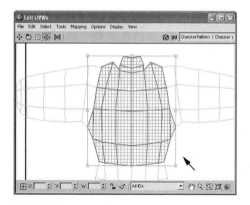

Figure 3.15

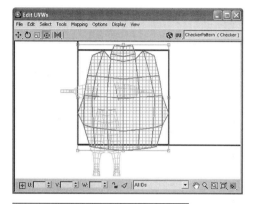

The Back

We are going select the back faces a little differently from the way we selected the front. Instead of selecting the faces in the 3ds Max viewport, we are going to select them in the Edit UVWs window.

In the Edit UVWs window, zoom in on the body, using the middle mouse wheel and button to pan.

Select the faces in the chest area; because we have already moved the front polygons, only the back faces remain.

Click on the Planar button and then on the Fit button. The faces should expand and detach from the rest of the body. Finally, zoom out a little and move them back up and to the right of the front polygons. Now is a good time to save your project with a new name.

Arms

The next part to be unwrapped is the arm. It will be a little different because of the area's shape. An arm is not as flat as the front or back of the body; it's more cylindrical.

In the Edit UVWs window, select the faces of the model's left arm. This time click on the Cylindrical button. Then, right below it, click on the Align X button.

Figure 3.16

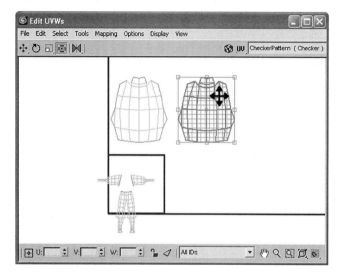

Figure 3.17

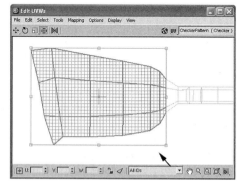

Figure 3.18

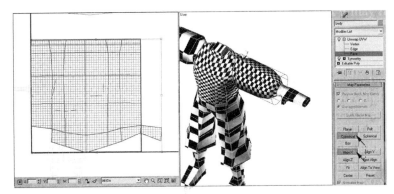

By default this will give you a fairly good layout, but you may have a polygon or two that could be placed better. In Figure 3.18 you can see that I have one polygon on the right side of the patch that needs to be on the left side.

The Seam

However, we are not done yet. By letting 3ds Max determine how the flatting happens we are left with an extra polygon on the wrong side of the patch. What we need to change is the seam or where a cylindrical mesh will be cut in order for it to be flattened. An easy way to think about it is that we are taking the label off a soup can and flattening it out. The problem we need to fix is the seam's location. We want to put the seam somewhere that will be less visible to the player and will create a good patch for texturing. For this model, that would be on the bottom of the arm.

The Cylindrical gizmo shows where the seam of the map will be with a green line on the gizmo. We can use this line to place our seams where we want them. We can also watch in the Edit UVWs window to see the effects of our manipulation of the gizmo. By default, the green line will be on the bottom of the arm. Because the vertices along the bottom of the arm are not exactly in a straight line, the splitting of the UV is not perfect, but it's an easy fix.

In 3ds Max activate the Select and Rotate button. Then, in the 3ds Max viewport, rotate the gizmo on the X-axis only—approximately −4 degrees or until the UVs look like Figure 3.19. Click on the Cylindrical button so that you can move the faces. Zoom out a little and move the arm up and to the right of the back. Now is a good time to save your project with a new name.

Figure 3.19

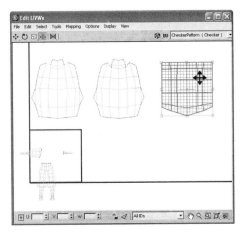

Figure 3.20

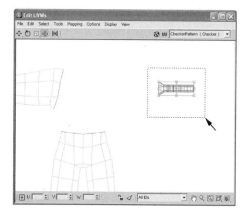

The Hand

The hand is a more complex shape than the ones we have done before. The hand is like a box, but because of the thumb, the default unwrap will not be as clean as the previous ones.

In the Edit UVWs window select the polygons of the hand. Click on the Box button and then click on the Fit button. Zoom out in the Edit UVWs window. Change to the Select and Scale tool, and scale the box gizmo in the 3ds Max window on all three axes individually until the checkers are square. Then, scale the gizmo on all three axes at the same time until the checkers are about the same size as the arm checkers. Finally, click on the Box button so that you can move the UVs up and under the back and arm patches. Now is a good time to save your project with a new name.

Figure 3.21

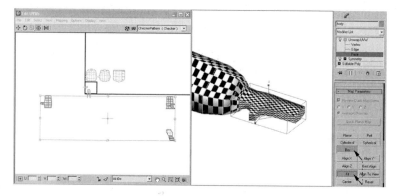

Figure 3.22

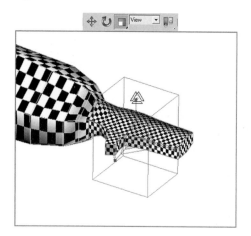

The Next Leg

For the character's leg we are going to use the same procedures that we used for the arm.

In the Edit UVWs window, select the polygons of the model's left leg. Click on the Cylindrical button and then on the Align Y button.

Notice that the green line of the Cylindrical gizmo is along the outside of the leg. This would put the seam of the texture map clearly visible on the outside of the leg. Let's rotate the gizmo so that the seam is hidden on the inside of the leg.

Change to the Select and Rotate tool and, in the 3ds Max viewport, rotate the Cylindrical gizmo approximately

Figure 3.23

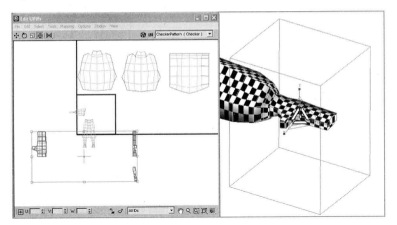

Figure 3.24

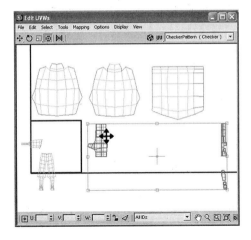

Figure 3.25

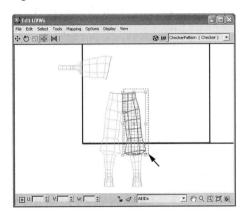

Figure 3.26

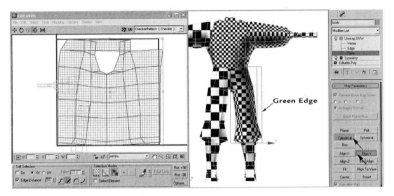

Figure 3.27

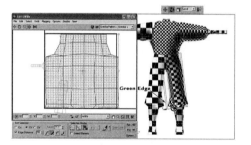

Figure 3.28

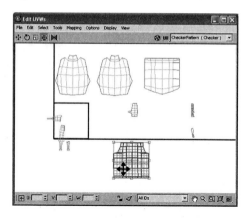

Figure 3.29

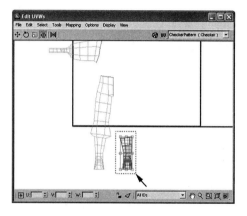

180 degrees until the seam is on the inside of the leg and your UVs look similar to the ones in Figure 3.27. Then rotate the gizmo on the Y-axis only until the checkers run straight down the leg, as shown in Figure 3.27.

Zoom out in the Edit UVWs window and move the patch down and under the hand polygons. Now is a good time to save your project with a new name.

The Boot

We are going to unwrap the boot using a similar method to the one that we used for the hand.

In the Edit UVWs window, select the polygons of the boot. Click on the Box button and then click on the Fit button.

Change to the Select and Scale tool, in the 3ds Max viewport, and scale the gizmo on each axis, individually, until the checkers are square.

Then scale the gizmo on all three axes at the same time until the checkers are roughly the same size as the legs.

Click on the Box button so that you can rotate the patches 90 degrees. Finally, move them down.

Figure 3.30

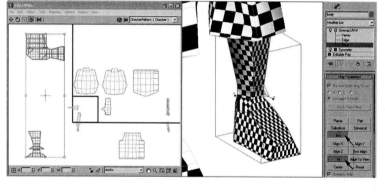

Figure 3.31

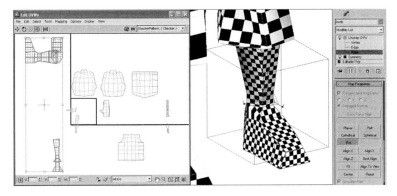

Figure 3.32

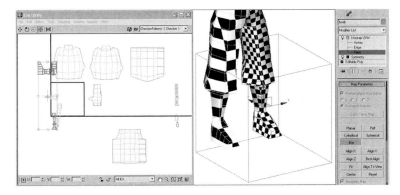

Figure 3.34

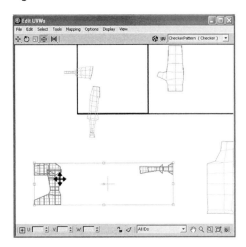

Figure 3.33

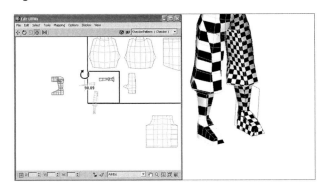

Figure 3.35

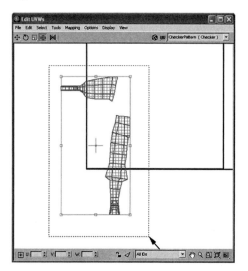

Figure 3.36

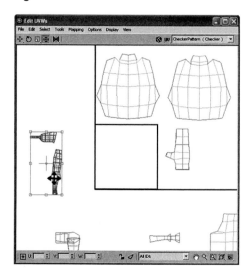

One more little cleanup job is to move the remaining UVs on the right side of the model off to the side. They will not be needed; we will copy the ones from the left side to the right.

In the Edit UVWs window, select the remaining UVs and move them away from the blue square.

Now that we have separated all the parts of the body, we are going to flatten them. It's a good time to save your project with a new name.

Flatting It Out

In order to fix the distortions at the shoulder and under the arm and elsewhere on the model, we will change the positions of the vertices in the Unwrap UVW modifier. This lets us change how much map is placed on each polygon.

The tricky part of the next step is that we need to see the distorted part of the model in our User Viewport and move vertices in our Edit UVWs window at the same time.

It's important to keep in mind that we need to fix only the right-hand side of the mesh's mapping coordinates because, toward the end of the tutorial, we are going to cut the mesh in half and mirror one side to the other, and the UVs will follow.

Point by Point

Let's start unwrapping the chest, but let's jump ahead a bit and look at some finished mapping coordinates. See Figure 3.37. As an example of corrected UVs, take a look at the size and shape of the polygons around the waist to the armpit of my model. Note that this strip of polygons, as seen on the model in Figure 3.38, looks similar to the way my final unwrap of that area looks. Now let me tell you how it was done. It's actually relatively simple.

First, change the Selection Mode of the Edit UVWs window to Vertex, and then you just move the vertices around in the Edit UVWs window.

Nothing needs to be done to the front centerline polygons because they have no stretching, so start by moving the outside vertices.

Start at the lower right-hand corner of the patch and, one by one, move the vertices out in the Edit UVWs window. At the same time, keep one eye on your model and how the checkers look on it. Then work your way up and down the UVs until you see nice squares everywhere. It takes a little practice, but you should get the hang of it quickly.

One thing that helps is to rotate your viewport a lot to check your work because, each time you move a vertex, the texture on all sides of that vertex changes.

Remember that only the right-hand side UVs need to be done because we are eventually going to cut the entire model in half again so that we don't have to unwrap both sides.

It is possible to use the UV layout from my model as a template for yours. If you want to know how it's done, see Appendix B.

Now we are going to place the UVs into the blue box. This box represents the actual mapping area. The pattern of checkers outside the blue box is just repeated tiling of the same mapping coordinates. Eventually, our entire model's UVs will need to fit into that blue box.

Select all of the vertices of the chest and, using the freeform tool, scale uniformly by holding the Ctrl key. Then move the patch into the upper left-hand corner of the blue box.

Figure 3.37

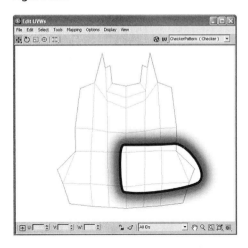

Figure 3.38

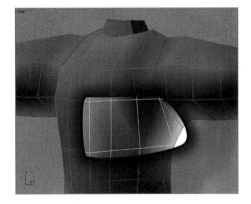

Figure 3.39

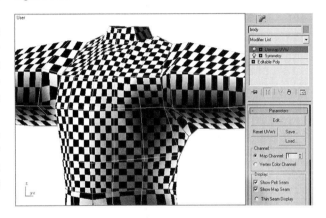

Figure 3.40

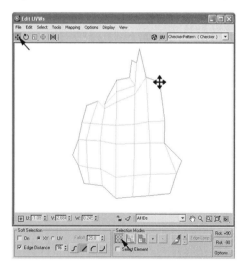

Figure 3.41

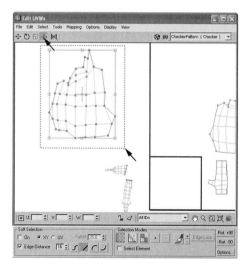

Figure 3.42

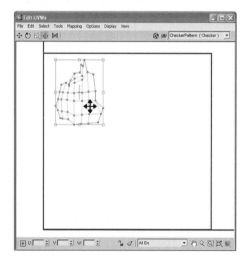

There is one connection I want you to understand: The UVs are a representation of the mesh, so each UV vertex knows all the other vertices that are connected to it in the mesh. Therefore, if you select one vertex, all the other vertices that are attached to it in the original mesh will highlight in blue in the Edit UVWs window. You can see that when you select all the vertices of the front patch of UVs a bunch of vertices will become blue.

Unwrapping the back side is about the same process as the front except that the UVs are actually backward. To fix it, all we have to do is flip all the UVs horizontally.

Select all the vertices' or polygons' UVs of the back patch and then click on the Flip Horizontal button.

Stretch out the left-side edge vertices, and then move the inner vertices out.

Keep rotating your viewport so that you can see the effects of the manipulations. You should be able to do it a little bit more quickly than you did the front half.

Select all of the vertices of the back and, using the freeform tool, scale uniformly by holding the Ctrl key. Then move the patch into the upper middle area of the blue box, next to the front patch.

The process to flatten the arm UVs will be a little more involved than were the first two. First, you will see that there is not a solid green line around the outside of the patch.

Figure 3.43

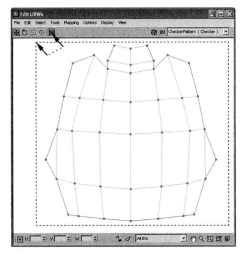

Figure 3.44

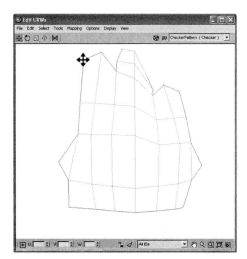

Figure 3.45

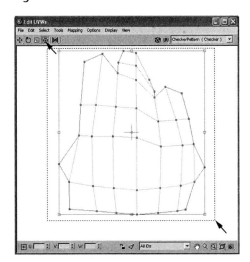

Figure 3.46

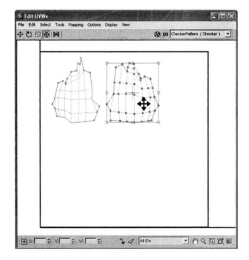

The reason we see a green zigzag or lines inside and not a solid green line along the outside is that the vertices are not welded together. "Why," you might ask, "did the unwrap not do this automatically for us?" Well, there is no answer. That's just the way it happens sometimes. It seems to happen more often with the cylindrical unwrap. This is not currently a big problem, but eventually it will become one. So it's best to take the time and weld them now, because the optimal shape for an unwrapped patch would be a square with a solid green highlight all the way around the outside.

If there are any green lines on the inside of the patch, it's a problem. First, a square or a triangle in the middle of any patch in the Edit UVWs window means that you missed a polygon during the Polygon selection procedure. In order to fix this, you have to select the correct polygons and reapply the flattening tool (Planar, Cylindrical, etc.); it will add the missing polygon to the patch. It's best to find these kinds of errors before the rearrangement of vertices begins because this process will reset any changes made to the patch.

When an obvious edge is broken up, creating a zigzag or T pattern, it needs to be fixed because the nonwelded vertices will make gaps between the polygons and a lot of extra seams.

This creates all kinds of distortions of the image along that edge. Even if you get the vertices close to each other, it still won't work right. We have to actually weld the vertices together to eliminate any distortion.

Welding UV vertices can be done in two ways. The first is just to select the two or more vertices you want to weld, right-click, and, from the quad menu, choose Weld Selected. The second, Target Weld, is my favorite; it is right above Weld Selected in the quad menu. You select a vertex and drag and drop it onto another, and they weld. We will use that a little later.

This time, just select all the vertices on the right side of the patch, right-click, and, from the quad menu, select the Weld Selected option.

Figure 3.47

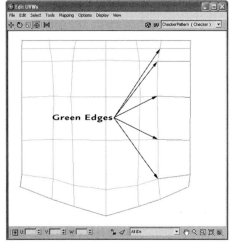

Breaking the Mold

Unfortunately, there is a problem with the wrist, and it's inherent in the geometry. A dilating cylinder cannot be flattened properly with a solid edge. So if you try to get the checker correct on the wrist area, you could try all day long and never get good results. The wrist edge of the patch needs to be broken up so that it can be flattened. What we have to do is break the vertices and open the polygons, as shown in Figure 3.47, but that's more quickly said than done. Breaking the vertices is actually just separating them. When you break a vertex, a copy is created for each edge that leads into it. So if there is a vertex with five edges leading into it and you break that vertex, it will turn into five individual vertices and five individual faces. See Figure 3.50.

First, start by rotating the UVs 180 degrees. Hold down the Ctrl key while rotating with the Freeform gizmo; it will snap right to 180. Then select the bottom row of vertices,

Figure 3.48

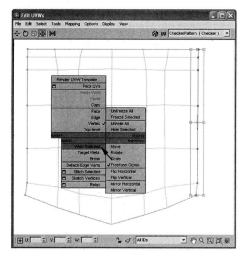

Figure 3.49

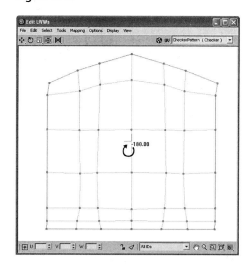

Figure 3.50

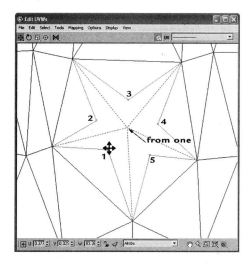

Figure 3.51

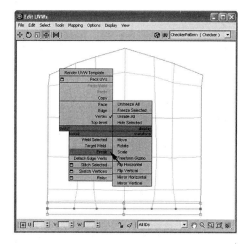

right-click, and, from the lower left-hand quad menu, select the Break option. Now that the vertices are broken apart, change to the Move tool in the Edit UVWs window and separate them. Watch the checker around the wrist as you move them apart and get them as square as possible. Finally, select the entire patch and change to the Freeform gizmo. Then, scale the patch down and move it into the lower right-hand corner of the blue box.

You may notice that the checkers may not be entirely square on the arm. You can move the vertical rows of vertices left or right a

Figure 3.52

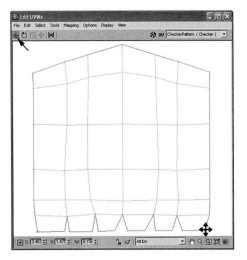

Figure 3.53

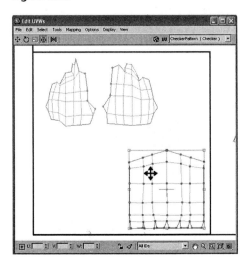

Figure 3.54

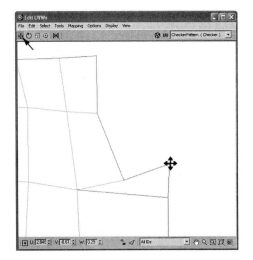

little to even them out, but since the texture of the arm is less defined, a little bit of stretching won't show.

Let's jump to the leg before we do the more complex hand and boot.

The leg has two other problems in common with the arm. The first is the seam, but before we can weld, there is a vertex that has to be moved away from its neighbor.

Zoom in on the top right-hand side of the patch and you will notice that there are a couple of vertices close together; select the one shown in Figure 3.54. Move it up and don't worry about the checkers right now. Select the vertices on the right-hand side of the patch and then right-click in the Edit UVWs window. From the lower left-hand quad menu, choose Weld Selected.

The second common problem is around the bottom of the leg. This needs the same adjustment that we did at the wrist.

Start by selecting the bottom row of vertices. Right-click in the Edit UVWs window and, from the lower left-hand quad menu, select the Break option.

Now that the vertices are broken, move them apart one by one until they are all separate, as shown in Figure 3.57.

As you are rotating around, you might notice some stretching in the crotch area.

Figure 3.55

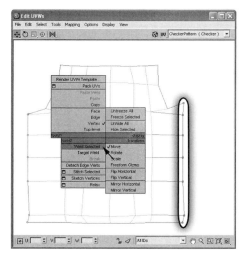

Figure 3.56

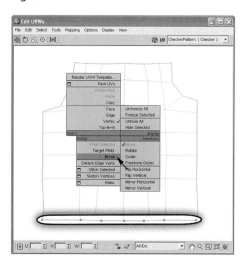

Figure 3.57

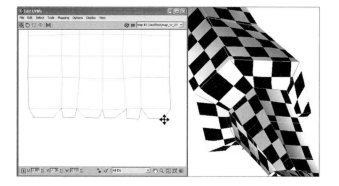

Figure 3.58

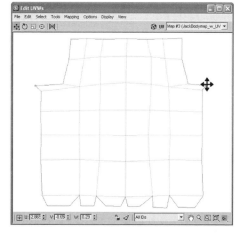

From the Front viewport, adjust the upper right-hand corner vertices until the checker pattern continues around the front.

Repeat the process for the back side, as shown in Figure 3.58.

Finally, select the whole leg patch and change to the Freeform Tool; scale it down and move it into the lower left-hand corner of the blue box.

You're done with the leg, so on to the boot. Now is a good time to save your project with a new name.

Figure 3.59

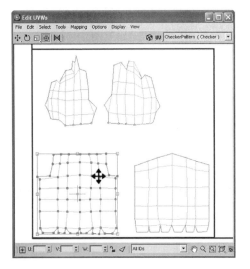

Figure 3.60

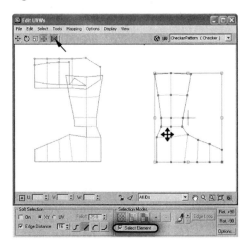

Figure 3.61

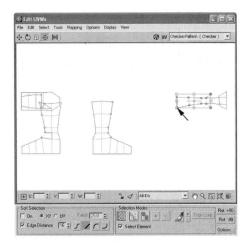

The boot is a little more complex than the parts we have done so far. Instead of one big patch, we are going to make five smaller ones that will be the front, left, right, back, and bottom sides.

Make sure that, in the Edit UVWs window under Selection Modes, Select Element is checked. Then click on one vertex in the boot UVs, move the selection to the right, and click the Mirror Horizontal button

Find the front of the boot patch, rotate it vertically, and move it close to the right-hand side of the boot patch.

Find the back side of the boot patch, rotate it –90 degrees, and move it between the left- and right-hand side patches.

Find the bottom of the foot patch and rotate it down 90 degrees. Move it to the left-hand side of the boot patches.

Now, to finish the front of the boot patch, there should be three small patches that have to be put together. Before we can do this, however, there is one small polygon in the wrong place that must be moved.

Change to the Polygon Selection Mode, uncheck the Select Element option, and select the extra polygon. Right-click and, from the lower left-hand quad menu, click on the Detach Edge Verts option. Now you can move it to the side of the boot missing polygon.

Figure 3.62

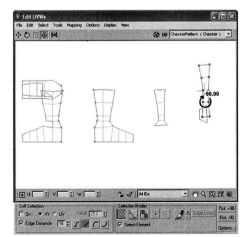

Figure 3.63

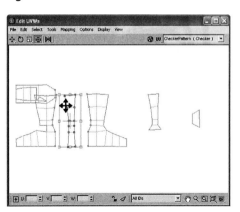

Figure 3.64

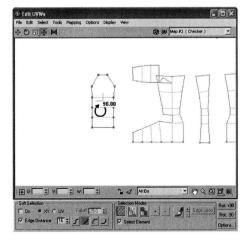

Figure 3.65

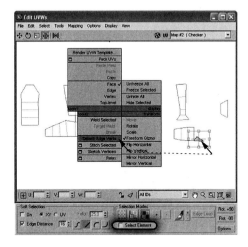

Figure 3.66

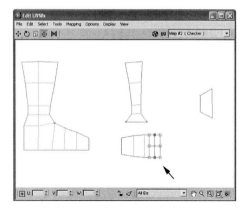

Figure 3.67

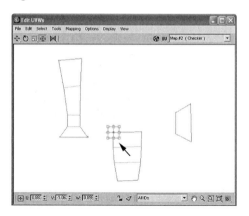

Figure 3.68

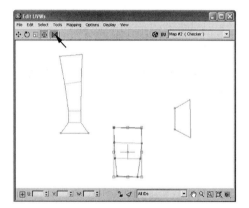

Figure 3.69

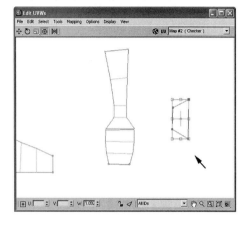

To figure out how to attach the three pieces, select the pair of vertices shown in Figure 3.66 and look to see what vertices and edge turn blue. Select the entire patch and rotate it so that it can be welded to the corresponding vertices. This little patch is tricky. Select one vertex on the connecting side and notice that its geometric neighbor is on the wrong side. To fix this, select the entire patch again and click on the Mirror Horizontal button; now the two patches can be welded together. Move the patch under its geometric neighbor and get the vertices close together.

It's always a good idea to check the individual vertex—not just pairs or patches.

Finally, select the toe patch and rotate it until the connecting edge is up, then move it under the other two.

The patches can be welded together fairly quickly using the Target Weld tool.

Right-click in the Edit UVWs window and, from the lower left-hand quad menu, click on the Target Weld option. In the window, zoom in on the middle patch, select a corner vertex, and then move it onto its blue neighbor. When you see the W, let go of the mouse button and the two should be welded together. Continue around until all the corners are welded and the green line continues around the outside of the patch.

Figure 3.70

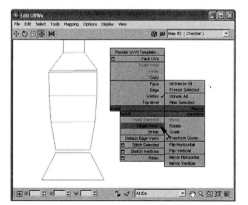

Figure 3.71

Figure 3.72

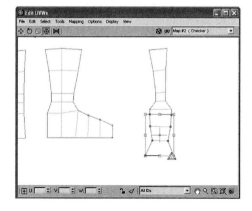

Figure 3.73

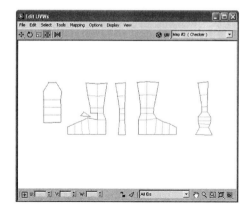

This patch needs to be squished up a bit, so select the bottom vertices, as shown in Figure 3.72, and move them up a little. Deselect the top row and move the remaining up, repeating until the patch looks like Figure 3.73.

We are almost done; there is just one arrant polygon to weld up in the boot.

Figure 3.74

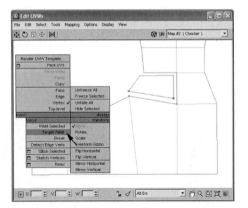

Figure 3.75

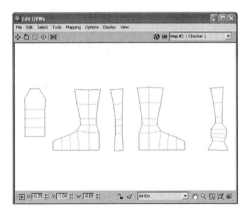

Figure 3.76

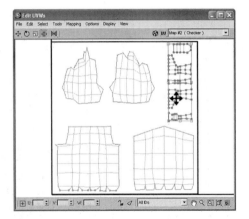

Figure 3.77

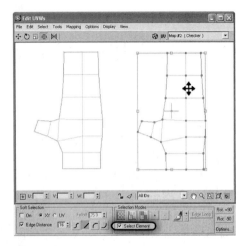

Zoom in on the side of the boot patch missing a polygon. Move each vertex of the polygon next to its blue geometric neighbor. Then right-click and, from the lower left-hand quad menu, select the Target Weld option. One by one, select the vertices of the polygon and move it onto its blue geometric neighbor, welding it.

The last thing to do is to select the five patches and rotate them and move them into the blue box, as shown in Figure 3.76. Now is a good time to save your project with a new name.

The hand will be the most complicated flatting procedure because of its shape. We are going to start by separating all the little bits; then, we will put them all back together into one patch.

Start by checking the Select Element option and clicking on one of the vertices of the hand patch. Move the selected patch and look in the 3ds Max viewport to see which side you have selected. My first selection was actually the bottom of the hand and it's facing the right way. Select the top of the hand patch and click on the Mirror Horizontal button so that the thumb is pointing to the right side. Then, move it to the right side of the bottom of the hand patch.

The next patch to look for is the outside of the hand; it should be one of the longer patches. Select it and move it between the top and bottom patches. This is one of the tricky ones. Uncheck the Select Element option and select one or two of the corner vertices; notice that they may

Figure 3.78

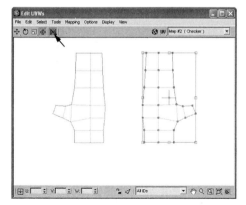

Figure 3.79

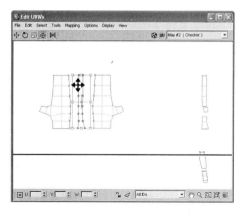

Figure 3.80

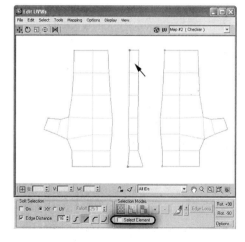

be on the wrong side. It's an easy fix, by selecting the whole patch and clicking on the Flip Horizontal button.

The next patch to place is the tip of the fingers; it should be a flattened hexagon shape. Select it and move it on top of the outside of the hand patch. Select the vertices on one end of the patch and rotate if necessary so that the connecting edge is in the right place.

The next patch is the inside of the hand. It should be the other long, straight patch. Move it to the left of the bottom of the hand patch; select the corner vertices to make sure the patch is in the correct orientation.

The next patch is the tip of the thumb. It should be only a single polygon. Select the whole patch and move it to the bottom of the hand patch's thumb area. Select a couple

Figure 3.81

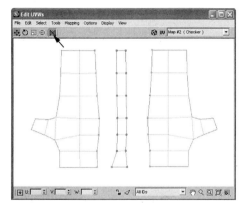

Figure 3.82

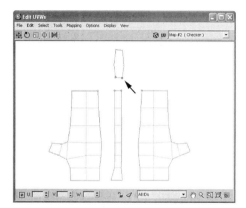

Figure 3.83

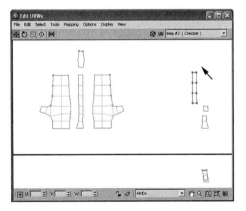

Figure 3.84

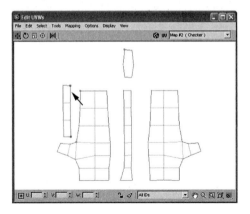

Figure 3.85

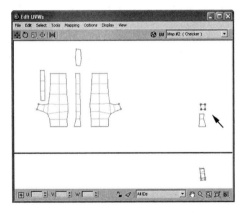

Figure 3.86

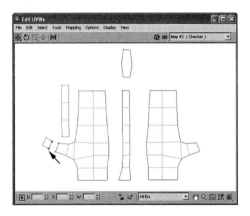

Figure 3.87

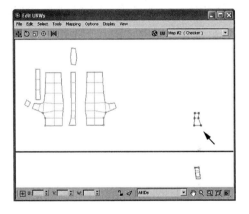

Figure 3.88

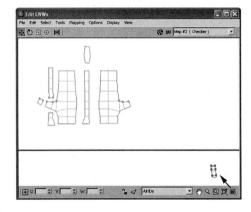

Figure 3.89

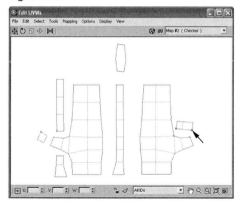

Figure 3.90

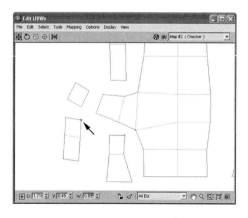

of the vertices to find the correct orientation. Rotate or flip it if necessary to get the correct vertices aligned.

The next patch is the inside of the wrist area. Find the patch and move it to the outside of the bottom of the hand patch. It's a good idea to check the orientation just in case.

The next patch is the inside of the thumb area. Find the patch and move it to the inside of the thumb of the top of the hand patch. Again, it's a good idea to check the orientation of the patch just in case it's flipped.

The last free patch is the outside of the thumb. It will need to be flipped horizontally and rotated to correct the orientation. Check by finding the one vertex shown in Figure 3.90 so that you get the correct orientation.

Now we are going to move all the patches together.

Start by checking the Select Element option and move the patches together, as shown in Figure 3.92. Then, uncheck the Select Element option and move pairs or individuals closer together.

Finally, right-click in the Edit UVWs window and click on the Target Weld option. Start welding the patches together until it looks like Figure 3.95. Then, select the whole patch, scale it down, rotate it upside down, and place it in the center of the blue box. Now is a good time to save your project with a new name.

Now that we have unwrapped the whole model, it's time to copy the UVs from the left-hand side of the model to the right. There is no way to do this at the UVW level, but it can be done at the geometric level.

Figure 3.91

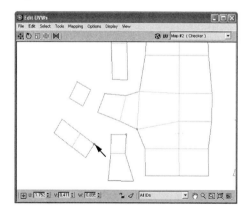

Figure 3.92

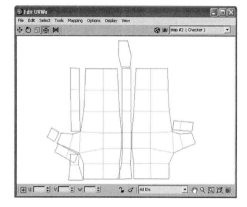

Figure 3.93

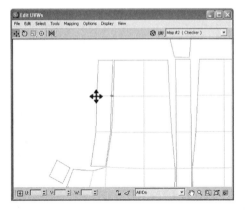

Figure 3.94

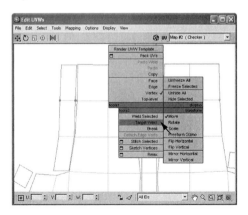

Figure 3.95

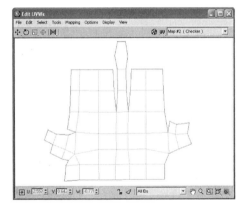

Right-click in the white area of the modifier stack area and select the Collapse All option. If you get a warning popup, just click the OK button. Now that the modifiers have been collapsed to an Editable Poly, change to the Polygon sub-object level. Select the right-hand side of the model and delete it. Then add a new Symmetry modifier.

Once you add the Symmetry modifier, it should be a perfect mirror. If not, then repeat the process we went through the first time we added the Symmetry modifier.

Add a new Unwrap UVW modifier and click on the big Edit button. There are all of your UVs—and you thought they were gone!

Figure 3.96

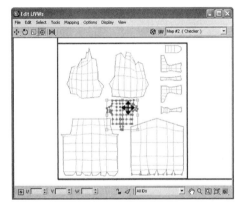

Figure 3.97

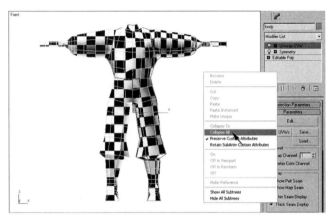

Figure 3.98

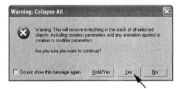

Figure 3.99

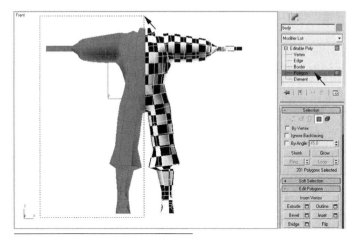

Figure 3.100

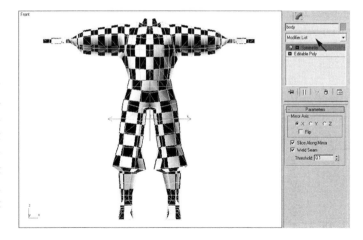

They were just hiding. When you collapse the stack, it bakes the Unwrap UVW modifier down to the face level. So, even without the Unwrap UVW modifier on, your models UV setup is preserved.

You might notice that the chest and back are only halves. Actually, the two halves are right on top of each other. Now all we have to do is separate the halves, flip one side, and weld them together to get a whole patch.

Start by checking the Select Element option and the Constant Update option. Then click on one of the vertices of the front patch. Make sure your 3ds Max viewport is in the Front viewport and zoomed in on the front of the model. Move the patch in the Edit UVWs window and watch your model at the same time. Find the half that

Figure 3.101

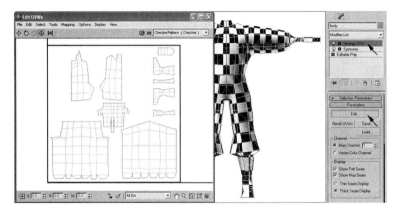

Figure 3.102

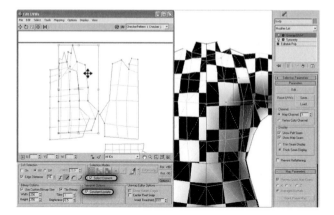

Figure 3.103

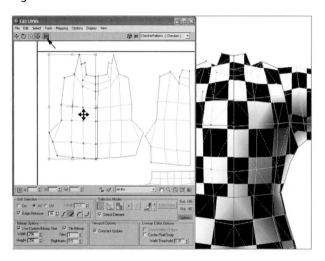

does not have the correct orientation and click on the Mirror Horizontal button. Put the two halves together as closely as you can. Uncheck the Select Element option and select the centerline vertices of both UV patches. Right-click and, from the lower left-hand quad menu, select the Weld Selected option.

Now you should have one whole chest patch.

The process is the same for the back.

First, change your 3ds Max viewport to the back by right-clicking on the viewport label and selecting the Views>Back options.

Figure 3.104

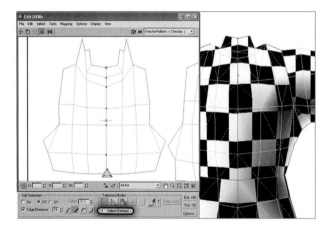

Then, check the Select Element option and click on one of the vertices of the back patch. Zoom in on the back of the model. Move the patch in the Edit UVWs window and watch your model at the same time. Find the half that does not have the correct orientation and click on the Mirror Horizontal button. Put the two halves together as closely as you can. Uncheck the Select Element option and select the centerline vertices of both UV patches. Right-click and, from the lower left-hand quad menu, select the Weld Selected option.

Figure 3.105

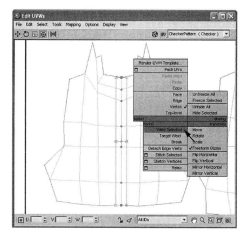

Figure 3.106

Figure 3.108

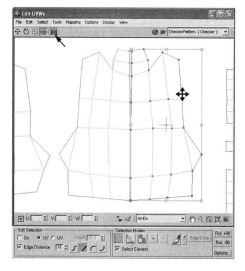

Figure 3.107

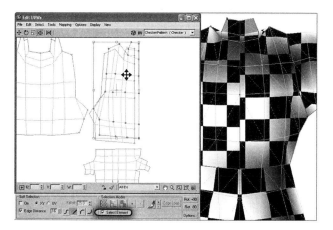

Figure 3.109

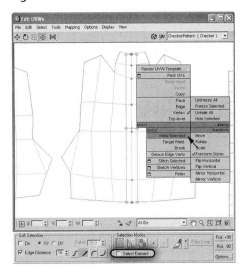

Figure 3.110

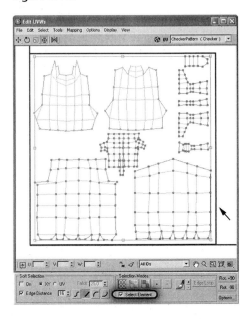

Figure 3.111

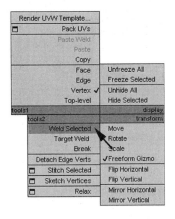

Figure 3.112

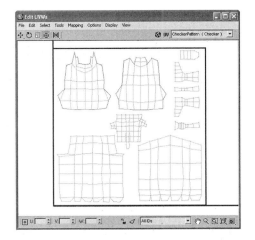

The final step is not totally necessary, but it does make editing easier. We are going to weld the left- and right-side patches together.

First, check the Select Element option and then, using the marquee window, select all the patches except the front and back. Right-click and, from the lower left-hand quad menu, select the Weld Selected option.

Notice that the green line around the outside of the patches is gone. That's because the left- and right-side patches are now welded together. Now is a good time to save your project with a new name.

Figure 3.113

Figure 3.114

Figure 3.115

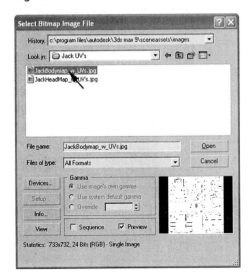

Figure 3.116

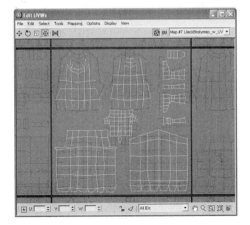

For the most part, we have a completed unwrap of the body. There are some patches that could use some more work. The reason we are not doing more is that the process is usually done in conjunction with the map or texture maker. The final adjustments are made as compromises to the way maps have to be made.

If you want to, use my map and complete the project, rather than make your own. You will have to change your UVs to match my map. This is not too difficult; it just takes a little time.

In the upper right-hand corner is a drop down; click on it and select the Pick Texture option. From the Material/Map Browser,

Figure 3.117

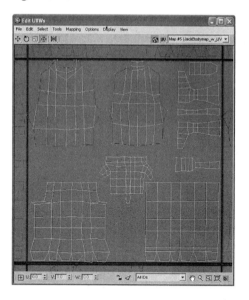

Figure 3.118

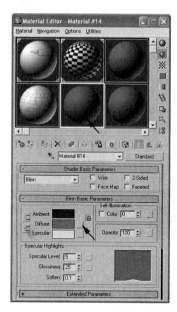

Figure 3.119

Figure 3.120

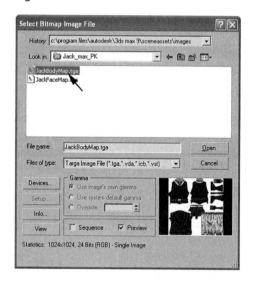

double-click on the Bitmap option and then navigate to the DVD that came with the book. From the Jack the P folder, find the Jack UVs and open it; you should see two files. Select and open the JackBodymap_w_UVs.jpg and it should show up in the background of the Edit UVWs window. Then, you can move the vertices of the patches around until it looks like the background image.

Figure 3.121

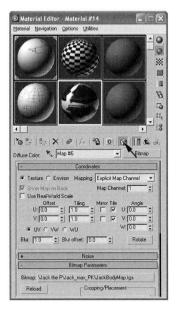

Figure 3.122

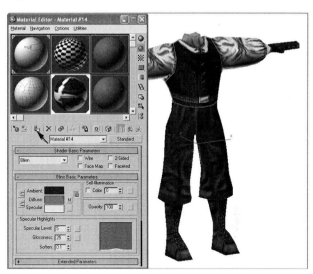

Now let's see what all our hard work has done for us.

Open the Material Editor by pressing the M key on the keyboard and select a blank material sample. Click on the little gray square next to the Diffuse color sample. From the Material/Map Browser, double-click on the Bitmap option and then navigate to the DVD that came with the book. From the Jack the P folder, find the Jack_max_PK; open it and you should see two files. Select and open the JackBodymap.tga and it should show up in the material sample. Click to activate the Show Map in Viewport. Click on the Go to Parent button and then you can apply the material to the body.

Now you should see material on the body. That's it for the body, so on to the head.

The Head

Take your time on this next part. It takes some time to unwrap a head properly. The complexity of the surface of the face is the problem. There are two ways you can do this. The first is to follow me, take your time, and do the best you can.

If you want to use a shortcut, see Appendix B for help.

Unwrapping the head starts the same way as for the body, but it will be a much shorter process because there are only three parts to separate. The face, however, will take much longer to flatten properly.

Let's start by hiding the body and unhiding the head.

Figure 3.123

In the modifier stack, right-click on the Symmetry modifier and cut it.

Make sure you close the Editable Poly by clicking the word until it turns gray.

Open the Material Editor by pressing the letter "M."

Change the name of the existing checker material and apply it to the head. It will turn white or some other color because it has no mapping coordinates.

From the modifier list, add a new Unwrap UVW modifier and click the Edit button.

Figure 3.124

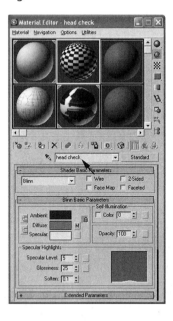

Figure 3.125

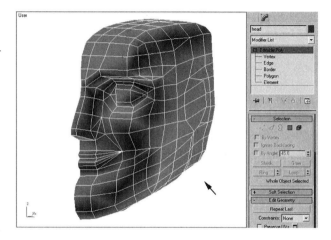

Figure 3.126

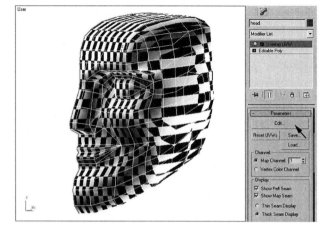

Figure 3.127

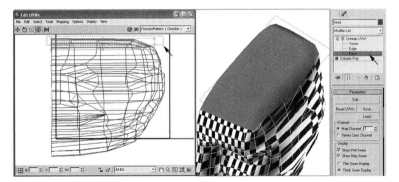

Figure 3.128

Change to the Face Selection Mode and, in the Edit UVWs window, select the top of the head polygons, as shown in Figure 3.127.

In the Modifier panel Map Parameters area, click on the Planar button and then click the Align Y button.

Then click on the Planar button to deactivate it and, in the Edit UVWs window, move the patch up.

The bottom of the head requires almost exactly the same process as the top of the head did. This time, the face selection cannot easily be made in the Edit UVWs window, so we are going to make it in the 3ds Max viewport.

Rotate your view so that you can see the bottom of the head and select the polygons, as shown in Figure 3.130.

Figure 3.129

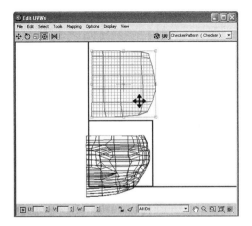

Figure 3.130

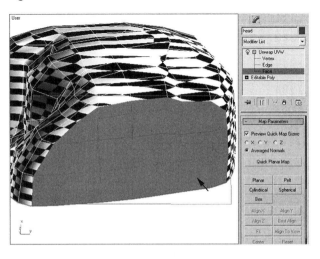

Figure 3.131

Figure 3.132

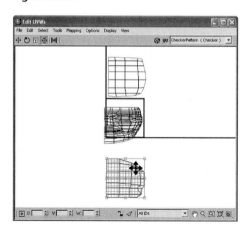

In the Modifier panel Map Parameters area, click on the Planar button and then click the Align Y button.

Then, click on the Planar button to deactivate it and, in the Edit UVWs window, move the patch down.

Figure 3.133

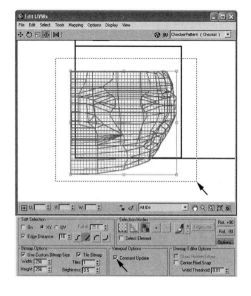

Face

The face is the hardest part of the body to unwrap. This is because there are lots of vertices to move and the face geometry is complex.

In the Edit UVWs window, click on the Options button and check the Constant Update option.

Then select the remaining faces inside the blue box.

Click on the Cylindrical button and then the Fit button. Notice that the seam is down the side of the face.

We have to deal with that pesky seam in the same way that we did with the arms and legs.

Change to the Rotate tool and, in the 3ds Max viewport, rotate the gizmo so that the green line is on the open side of the face.

Figure 3.134

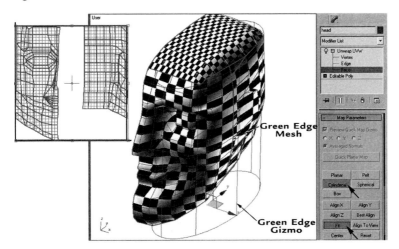

Figure 3.135

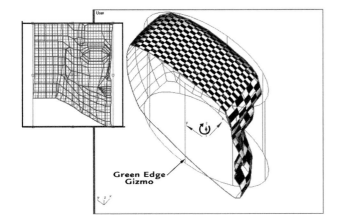

Figure 3.136

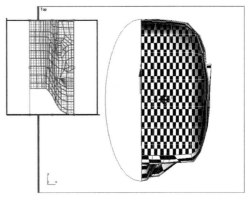

Change to the Top view and move the gizmo toward the center of the head. Then click the Cylindrical button to deactivate the gizmo.

Notice the difference between the left and right edges of the patch in Figures 3.135 and 3.136. After moving the gizmo to the actual center of the head, the seam edges have fewer overlapping polygons. This will help you a lot in the face-unwrapping process.

Before we start unwrapping, we have to make the checks smaller. The geometry of the face has finer detail, so we want smaller checkers to show it.

Figure 3.137

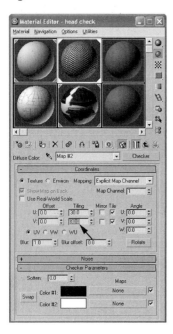

Figure 3.138

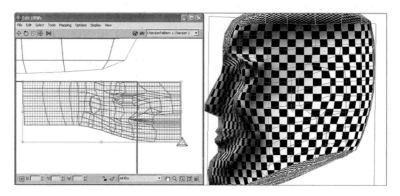

Figure 3.139

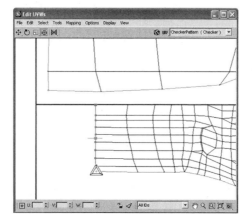

We will now move groups and individual vertices around in the Edit UVWs window to regularize the mapping coordinates.

Press M to open the Material Editor and click on the M button next to the Diffuse color sample. In the Coordinates rollout, change both Tiling values to 30. This will give us small enough checkers to unwrap the nose area. Since we have the face polygons selected, let's start with it.

Using the Freeform mode, scale the polygons until the checkers on the side of the head are square.

Don't worry about fitting it into the blue box just yet. Sometimes it's easier to work a little bit bigger then scale it down later. Now is a good time to save your project with a new name.

Figure 3.140

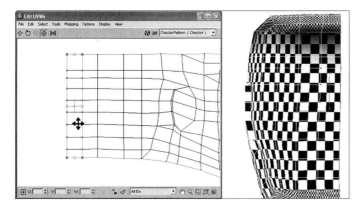

Figure 3.141

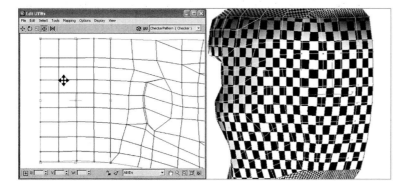

Change to the Vertex Selection Mode and, starting at the back of the head, select one vertical row of vertices at a time and scale them horizontally until they are vertical, using the Freeform mode.

Don't worry about moving them just yet; first, get the rows vertical.

Then, watching the back of your model's head, move them to the right until the checkers become square on the model. Starting with the outermost row, add the next row and move both to the right and so on until you get to behind the ear.

You now have most of the head done; the face is next.

The area that will need the most work will be that selected in Figure 3.142.

Change to the move tool and dive in.

Figure 3.142

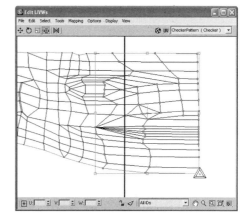

Figure 3.143

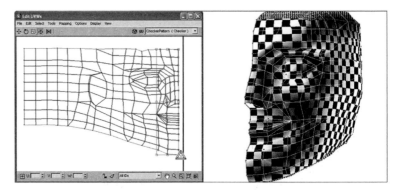

Select the vertices as shown in Figure 3.142 and, using the Freeform mode, scale them down toward the eye.

Then select the first vertical row of vertices and move them out a little.

Select the vertices under the mouth along the chin and move them out until the checkers are square on the model.

Zoom in so that you can tease apart the vertices in the corner of the eye.

Always keep one eye on the User viewport and the shape of the checkers.

Select the first three rows of vertices, as shown in Figure 3.147, and move them out to give you some space to expand the eye.

Keep working your way across the face, working on one vertical strip at a time. Around the eye will be the hardest. It can take an hour or more to adjust the eye and

Figure 3.144

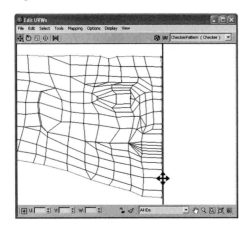

Figure 3.145

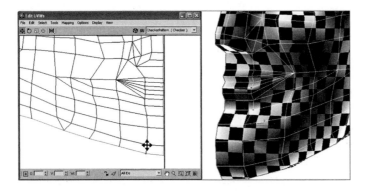

Figure 3.146

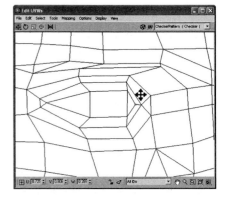

Figure 3.147

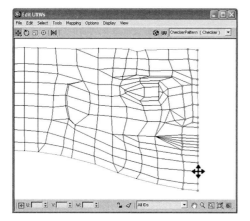

Figure 3.148

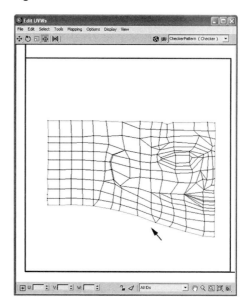

nose areas. Don't worry about it if you can't quite get the face perfectly unwrapped. There is a little bit of room to wiggle between the painting and unwrapping processes. We can fix a few things with the map. So take your time and remember that it is possible to use my UVs to help you lay out yours. See Appendix B.

When you are done, make sure you save your project with a new name.

Putting It Together

Now we'll put all the patches together inside the big blue square in the middle of the Edit UVWs window. We want to arrange them in order to create a surface as easy to paint as possible.

Zoom out in the Edit UVWs window so that you can see the top and face patches.

Select the face vertices and, using Freeform Mode, move and scale the patch into the middle of the blue box. Remember to use the Ctrl key for uniform scaling.

Now we are going to move the top of the head patch into place.

Select the vertices on the right side of the patch and look for the blue vertices on the face patch. Rotate the patch clockwise 90 degrees and scale it until the checkers are square. Move it into place on top of the face patch and then, holding the Ctrl key, scale it down to fit.

The same steps can be used on the bottom of the head.

Figure 3.149

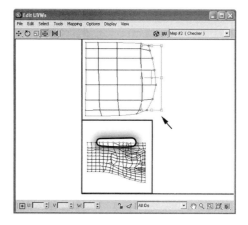

Figure 3.150

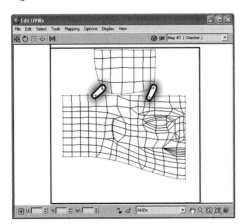

Figure 3.151

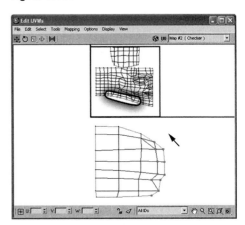

Figure 3.152

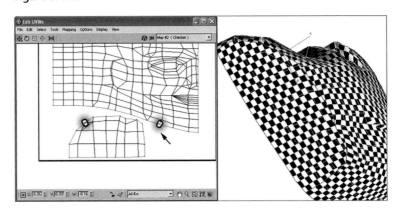

Figure 3.153

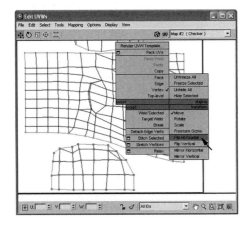

Figure 3.154

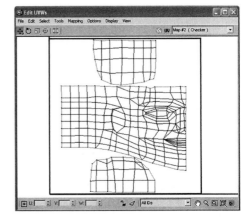

Select the vertices on the right side of the patch and look for the blue vertices on the bottom of the face patch. Rotate the patch counterclockwise 90 degrees and scale it until the checkers are square. Move it into place on top of the face patch and then, holding the Ctrl key, scale it down to fit.

This is one of those tricky patches. Select the upper left-hand corner vertex of the bottom of the head patch and notice that the blue vertex on the face patch is in the front. To fix this, select the whole bottom of the head patch and right-click anywhere in the window. From the lower right-hand quad menu, select the Flip Horizontal option. Then move it in closer to the face patch.

Now we have created usable UVs; if you want to use my map for your head, see Appendix B.

If you want to create your own map from scratch, you have to export your UVs so that they're usable in a painting or Photoshop type program; see the following *Exporting UVW Maps* section.

If you followed Appendix B, you should be able to put the JackFaceMap.tga into a material and apply it to the head. Make sure to press the Show Map in Viewport button so that you can see the map in the viewport.

Paste the Symmetry modifier back on to create a whole head.

Right-click in the Modifier Stack area and select the Collapse All option. If you get a warning popup, just click the Yes button. Now is a good time to save your project with a new name.

That's it; you're now ready to go on to rigging.

If you want to make a different character and new maps, there is one more step to take. That is to export your model's UVs to an image format so that they can be taken into a paint program and used

Figure 3.155

Figure 3.157

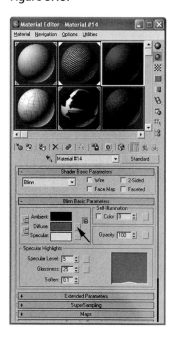

Figure 3.156

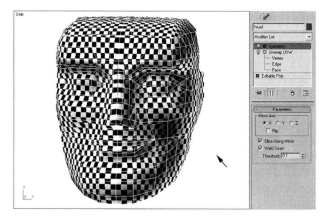

Figure 3.158

Figure 3.159

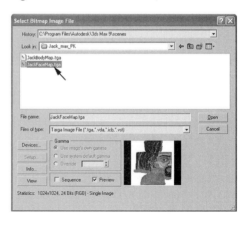

Figure 3.160

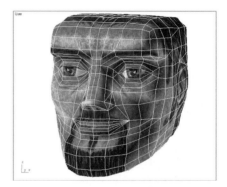

Figure 3.161

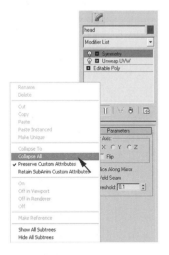

as a template for texture map creation. This is how I generated the JackBodymap_w_UVs image.

Exporting UVW Maps

To export your UVs is fairly easy. Remember that only the area in the blue box will be rendered.

Once your UVs have been laid out in the Edit UVWs window, click on the Tools pull-down menu and select the Render UVW Template option.

In the Render UVs popup, click on the Render UV Template button at the bottom.

From the Render Map window, click on the Save button in the upper left-hand corner. Save the file with a .TIF image format.

Now that file can be opened in any image editor and used as a template.

Figure 3.162

Figure 3.163

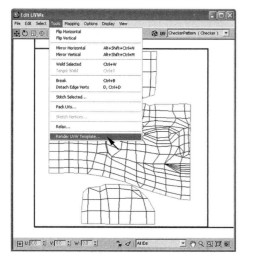

Figure 3.164

Figure 3.165

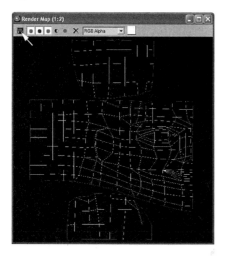

Figure 3.166

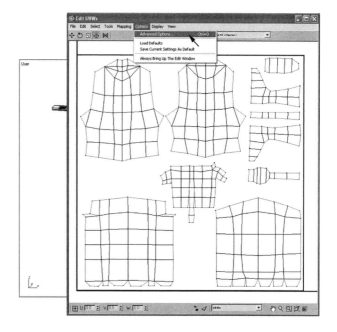

Another Option

For older versions of 3ds Max, we have to do it a little bit differently. It's not too hard; all we have to do is take a screen grab.

Unhide your body and select it. In the modifier stack area, select the Unwrap UVW modifier and click the Edit button.

Figure 3.167

Figure 3.168

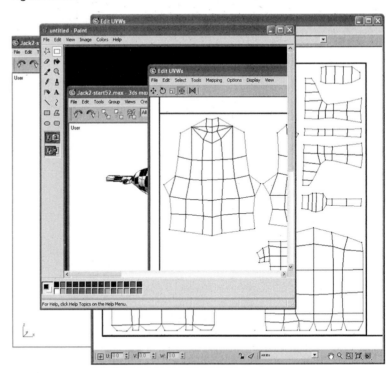

In the Edit UVWs window, choose Options>Advanced Options, or in 3ds Max 9, choose Preferences. In the Unwrap Options dialog box, change Line Color to black and Background Color to white. Uncheck the Show Grid box. This will give you the cleanest image to use for a template. Click OK.

From the bottom right-hand corner of the Edit UVWs window, drag out the window size as big as you can and press the Print Screen button on the keyboard.

Print Screen copies the screen to the Microsoft Windows clipboard. The clipboard can store only one image at a time, so we have to open Photoshop or Microsoft's Paint program and save our template.

Let's use the Paint program to keep it simple.

From the Windows Start menu, choose All Programs>Accessories>Paint.

In the Paint program, choose Edit>Paste. You can now see a snapshot of your computer screen. Save the file as a .TIF, with a name like "body_unuvw_temp." Then choose File>New to clear the old image.

Figure 3.169

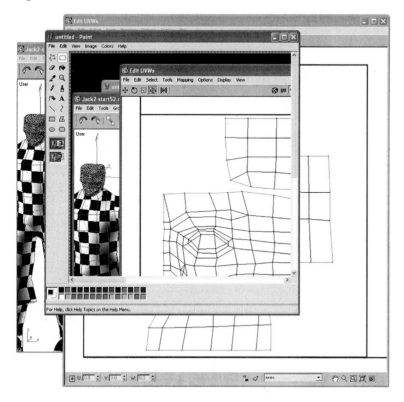

Repeat the process for the head and give it a name like "head_ unuvw_temp."

Unfortunately, you can't use Paint to create texture maps. LOL! You have to use a program like Photoshop, Painter, or Corel Paint.

4

Photo-Realistic Map Making

In this chapter we are going to create part of a map that could be used on a character. In the tutorial section I will be using a technique for mapping I call photo-manipulation. This method involves using Adobe Photoshop CS to manipulate multiple photographs to create a custom-made map. Because this method can be used to map any model, it's a universally useful tool for any 3D artist. There are, of course, many other ways to create maps, or skins as they are sometimes called. The other methods usually involve digital painting mixed with image manipulation to create original maps. For a minute, let's take a look at the subject of mapmaking in a larger context.

Photo-Realistic, Realistic, and Cartoon Detail

There are three basic levels of detail by which an image can be classified. The highest level of detail and realism is called photo-realistic. If you did the leaf tutorial in Chapter 2, you have already used a photo-realistic map as part of a material. By using high-resolution photographs as source material you can create photo-realistic maps for any model. To create a photo-realistic material, however, needs more than just a good color map. It requires a surface simulation.

This will push a 3D model into the photo-realistic realm. There are some special effects that can be used at render time to create more realistic surfaces—things as small as the pores of the skin, surface properties like the oiliness or dryness of the skin, and the different depths of translucency that different areas of the body have. For even more detail, the inner workings of light in the eyeballs can be simulated. At this point in time, most games do not require that much detail. However, the next generation of real-time game engines will be able to take advantage of some of the additional information that can be generated by 3ds Max. So I am sure someone will find a use for it. I can easily predict that the next generation of Sims games will be using some of the new rendering technique, such as normal bump mapping. A little further into the future I would bet that the quality of real-time games will approach film-quality renderings.

Most of the trailer movies made for video games fall in to the realistic realm, the middle ground between photo-realistic and cartoon. One of the best trailers for a game made with 3ds Max is Onimusha 3; you can download it at gamespot.com or gametrailers.com. This is a great example of the upper end of realistic rendering. You might even notice one of the characters as the actor Jean Reno, of the cult classic film *The Professional*. His image was used to create the model and texture of the character. It's not good enough to be a film body double, but it looks great in its context, and it's about the same level as the next generation of game assets will be. By the time you read this, Onimusha 4 should be out. The HD trailer for it was done with game rendering. It looks great for what it is, but I still like Onimusha 3's trailer better.

The last level of detail is not actually of a lower quality, just a different style. The characters that are cartooned are usually the more traditional real-time kids games. The evolution of Sonic the Hedgehog from a two dimensional one-button game into a great-looking 3D game is a good example. The makers wanted to keep the branding created by the original game but had to bring it into the 3D world. So they kept the simple cell-shaded look of the 2D character for the character and made a rich 3D world to play in. Eventually a true 3D character replaced the 2D character. The Mario Brothers game Empire evolved along the same lines. If you want to see screen shots and details of the evolution check out gamespot.com. They have the complete historical documents.

One way that the 2D world and the 3D world have combined into one is in a game called Simpson's Road Rage. The game engine is designed to render the 3D world in a process that is called "tooning" or cell shading. At render time, the 3D quality of the models is removed by drawing a black line around the outside edges of the objects. This traditional process is called inking. Then, the inside of the black line is filled in with one to three shades of one color. This creates a 2D look while still using the 3D game engine's advanced technology. 3ds Max has a material type called Ink and Paint. That can give you a similar effect as seen in the game, but not in real time. This is for pre-rendered movies only.

In a nutshell, there is a connection between the end result and the tools necessary to achieve it. If you want a photo-realistic material, you have to use high-quality photos and Photoshop. If you only need your material to be realistic, then you can use normal photos and a little bit of manipulation in Photoshop to create the detail. Creating realistic maps by painting is a technique reserved for the artistically inclined advanced Photoshop users and is a subject that deserves a book of its own. The easiest way I know to make great photo-realistic or realistic maps is by photo manipulation.

So let's take a look at how I implement the photo manipulation method. First we need to find or make a lot of reference images of the subject matter and then manipulate them into a map. The best reference images are those you take yourself, for example, if you were making a model of a specific car. You could find some pictures on the Internet, but they might not work for a number of reasons, such as reflections of the environment in the surface or the image resolution being too low.

If you go down to your local car dealership and take a bunch of pictures yourself, you can get exactly what you need. When taking your pictures always keep in mind how you might have to unwrap the model. I also carry around a cheap digital camera with me so that any time I find a cool wall or a sign, I can take a snapshot. This way I can build up my texture library for use in future projects.

There is one other method that can be used to create maps: paint one. Using Photoshop's painting tools, a skilled texture artist can paint a skin from scratch. Photoshop has some good painting tools, but its main focus is image manipulation. There are other programs like Metacreations' Painter or Corel Painter that have tools specifically designed for digital painting. You could use Window's Paint program to create a map, but I would not suggest it. The tools are too primitive to create anything beyond a cartoon type of map. There is a folder called "assorted UT assets" on the included DVD with the skin maps of some the characters in Unreal Tournament. It will give you an idea of the current level of quality.

Other tools for making maps are the 3D paint programs, Pixologic's ZBrush 2 and Right Hemisphere's Paint 3D v2. Both are quite expensive programs that have some incredible power.

They both allow you to paint directly on your 3D model, and they create the UVW unwrap for you. Zbrush has some additional tools to create normal bump maps. You should check out the gallery of images on both programs' web sites. The level of detail in the models generated by Zbrush will become the game industry standard soon enough. If you check out the Unreal Engine 3 web site you can see that the new characters look similar to Zbrush models.

As I said in the introduction, you don't need Photoshop to complete the project. I have given you two complete maps to finish the project. There is one map for the body and one for the head. So you can use them to finish the project. If you want to make your own character skins however, you will have to invest some time in learning Photoshop or one of the other painting programs. Photoshop is one of the most complex programs available for image manipulation today. It has many tools that can be used in conjunction with filters to give you an almost infinite tool set for image manipulation. The next thing to do is to decide what level of detail our map will have.

Creating a Realistic Map

So we are going to make one part of a body map. This will show you how to use Photoshop's tools and some of the techniques used to make maps. We are going to make some blue jeans. The first thing to do is to get some reference material. One of the easiest ways to get reference material is to use Yahoo's image search. All you have to type is the word "jeans" and you get tons of results. With a little manual searching I collected about 20 images. These included a bunch of front, back, and side shots of jeans.

It's also good to get pictures of close-ups of individual parts of what you're trying to create. For our jeans example, get things like buttons, pockets, belt loops, zippers, and whatever you can think of. It's easy to download images. Unfortunately, it's a little bit trickier when it comes to using them in a commercial production. The first big issue is one of copyrights. Most of the time you might only use a small part of an image, but it's better to be safe than sorry. Fortunately, there is no problem in using downloaded images as reference material, as long as you don't use the actual image in your map. The other is a question of image quality. Most images used for the web are about 200 × 200 at 72ppi. This is much too low to be used in production.

I will now walk you through the process I followed to create the maps included on the DVD. I started by laying out a white sheet in the noonday sun and took pictures with my cheap 1.33 megapixel digital camera. The more light you have, the better a low-megapixel camera will work. Close-up shots will also help in improving the quality. I took about 10 shots and used only six of them. Just take a look at my source files to see how I shot them and try to take similar ones.

Before we get started on this process, we need to edit our body's UV template image. To start in Photoshop, open the template image we created at the end of the last chapter. You can also open mine, "JackBodymap_w_UVs" from the Jack the P/Jack UV's folder.

If your images have not yet been edited and have more than the UV's bluebox, select the Crop tool from the tool palette. Click and drag a window selection around the blue box that encloses your flattened UVs. Confirm the crop by clicking the Commit button in the toolbar (the checkmark icon).

As I said before, we need a 1024x1024, 72ppi image in the end, so let's check the image size. When cropping by hand, it's almost impossible to do exactly down to the pixel.

Choose Image>Image Size. In the Document size area, change the resolution to 300ppi.

If your images' width and height values are different, you have to first uncheck Constrain Proportions. Then all you have to do is type 1024 in both the Width and Height areas in the Pixel Dimensions area.

If you use mine, all you have to do is change the resolution of the image to 300ppi and the width and height to 1024.

Now we are ready to start making jeans for our pirate. First open all six images I included as reference material in the Chapter 4 assets folder. We will take small parts of each and put them into

Figure 4.01

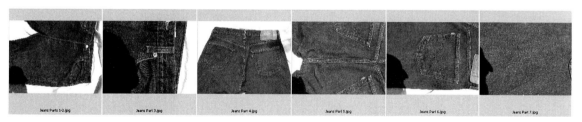

Jeans Parts 1-2.jpg   Jeans Part 3.jpg   Jeans Part 4.jpg   Jeans Part 5.jpg   Jeans Part 6.jpg   Jeans Part 7.jpg

Figure 4.02

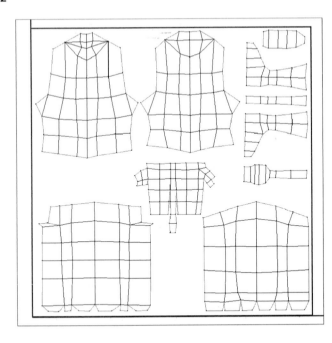

Figure 4.03

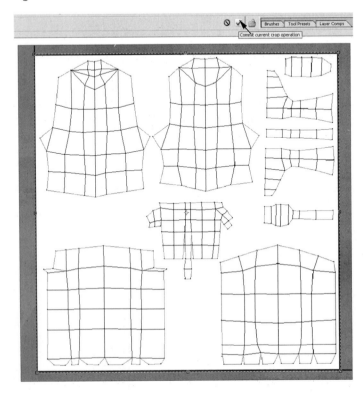

a master map file. Let's start with the Jeans Parts 1-2 file. First choose the Marquee tool in the tool palette. Then select the fly and pocket area as shown in Figure 4.05.

To move the selected area to a new image, we will use the Move tool, so choose it from the tool palette (it's just to the right of the Marquee tool). The trick to using this method is to have both images visible so that we can drag and drop from one to the other. In the Jeans file, as soon as you put the cursor inside the selected area, the cursor will automatically display a small scissors icon. Click with the left mouse button, drag the selection to the "body_unuvw_temp" image, and let go of the mouse button to drop.

You should see the section you selected now on top of the unwrap

Figure 4.04

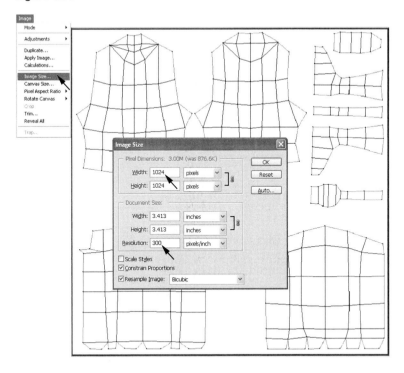

Figure 4.05

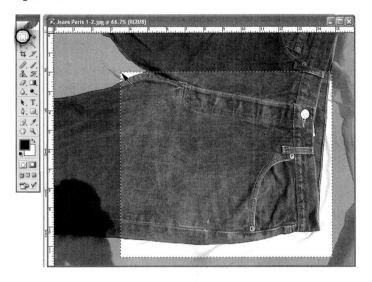

Figure 4.06

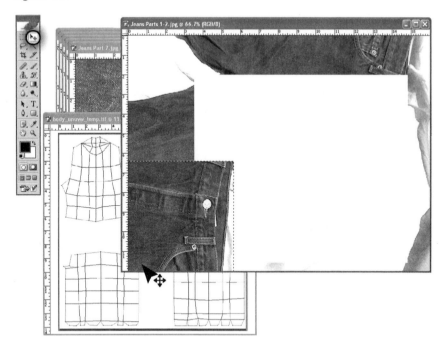

Figure 4.07

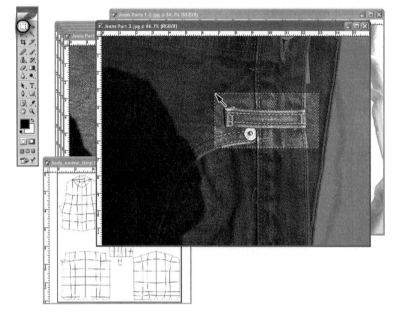

Figure 4.08

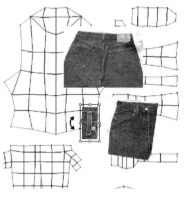

Figure 4.09

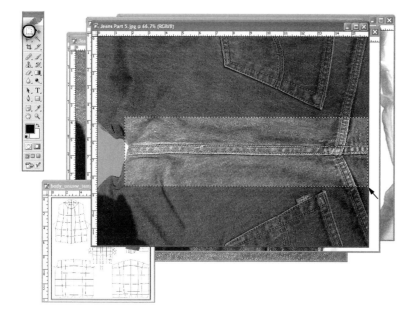

image, but it's not oriented in the right direction. It needs to be rotated and flipped horizontally, all things we can do using Free Transform. There is a menu choice for choosing Free Transform, but it's better if you get into the habit of using the keyboard shortcut Ctrl-T. Once you do, a rectangle will appear around the edges of the layer. To rotate the layer, move your cursor just outside of the rectangle (you may have to expand your window to make it larger than the canvas), and the cursor will change to a curved double-headed arrow to indicate that you can rotate the rectangle. Click and drag until the fly is vertical. Now all our transforms are done. Either click on the Commit button in the toolbar, or double-click inside the rectangle. This will apply the changes to your layer. If you don't like the changes, then click the Cancel button just to the left of the check button. We are going to have to make some more changes to this layer in order to use it, so for now just move it over to one side, and we will come back to it later.

Now on to the Jeans Part 3. Use the same process to extract the belt loop from this image. Select the Marquee tool and select the area as shown in Figure 4.07. Then select the Move tool. Cut and drop the image into your master map file. Again, we need to transform the layer's orientation. Use Free Transform to rotate the layer

Figure 4.10

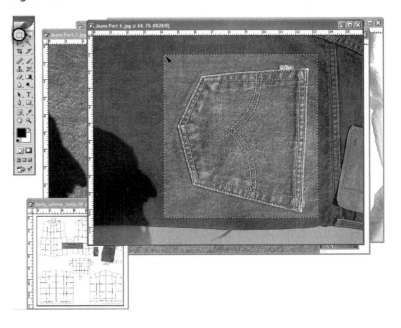

Figure 4.11

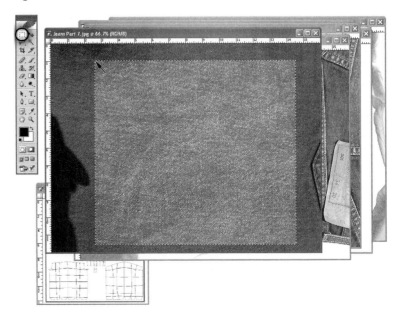

around until the belt loop is vertical, and move it off to the side. You will notice that the scale of the two layers is not the same. We will decide what scale they should be in a little bit using our model and the back pocket as guides.

We are actually going to use a lot of Jeans Part 4, so just copy the whole image to the master map file using the Move tool. Then move it to off to the side.

In the Jeans Part 5 file, we want to select just the stitching as shown in Figure 4.09. Drop the selection into your master map file and move it off to the side.

For the Jeans Part 6 file, we want just the pocket. Select the pocket area as shown in Figure 4.10. It will need to be transformed so that it's oriented correctly and moved off to the side.

In the last Jeans Part 7 file, select the middle area of the image as shown in Figure 4.11 and drop the selection into the master map file.

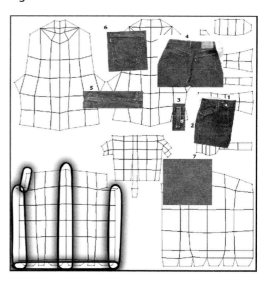

Figure 4.12

We now have all the parts we need to create a pair of jeans for our pirate. Now is a good time to save your file with a new name. Just add a "_working" postfix and save it as a Photoshop file. Even though the TIFF format can have layers, we will be using layers later on that cannot be saved in the TIFF format.

Let's start by creating all the stitches around the outside of the pants. We are going to use part number five, the stitches, and lay it on the edges circled in Figure 4.12. We will actually need a bunch of copies of this same layer. To keep track of them, we are going to create a layer set. This is like a folder that can hold any number of layers. This gives us the ability to manipulate them as a group.

So at the top right corner of the Layers palette is a little button with a right-facing triangle. Click on it and choose New Layer Set and name it Seams. Click and drag Layer 5, or whatever your seam layer's name is, and drop it on the word Seams. It will now appear indented just a little. Right-click on Layer 5. From the pop-up menu, select Duplicate Layer and confirm. In this case, it's okay to leave the name unchanged, because were using the Layer Sets to control the copies.

The middle edge of the leg patch is along the outside of the leg, so we can start there. Move the copy somewhere off of the original. Along the outside of the leg, we don't need the "T" section of the image, and the opposite end is looking a little ragged, so let's erase them both.

Figure 4.13

Figure 4.14

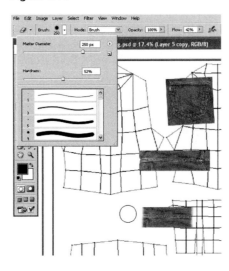

Select the Eraser tool from the tool palette. To change the brush size, click the second button in the toolbar, the Brush presets picker. From the pop-up menu, change the Master Diameter, then erase both ends. Also take a swipe at the top and bottom of the layer; this will soften the edges all around. Then we need to rotate the layer using the keyboard shortcut Ctrl-T. While holding the Shift key, rotate the seam vertical.

Hint: If you hold the Shift key down while you're rotating, it will snap at 25-degree increments. It will also constrain the scaling aspect of the Free Transform operation so you can scale uniformly.

We also need to reduce the scale of the layer by 50 percent. Still in Free Transform mode, put your cursor on one of the corner boxes,

Figure 4.15

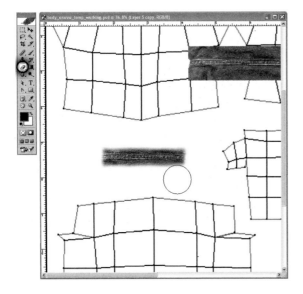

Figure 4.16

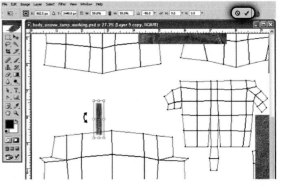

hold the Shift key, and drag down and to the left. Then move it to the top and center of the pant patch.

Now we're ready to move and copy the layer around, creating the seams. Right-click on the first copy and duplicate the layer. In the window, move the copy down. Don't worry about overlapping the layers; that will help to reduce the tiling effect. Repeat the process three more times, so that you have a seam all the way down past the edge, as shown in Figure 4.17. Then save your file.

It's a good time to apply our map to the model so we can see what it looks like on the model. So open 3ds Max and open your last project (or load the JackAfterUnwrap.max from the Chapter 4 assets folder). If your biped is visible, you can hide it, but don't delete it. We still need it for export. Open the Material Editor and select a blank material. Click on the little gray button next to the Diffuse color sample. From the Material/Map Browser, select the Bitmap option. Navigate to your working Photoshop file and click the Open button. Click OK to collapse the layers. Assign the material to the body, and remember to click the Show Map in Viewport button so you can see the map on the body. Now, every time we save our file we can go back to 3ds Max and see the results.

Back to Photoshop. The next step is to create the stitching for the inside of the legs, which would be the left and right sides of the patch. We actually need only the inside half of both sides, but instead of trying to cut the seam in half, all we have to do is put the

Figure 4.17

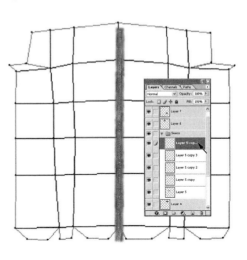

Figure 4.18

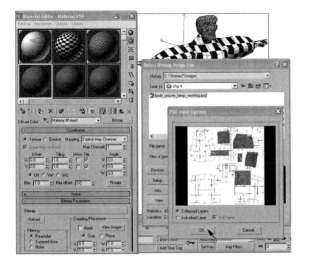

Figure 4.19

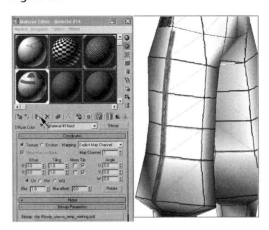

Figure 4.20

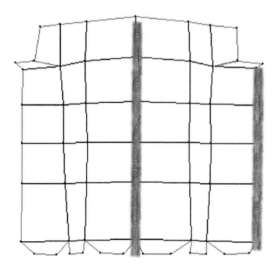

Figure 4.21

Figure 4.22

Figure 4.23

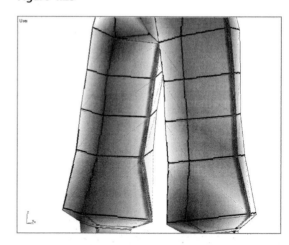

seam on the line and let the UVs cut it for us. That way, any little mistakes will be covered up.

Now let's repeat the process for the inseam. Right-click on the last Layer 5 copy and duplicate it. Then Move the copy right on top of the right green edge of the patch. Duplicate and move more copies up until it looks like Figure 4.20. Repeat the process for the left side of the patch until it looks like Figure 4.22. Don't be afraid to zoom in to get the seam image centered right on the green line.

Figure 4.24

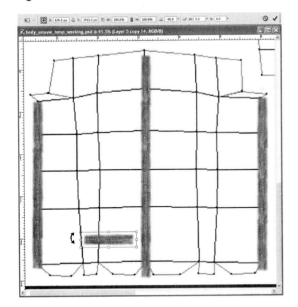

Figure 4.25

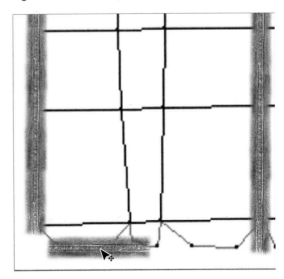

Figure 4.26

Then save your file with the same name, go back to 3ds Max and rotate your viewport until you can see the inseam.

If your green edge around the ankle or hemline area is not exactly where it should be, don't worry. We'll fix this later.

Back to Photoshop. The next part is to work the seam around the ankle. Copy the last Layer 5 and move it to the middle somewhere. Using Free Transform, rotate it horizontally, then move it down to the bottom edge of the patch. Duplicate the horizontal seam layer, and then move it across the whole bottom of the patch. Repeat until the bottom is covered.

As we start to add more layers to the image, it will get harder to see the UVs layer. So we are going to delete the white or black area of that layer, leaving only the edges. In the Layers palette, scroll down to Layer 1 (or whatever your UV layer's name is) and select it. You can also change the name of a layer by double-clicking on the name of the layer. Then choose the Magic Wand tool; it's right under the Move tool. At the top of the interface change the Tolerance value to 5 and uncheck the Contiguous box. All you have to do is click once in a white area and it should select all the white of the layer. Press the Delete key. It won't look like anything happened, but trust me, something has.

Figure 4.27

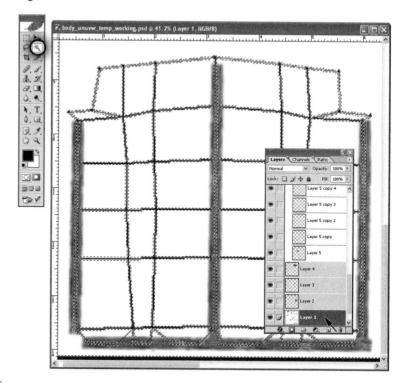

Figure 4.28

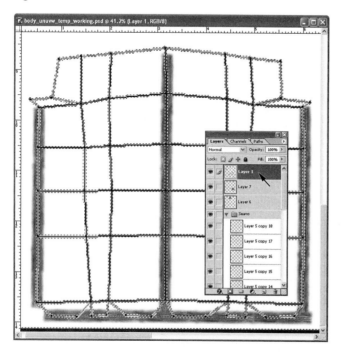

Note: Photoshop is a top-down program. That means the layer on the top is laid on top of the lower layer.

To move a layer up in the stack, select the layer and drag it up. You will see a black bar where the layer will be inserted. If you need to move it farther up the stack than you can see, then put your cursor all the way at the top and it will automatically scroll up. Or you could click on the down arrow next to the Seams folder icon. That will close the folder and make it smaller.

Now move the UVs layer up to the top of the stack. This way we can see the UVs on top of our jeans.

We're almost done with the seams, but the hemline is not finished. There are four more edges that need a seam. They are all at slightly different angles, and yours may be different from mine. You

Figure 4.29

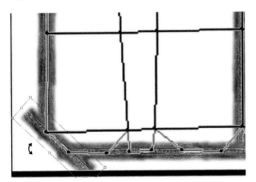

Figure 4.30

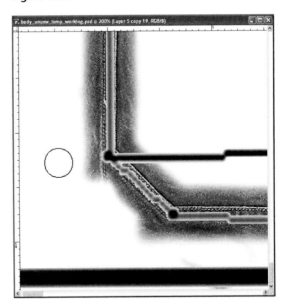

Figure 4.31

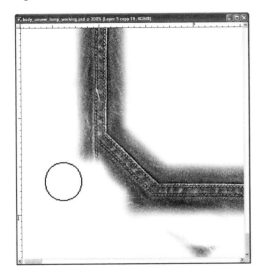

know the drill. In the Seams folder, select the last Layer 5 copy and duplicate it. Move the copy off the original. Using Free Transform, rotate it and move it until it looks like Figure 4.29.

Now there is a little bit of extra seam on both sides, so select the Eraser tool. Adjust the brush size down to around 50 and erase both ends as shown in Figure 4.30. Let's make the UVs layer invisible by clicking on the eyeball icon to the left of the Layer 1. Now you can see your eraser work a little bit easier. There are three more edges to make.

Copy the last Layer 5 copy and move it over to the center of the patch. Using Free Transform, rotate and move the copy into place at the right of center. Once the seam is aligned to the UVs green edge, you can make the UVs layer invisible by clicking on the eye icon. There may be a little bit of modification necessary using the Eraser tool. In my case it's an almost perfect match.

Figure 4.32

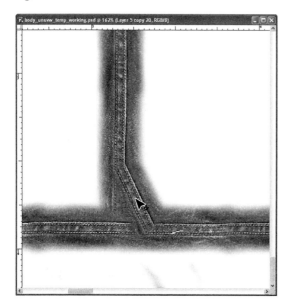

Figure 4.33

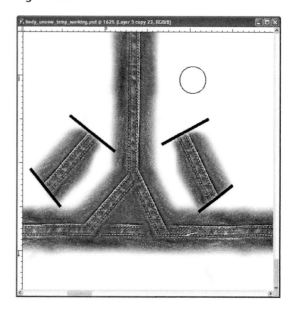

Figure 4.34

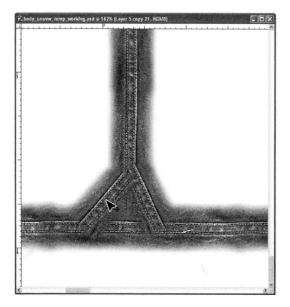

Figure 4.35

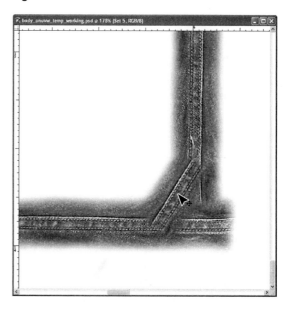

Repeat the process for the other side. First copy the last Layer 5 copy. Turn back on the UVs layer. Using Free Transform, rotate and move the copy until it looks like Figure 4.33. I would suggest rotating counter-clockwise or right-clicking and choosing Flip Horizontal. That way the erasers are at the same angle and will work

Figure 4.36

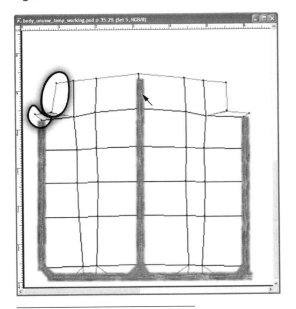

Figure 4.37

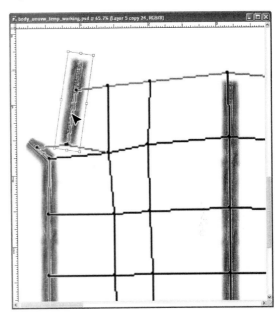

Figure 4.38

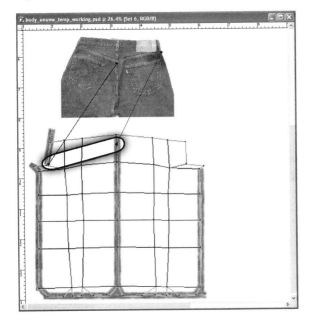

Figure 4.39

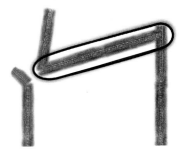

even if they are rotated unequally. Re-hide the UVs layer and erase to fit. If you don't have enough image to work with, you can always copy one of the earlier layers to use.

Turn on the UVs Layer. Then one more time, copy the last Layer 5 copy. Using Free Transform, move the layer over to the left side

Figure 4.40

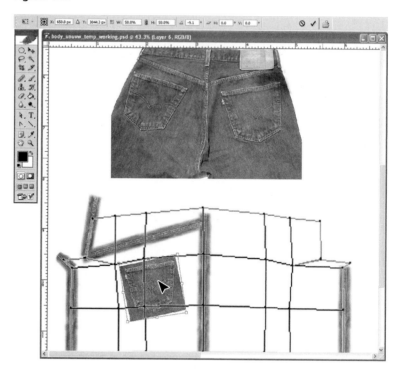

of the patch and rotate it to match the angle of the right side's bottommost segment. That will finish the hemline, but there is a little more to do.

There are two more seams we need to add in the top left corner of the patch. So one more time, duplicate the last copy of Layer 5. Using Free Transform, move the new layer up to the top left corner and rotate it to match the lower green edge.

Now we want a longer seam than the last Layer 5 copy, so if you select Layer 5 copy 17 or less, then right-click on it and duplicate it, you will have a seam longer than the last. To find the copy, activate Free Transform by pressing Ctrl-T, and the rectangle will show up. Then just move it up and rotate it until it looks like Figure 4.37.

There is one more seam that you might not notice. It is a signature of Levis jeans, the V on the back panel. It's a little confusing exactly how to make this happen in the right way, so check out Figure 4.38. The left side of the patch is down the center of the backside, so the seam needs to start lower than the outside edge. The seam connects to the outside edge's belt loop that's almost at the top. So the end needs to be toward the top of the center of the patch. It may take a couple of copies, but it should be quick and

Figure 4.41

Figure 4.42

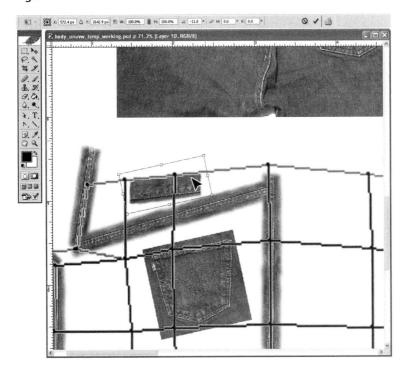

Figure 4.43

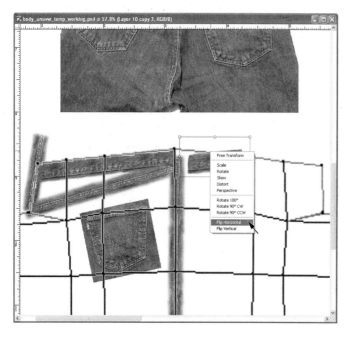

Figure 4.44

easy. Then using the Eraser tool, clean up both ends so the layers blend better.

Now we can place and scale the pocket layer. Select the Move tool and make sure the Auto Select Layer box in the toolbar is checked. Select and move the pocket layer into place on the left side of the patch. Then using Free Transform, scale the layer down around 50 percent using the Shift key to make the scale uniform. Then rotate it counter-clockwise about nine degrees. If necessary, move it into place so that it looks like Figure 4.40.

Now we are going to make the waistband and belt loops. Using Layer 4 or the two back pocket images we are going to copy the waistband out of the top section of the image between the belt loops. Then copy it across the top of the patch to create the waistband. So before we get too far, let's make a new folder for our copies. At the top of the Layers palette, click on the right-arrow button and select New Layer Set. Enter the name "Waist." Then move Layer 4 into the Waist folder.

With the original Layer 4 selected, activate the Rectangular Marquee tool and select the area as shown in Figure 4.51. Now I want you press a series of keyboard shortcuts, first Ctrl-C to copy, then Ctrl-V to paste. Photoshop will paste the contents of the clipboard into a new layer for you.

Select the Move tool and move the copied area to the top of the patch. It needs a little cleaning before it's usable. Select the Eraser tool and remove the top and bottom areas so that just the waistband area is visible. Then take a little off both ends so that you get just a nice straight piece of waistband.

Using Free Transform, rotate the layer about 10 degrees or whatever matches your UV's top edge. Then move it so that the top edge of the layer is just under the green edge of the UV's. Duplicate the layer and move them across the top of the patch until it looks like Figure 4.43. Remember, you can always use Free Transform and flip an image or layer horizontally or vertically.

Now to create the belt loops. Select Layer 3 or whatever layer your belt loop image is. Of course, it's going to take a little clean-up to make this a usable image. Before we start let's make a new folder for our belt loops and call it "Bloops." Then move Layer 3 into it.

First we have to get rid of the rivet by using the Clone Stamp tool. The Clone Stamp tool is the fifth tool down on the left side of the tool palette. It is actually a two-part tool; first we have to select the cloning area. To do this, first change the brush size to about the rivet's diameter. Press Alt and sample the area in the left corner of the image by clicking once with the left mouse button. The second step is to paint (clone) in a new area. In this case, I want you to uncheck the Aligned box so that when you click somewhere, it clones from the same place. Place your cursor over the rivet and click around until the image looks like Figure 4.46. Change your brush size down to get into the corners and back up to fill in the larger areas.

The belt loop is obviously a little large, so we will have to reduce the scale. The Bloops folder is lower in the stack than the Waist layer. We need the belt loops to be on top of the waistband. So let's move the Bloops folder up in the stack above the Seams folder. Now select

Figure 4.45

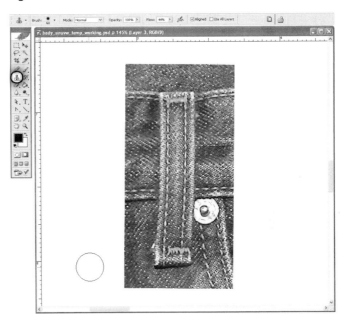

Figure 4.46

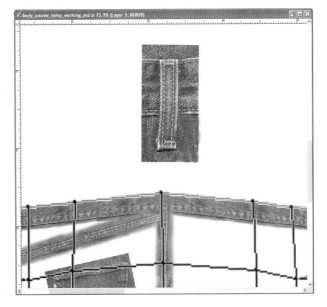

Figure 4.47

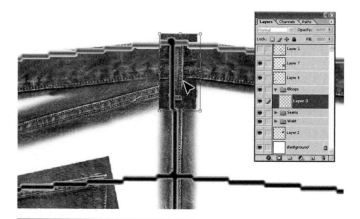

Figure 4.48

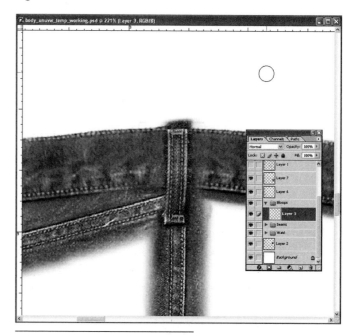

Figure 4.49

Figure 4.50

Figure 4.51

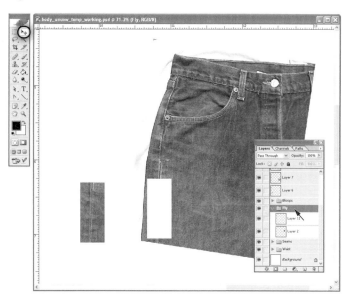

your belt loop layer and use Free Transform to first scale it down uniformly to around 33 percent and then move it into place at the middle of the waistline.

Make the UV's layer invisible and use the Eraser tool clean up around the lower part of the belt loop until your image looks like Figure 4.48.

Normally a pair of Levi's has one belt loop at the center of the back, two on the left and right sides, and two on either side of the fly. Because we have only one-half of the pants UVs to map, it's not going to be easy to make the left and right side of the pants different from each other; in fact it makes it impossible. The front loops are no problem. Copy Layer 3 and move it to the right side of the patch. Using Free Transform, give it a slight rotation to match the angle of the waistline. Then do the same for the backside belt loop until it looks like Figure 4.49. It will give us two loops in the back, but that's okay for this tutorial. If we really needed to have the left and right sides of the map, then we would have unwrapped it differently. Now is a good time to save your file.

The next area to work on is the front of the pants, including the front pocket.

Using the Layer 2 image we are going to create the fly and front pocket area.

Select the Move tool and select the front of the pants image. It should be Layer 2.

Figure 4.52

Figure 4.53

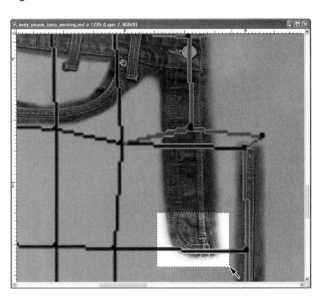

We need to erase most of the image, but before we do, let's copy a small section into a new layer.

To keep track of the layers, let's make a new layer set and name it "Fly." Move Layer 2 into it.

Use the Marquee tool to select the area as shown in Figure 4.60. Activate the Move tool.

Press Ctrl-X to cut and Ctrl-V to paste. The new layer will be in your Fly folder.

Move the new layer off to the left. In the Layers tab, select and move the Fly folder above the Seams folder.

To do the erasing, start by selecting the original layer and activating the Eraser tool.

Erase most of the image except the pocket, fly, and button area, similar to Figure 4.52.

Move the layer into place as shown in Figure 4.53, with the button split down the middle with the green edge.

One thing you might notice is that the fly area is extremely long. For our map, the whole fly area can be only as long as the first vertical green edge. So we are going to cut the bottom off and move it up a little.

Use the Marquee tool to select the area as shown in Figure 4.53.

Use the keyboard shortcuts for Cut and Paste to make the bottom of the fly a new layer.

Select the Move tool and move the new layer up so that the bottom of the fly image is at the bottom of the first edge as shown in Figure 4.54.

Select the Eraser tool and take a swipe at the top of the image. That should help it blend with the top half.

To finish up the fly, select the Eraser tool, select the original Layer 2, and remove the bottom half of the fly.

That's it for the fly; let's do a little more work on the pocket. We will use the small section that we cut out earlier to connect the lower pocket rivet to the waistline.

Figure 4.54

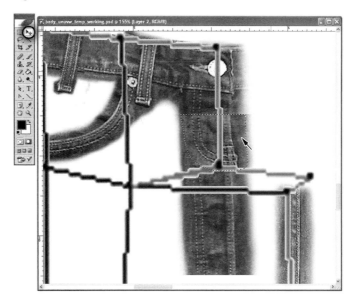

We are now going to add a small seam detail to the front pocket. It will need to be under the waistband and the rivet of the front pocket. Activate the Move tool and move the layer with the seam we cut out earlier into place. When I did, mine was covering both the waistline and the pocket rivet, so it needs to be moved down in the stack.

To make it easer on us, let's make sure to move this layer all the way down to the bottom and work with it there. So in the Layers tab, move the selected layer down below the Waist folder and drop it.

Using the Free Transform tool, rotate the layer counterclockwise about 10 degrees.

Now select the pocket layer and activate the Erase tool. Reduce the brush size and erase around the rivet until it looks like Figure 4.58.

Let's fill in the middle of the patch with our jeans material sample layer, which should be on Layer 7 (if it's not, you can change it to jeans or something similar).

The quick way to fill in the patch is to move Layer 7 to the bottom of the stack. Make a new layer set and call it "Jeans." Move Layer 7 into it. Duplicate the layer and move them around until you fill in the patch.

That's the basic setup for the jeans. Because we have created everything in parts, we can change those parts around. So if we want to change how many belt loops we have or where they are, it's easy.

Figure 4.55

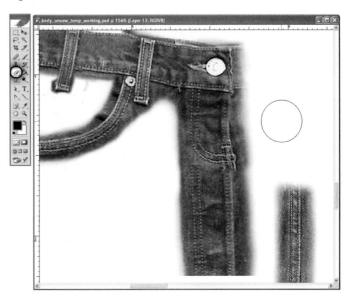

Figure 4.56

Save your file and take a look at your model in 3ds Max. Rotate your view around and see if things are the way you want.

The first thing that needs to be changed is that the mid-front pocket belt loop looks out of place and that maybe the seam that connects the bottom of the front pocket to the waistline could be more vertical.

After making those changes, save your file then take another look at it in 3ds Max. It should look much better.

Now is a good time to do a little bit of cleanup on several layers. For example, there is an extra seam sticking out the back of the patch that needs to be erased.

The back pocket could be better integrated by erasing around the outside. Also the seam that connects the pocket to the waistline could use a little trimming.

Tileable Textures

One of the reasons we are having some integration problems has to do with scale. The scale of the jeans material sample needs to be about 3/4 smaller than the size we first used it. To work at that scale we need to create a tileable texture.

To do that, first we need a new file with just the jeans material sample in it. From the Jeans folder, select the original Layer 7 (or the layer with your jean material sample) and move it up a little. Press Ctrl-A, which will select the whole layer.

Move it again, and the selection area will contract down to just around the image in that layer. Press Ctrl-C to copy the selection to the clipboard. Press Ctrl-N to create a new file, which will make a new file just to the size of your clipboard. Confirm the size, then press Ctrl-V to paste the clipboard image in.

Figure 4.57

Figure 4.58

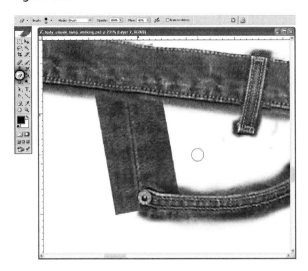

Figure 4.59

Figure 4.60

Figure 4.61

Figure 4.62

Figure 4.63

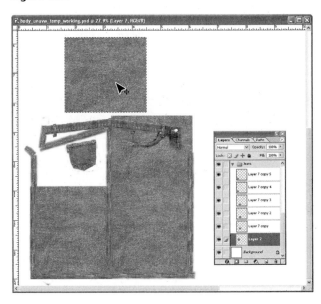

Figure 4.64

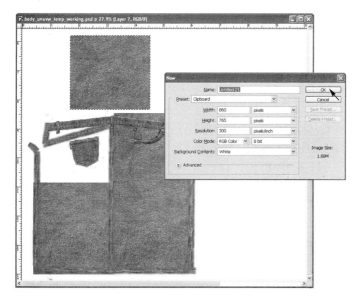

At the bottom of the tool palette is a button that starts a program called ImageReady, which is designed to help with generating images for web pages.

It has a feature that is used to create tileable background images for web pages. We are going to use it to make our jeans material a seamless tile.

From the Filter menu, select Other>Tile Maker. Click OK; the default settings work fine.

The new image is now tileable, so to get it back into Photoshop, click the corresponding button at the bottom of the tool palette.

Back in Photoshop, the layer will look a little different, but it's hard to tell exactly what's changed. First you can see that it's smaller than the original layer we took into ImageReady. This is because ImageReady has done it the old-fashioned way for you. That is, the edges of the image are cut off, flipped horizontally, moved to the opposite side, and blended with the new edge. That makes the left and right sides connectable without any seam. The same process is done for the top and bottom sides.

Make sure the Move tool is selected. From the Layers palette, select Layer 1. Drop it onto your working file.

It will drop it into whatever folder you have selected at the time, but we need to put it into its own folder so we can control all the copies.

Figure 4.65

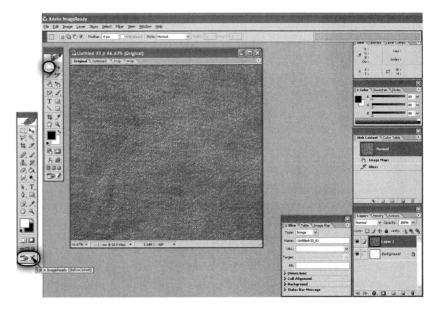

Figure 4.66

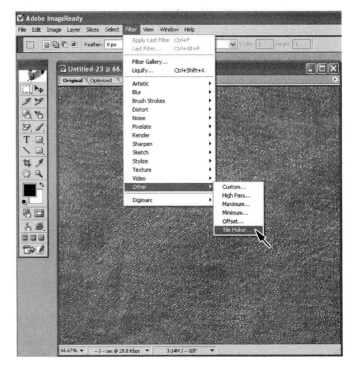

Figure 4.67

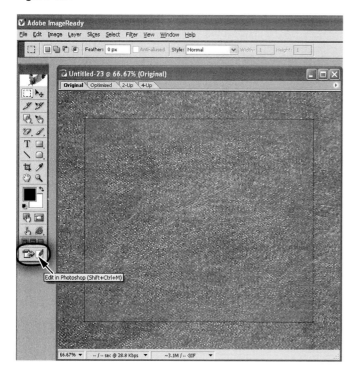

To move a layer out of a folder you have to move it up in the stack and above the folder it's currently in, then drop it.

Make a new layer set, calling it something like "Jeans Sml," and move the small jeans sample into it.

Using Free Transform, scale the layer to 50 percent of its original size using the Shift key to keep it square.

If you click on the eye next to the original Jeans folder, it will hide it. Then we can add the new smaller jeans sample in its place.

Duplicate the smaller jeans sample and move it around randomly. There can still be some tilling effects in the center of the image. Using Free Transform, you can flip the sample horizontally or vertically to break up any tiling effects from the center of the sample.

It took me about 35 copies to cover the area. Then I zoomed out and looked for any repeating image. If you find any, fix it by selecting any of the layers one at a time and flip them horizontally or vertically. Any tiling effect will disappear.

The last integration task is to even out the exposure levels of the different elements of our map. In the set of images included with the book, the button fly and front pocket layers are the ones that need

Figure 4.68

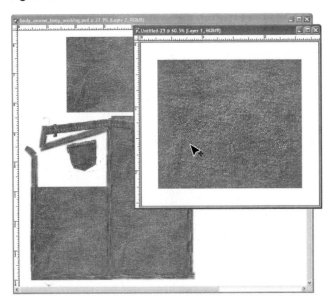

Figure 4.69

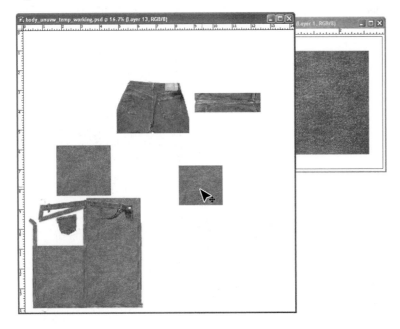

Figure 4.70

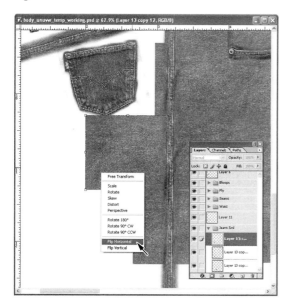

Figure 4.71

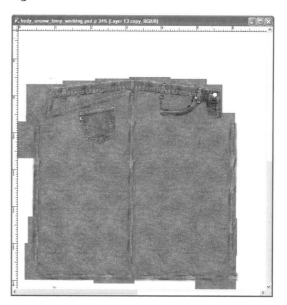

the most adjustment. They are a lot darker than the other parts of the image. So it might be easier to fix them rather than all the others.

To do this we need to change the layer blending mode of the Fly folder. Select the Fly folder. At the top of the Layers palette, there is a drop-down menu that says Pass Through. If you click on it and change the style to Normal, whatever we do inside this folder will affect only the layers inside of it. What we are going to add to this folder is called an adjustment layer. From the Layer menu, choose New Adjustment Layer>Levels. Click OK to confirm the name. If you'd like to reopen the Levels adjustment layer, double-click on it.

From the Levels dialog box, move the central gray slider to the left until the button fly area matches the waistline image. This will change the center of the contrast spectrum and not change the actual color of the layer. Now all of our parts look very close to each other in terms of contrast.

Figure 4.72

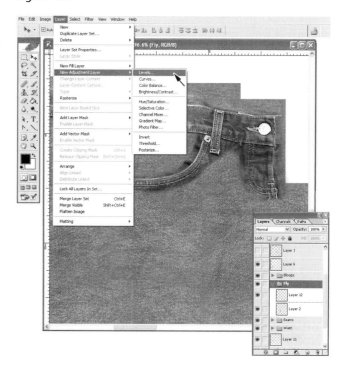

Figure 4.73

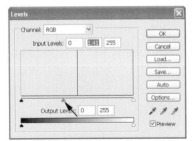

Figure 4.74

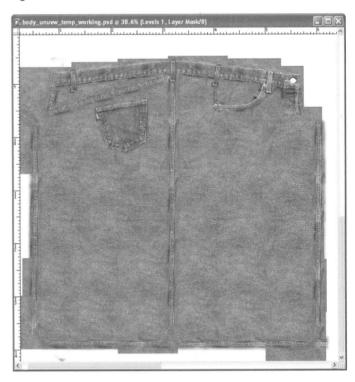

Figure 4.75

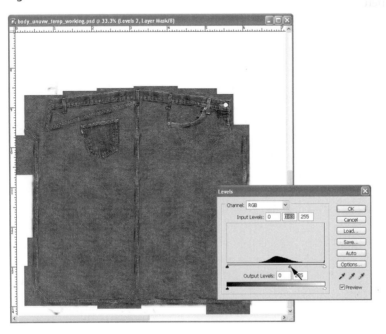

If you want to change the color or contrast of the whole patch, then you can add a new adjustment layer to the top of the stack, and it will affect the whole map. You can even change the color of the jeans by adding a Color Balance or Hue/Saturation adjustment layer to the top of the stack.

Add a new Levels adjustment layer, and this time move the center gray marker to the right to darken the whole pants patch. Make sure that it's at the top of the stack. Save your file with the same name and check it out in 3ds Max.

Exporting from Photoshop

Shadows and Creases

Now that most of the major problems are fixed, you might notice that the jeans look extremely flat. The problem is that there are no shadows and no creases anywhere on the jeans. As human beings, we have evolved a complex system for interpreting shadows. We have developed this ability so that we would not step in holes and break our ankles.

You might think that the game engine casts shadows, and it does, but only on the land. Current real-time game engines do not cast shadows on characters dynamically. The new generation of game engines are able to dynamically render shadows on characters. It won't be true shadows; it will be a rendering trick using a normal bump map to create the illusion of detailed shadows and creases.

Soon, having to create shadows and creases the way I will show you will not be used for game production. Creating the shadows for a map is more of an art form than a mechanical step-by-step process.

So I won't be doing a liner step-by-step tutorial on how to create the shadows and creases. Instead I will describe the setup and show you generally how the image might evolve. I will also explore and demonstrate some new Photoshop tools for you.

I am going to start with the large shadows. For the pants patch, the crotch area and the inside of the legs are where we can add shadows. If we were working the shirt area, then we would add shadows in the armpit area. Take a look at Figure 4.76 and compare it with Figure 4.77. The jeans in Figure 4.77 were laid flat when the picture was taken; notice that the crotch area is much lighter and more evenly lit than the next picture. The jeans in Figure 4.76 were being worn when the picture was taken; notice that crotch and inside of the leg are much darker than other areas. That's the effect I want to reproduce in my image.

The other effect we can work on is the wear pattern. The blue jeans fabric tends to fade over time, and sometimes it fades unevenly due to artificial damage. The examples show a couple of different ways they could be faded. Instead of copying one or the other exactly, I am going to mix the two, using the shadows and creases from one and the wear pattern from the other, creating a unique pair of jeans.

Before I can start to manipulate the jeans portion of the map, I need to take all the layers in the "Jeans Sml" folder and merge them into a single layer. To do this I need to turn off all the other layers, so that only the "Jeans Sml" folder is visible. By left-clicking

Figure 4.76

worn

on the right arrow button in the top left corner of the Layers palette, I selected Merge Visible. Notice that I also had the "Jeans Sml" folder selected before I merged. Now I have a single layer that I can modify, but first I will make a copy so that at any time I can start over.

I don't want to just paint black in those areas, but I want to make them darker. I am going to use a pair of tools called Dodge and Burn. The Dodge and Burn tools originated from black-and-white photograph printing process. It's the process of painting with light. Adding light to part of an image increases the contrast or makes that part darker. Denying light to part of an image decreases the contrast or makes that part of the image lighter. In photography, the art of printing great black-and-white images takes years to learn, and more to master. Luckily for us, the Dodge and Burn tools in Photoshop are super-easy to use. So which one is which? Well, Burn is adding light, so that makes it darken the image. Dodge is restricting light from the image, effectively lightening it. To paint shadows, I usually start with the Burn tool with a big brush size and a low exposure value.

Using the UVs to guide me, I burned the crotch area and saved the image with a new name.

Figure 4.77

flat

Figure 4.78

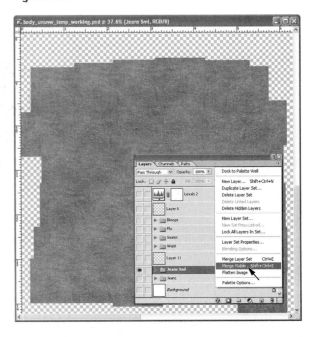

Figure 4.79

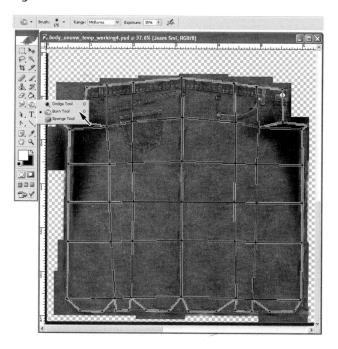

Figure 4.80

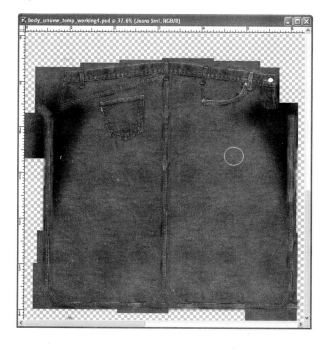

Figure 4.81

Figure 4.82

Then in 3ds Max I changed the bodies material diffuse map channel bitmap name to the new body file.

The other area that could use some darkening to add to the general relief of the material is on the outside of the pants. This will also serve to define an unworn area pattern.

Saving my Photoshop file, I looked around it from the front, bottom, and back in 3ds Max to see how it looks. Even these small changes have had a big effect on how the map looks on the model.

Now to do a little of the inverse, I changed to the Dodge tool, and with a large brush, I added some well-worn areas on the back side. Then I used the tool again to create the worn knee area. After I have made some major changes I usually make a duplication of the layer and continue working. That way if I don't like the next change I can always start again with the copy.

Now we will create some folds in the knee area, so that it looks like someone is wearing them.

To help me out, I separated the front part of the image of someone wearing jeans and added it to my map. Then I had to scale it a little and move it into the correct place on top of my image.

I turned down the layer's opacity to about 75 percent so that I could tell something was happening as I dodged and burned to match the picture.

After I did a little dodging and burning, I turned off the picture of the jeans by clicking on the eyeball next to the Layer and touched up the creases a little more.

To make it a little easier for you to see, I changed the model, removing the puffy bottom of the pants and making it straight-legged. Because I changed the mesh, I also had to fix the mapping a little to match it.

Figure 4.83

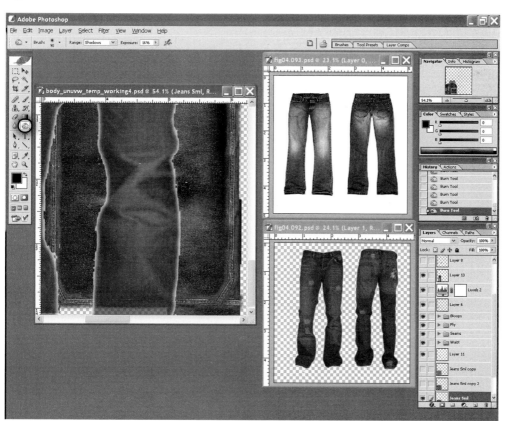

Figure 4.84

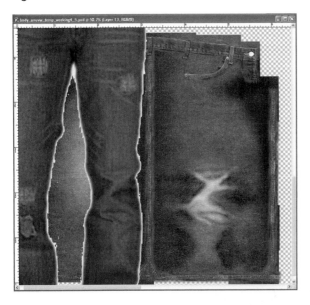

Figure 4.85

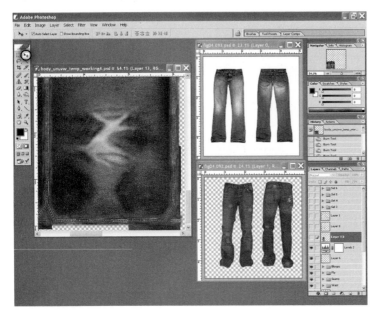

Figure 4.86

Figure 4.87

The next area I worked on is the waist area. Using both the Dodge and Burn tools, I created the wrinkles using the pants reference image.

For the back of the knee, I used the same technique as I did for the front of the knee.

From the "wearing jeans" reference image I copied the back side of the image into my map.

I had to scale and move it into place so that I could use it as reference. Then I turned down the layer opacity to about 75 percent. Using the Dodge and Burn tools, I created the wrinkles on the jeans layer.

This is about as far as I need to take this map. Of course, there are always things I could add like rips or additional wear patterns. I would not be using any new techniques, so that's it, all done.

The last step is to change the image size down to 1024 × 1024 at 72ppi and save my file as a 24-bit Targa. That way it's ready for use in the Unreal Editor.

This whole process is not easy. For me it's one of the hardest. It has taken years of research and practice in order to get good at creating

Figure 4.88

shadows on clothing. I learned how to effectively use the Dodge and Burn tools after hundreds of hours editing photographs. Another good reference are books on pencil figure drawing. This will show you how to draw clothing on a body. Remember, practice makes perfect.

| **Figure 4.89** | **Figure 4.90** |

5

Model Motion

In this chapter we are going to add a whole new level of detail to our character using part of 3ds Max called Character Studio. It is absolutely necessary for us to do this process so that our character can be used in a game. Without it our character is just a prop, not a player.

Introduction to Character Studio

Character Studio is a character animation system built into 3ds Max. It's designed to automate or simplify the animation of bipedal bodies. It can work for quadrupeds or more complex multipeds, but it takes a little more work to get them up and walking around.

Character Studio plugs into two aspects of the game industry. The first is for creation of the in-game action, which uses short pieces of animation that are later combined by the game engine. The second is to create animated characters in short films or stills for the game's advertising promos and for any pre-rendered movies shown in the game. This usually involves creating much longer animation sequences that incorporate a series of actions and hopefully some acting by the character.

If you don't know what motion capture is, I am sure you have seen actors in spandex with little white balls on it dancing around. There are special cameras that can track the little white balls and triangulate each ball's position over time. This information can then be applied to any biped making them dance.

Both the in-game animations and the pre-rendered sequences can take advantage of the two general strategies. Character Studio provides for creating motion. One way is to do it by hand, by moving the skeleton bone by bone. The other is to use pre-existing motion capture data to create the character's motion.

We will take a look at both methods, including special steps for exporting the animation to the game engine.

Character Studio includes a really powerful motion editor that offers some of the industry's best tools for editing raw motion capture data. One of the inherent problems with motion capture data is that there is a lot of extraneous information. Often files contain specific data about the transforms of every bone on every frame. At 30 to 60 frames per second this creates a huge data set, and with a keyframe on every frame, it's almost impossible to edit. To make that data usable, it has to be analyzed and refined into a few key positions. Then you can effectively edit the data, and an exporter specially designed for the game engine can convert this reduced data set into a format that can be utilized by that specific game engine. Many different exporters allow the reduced data set to be used for many different game engines to make different games.

Another issue with mo-cap is the difference between what you capture and what you actually use. In games you are usually going for actions between 12 and 120 frames long. It can be cost-prohibitive to use motion capture for such short sequences. I am not saying it's not done, but a motion capture session is usually a big production, with actors, directors, animators, and techs to run the recording system. Before it even starts all the sequences are preplanned, and the session is timed to get all the priority shots captured. Often, hand animation is the fastest, cheapest option.

Even if it is affordable, motion capture still takes a lot of work to make it usable. When the action is captured, there is extra data at the beginning and end of the file that needs to be removed, and the data set needs to be reduced. Character Studio does everything you need to work with motion capture except capturing the motion.

For those of you who aspire to be animators, don't worry. Motion capture has not replaced the animator, but it has expanded the role of the animator into a new arena.

Character Studio has a secondary function as a crowd simulator. The crowd simulator can be used to automatically animate multiple characters, their interactions with each other, and their interactions with objects, all at the same time. With Character Studio's crowd simulator you can script behaviors and animations for hundreds of characters and have them respond to external events. The main character can walk through a huge crowd and have all the extras react to him and his movement, without having to explicitly animate each one of them. This allows for crowd scenes that previously were too expensive to create.

That's not all, folks; it can also be used as a flocking simulator. This gives us an easy tool to create flocks of birds, swarms of insects, or schools of fish. The simulator can give each member of the group the ability to display a variety of animations and complex behaviors. You can even create an automated coral reef system, if you have the time.

This part of Character Studio is not directly applicable to in-game play, but it can be used to add greater detail to the pre-rendered aspects of game production, such as cinematic and stills. We will not be going over the crowd simulation in this book. If you are interested in furthering your education on the subject there are plenty of tutorials inside 3ds Max that can help you get a head start on creating your own simulations, as well as Michele Bousquet's book, *Character Animation with Biped*.

Biped

There are two parts of Character Studio that are used for character animation. The first is Biped; it's a skeleton simulation module. It allows you to easily create a skeleton. The second is Physique; it's the part that hooks the mesh to the Biped.

First let's take a closer look at the biped skeleton. It's not just any old skeleton but one that has a lot of automation built into it, including the ability to animate using user-defined footsteps as a baseline. One other system that does not get a lot of press is the automated balancing system. It allows you to change the center of mass of the character and have the footstep animation adjust automatically. This makes it easer to animate extreme characters.

To create a biped, all you have to do is click and drag. This will create an androgynous bipedal skeleton with parameters we can adjust later. Let's dive right in and make one.

In the Create tab, click the Systems sub-object category button and click the Biped button.

In the Perspective viewport, click and drag up with the left mouse button.

Figure 5.01

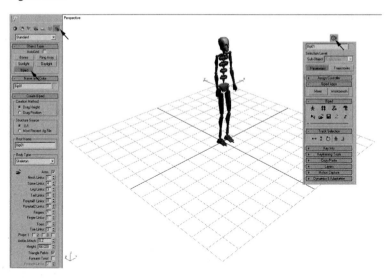

As soon as you have your biped created, change to the Motion panel by clicking the fourth tab over, the one with the icon of a wheel in motion on it. This is the area where all the adjustable parameters for the biped are. All you have to do is select one part of the skeleton, and the parameters will appear in this tab.

Figure

In the Biped rollout are four buttons that change the modes of the biped. The first button activates Figure mode. This mode is for modifying the skeleton shape and parameters, if you try to modify the shape in another mode, Character Studio won't let you. At the bottom of the rollout area is the Structure rollout. Click on the bar and open it up. You will see all the parameters that can be changed and some extra things that can be added to the bipedal skeleton. Play around with them to see how they affect the biped. Add a tail, increase the neck and leg links, just play and see what happens. At the very bottom of the palette there is a pull-down menu that can change the general shape of the bones or body type.

The selection of parameters allows you a good degree of flexibility in the kinds of characters you can rig with the default biped. You're not limited to the options in the Structure rollout; any piece of geometry can be used as extra bones. 3ds Max even has its own bones system that can be integrated into the biped system.

Figure 5.02

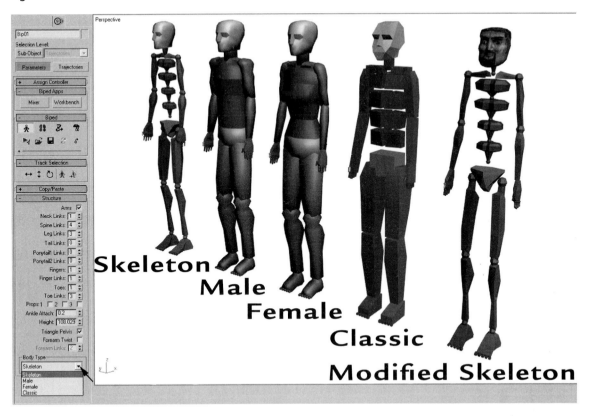

Figure 5.03

Figure 5.04

Just a little warning: Adding extra bones to a character that is going to be used for a real-time game can be tricky. Most game engines have very simple character rigs and may not support any extra bones. The Unreal Engine does, but you have to make a custom set of animations if you want your added bones to move. Check out Chapter 7 to see what that entails.

Note: If you unhide the biped in the included Jack-start.max project file it will have a long box linked to the right hand. This box will not control any part of your mesh but is just used to define where the gun will be linked to your character, so don't delete it.

Fitting In

Aside from changing the parameters, the other adjustment that needs to be made to the skeleton is to fit it inside your character's model. You might have noticed that when you first created your biped, the arms were down and the legs were together. This, however, is not the way our model is built. In our character's mesh, the arms are out and the legs are apart. There is a specific reason for this pose. In the rigging phase, it makes vertex assignment much easier, because each bone is automatically assigned to the vertexes in the immediate area.

You can imagine the influence area that a bone makes is in the shape of a football. The size and position of each bone defines the precise shape of the influence gizmo. The football shape gives the vertexes around the center of the bone the greatest amount of influence. Then it falls off toward each end, based on the shape of the gizmo. In the area where the two bones' influences overlap, they share influence over the vertexes. This works great when the thighbone and the shinbone share vertexes, but doesn't work when the thigh and hand share vertexes. You could hand-assign each vertex, but it's easier to position the mesh so you have the least possible overlap of bone influences. That's one of the reasons we have our character in that "DaVinci" pose. The other is that it's easer to model with the arms and legs in those positions.

Because Biped is a skeletal system and not just a skeleton, there are some limits on how you transform certain bones. Generally you can do all three transforms to a biped's bones, so that they can fit into any model. However not all bones can be moved, and some have restriction on what axis they can rotate on.

To rotate the bones of the arms up, first select one of the bicep bones, called UpperArm. Hold the Ctrl key and select the other bicep. Now you can rotate them both up on the Y-axis.

Each of the UpperArm objects are linked to a Clavicle object. Each Clavicle object in turn is linked to the top Spine object, and the bottom Spine object is linked to the Bip01 Pelvis object. In fact, all the bones are eventually linked to a root object called Bip01. To see the hierarchy of the biped, press H, and in the bottom left corner of the Select Objects dialog box, check the Display Subtree box. At the top of the list will be the Bip01 object. This is the root of the hierarchy. If you need to move the whole biped you can, by moving the Bip01 object.

I will provide you with a biped which is close in proportion to the skeletal size that the Unreal game uses. That way, the vertex assignments we will create in Character Studio will smoothly transfer into the game, and your character will deform properly in-game. When you're doing this for your own project or this one, you start the fitting process by moving your mesh so that the center of the world is between the feet. Then move the Bip01 object so that it's centered on the mesh. Remember that in order to move the biped, it needs to be in Figure mode first. In the Front viewport, zoom in and make sure it's centered on your mesh. Then from a side view, make sure it's positioned correctly in the center of the mesh. The Bip01 object is actually the center of mass for the character and it can be changed, but it doesn't matter in-game.

The next step is to scale all the bones to adjust the pivot point of all the joints. Start at the Pelvis object and work your way out, all the way out to the fingers and toes. We are adjusting bone length

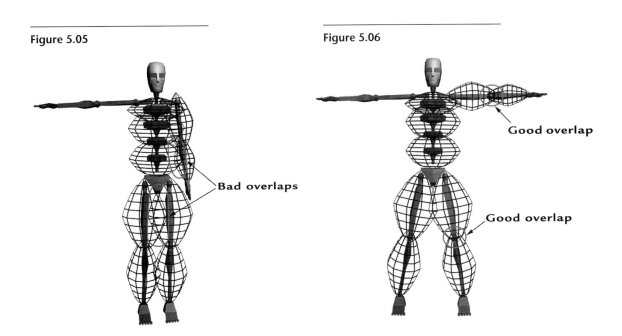

Figure 5.05

Figure 5.06

Figure 5.07

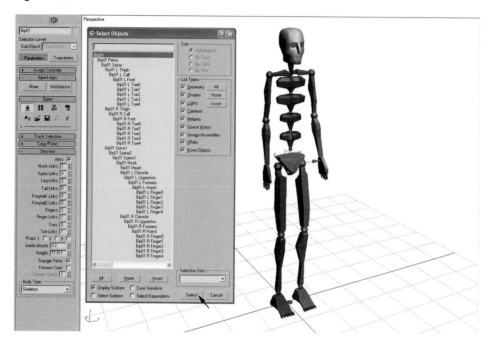

for the vertex assignment and also defining the pivot point of all the joints of the body. You want to work your way out from the pelvis so that you are adjusting parent bones before you adjust their children. If you try to scale the pelvis now, you might notice that it's not scaling correctly. Set the Reference Coordinate System menu in the Main toolbar to Local before you start scaling, or the bones won't scale correctly. Scaling the pelvis on the Z-axis adjusts the width of the hips' pivot points, creating a larger distance between the pivot points of the legs. That way, we can align the leg bones directly down the center of the mesh's leg. By scaling the length of the thighbones (parent) we are effectively changing the position of the knee (child). This goes for the same for either UpperArm object. The longer it is, the farther away from the body the elbow will be. Just to let you know—this is not a linear process. There is a lot of readjusting back and forth, scaling and rotating, again and again, until eventually your biped is completely inside your mesh and all the pivot points are in the correct place.

You should try to fit a biped into your model, but eventually I want you to use the biped included in the Jack-Start project, just

Figure 5.08

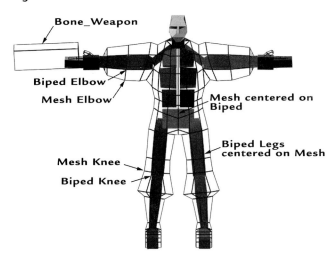

Bone_Weapon

Biped Elbow

Mesh Elbow

Mesh centered on Biped

Biped Legs centered on Mesh

Mesh Knee

Biped Knee

to make sure everything will go smoothly. If you accidentally delete the biped included in the Jack-Start project you can always choose File>Merge to import it again.

Funny Bones

Not all characters are bipedal. Even the ones that are may have extreme proportions. That's why there are some biped objects that can be moved away from the body. They are linked hierarchically but don't have to maintain a direct connection. The obvious ones are the Ponytail and Tail objects. You can move them anywhere on or even off the body.

However, they do maintain their hierarchical connection, so even though you can move the tail to the head, it will animate as if it were at the waist. The same goes for the Ponytail bones except that they follow the head. If your character were an alligator you might use the Ponytail bones for animating the mouth; using the Tail bone wouldn't work too well. The other bones that move are the shoulder bones, the neck bone, and the lowest spine bone. You can adjust these to fit characters that are shaped very differently from regular humans.

There are also three prop objects that can stand in for swords, sticks, and guns. One follows the left hand and one follows the right. The body controls the third.

Figure 5.09

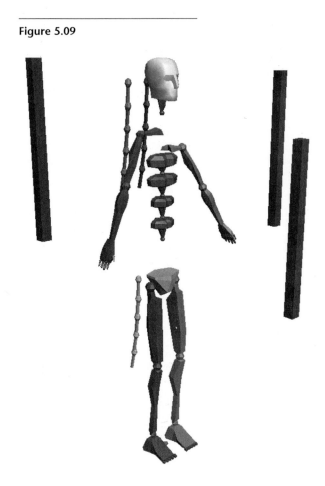

Before we move into biped animation, it's good to get a little background into how computer animation works. Then when we get into the details of Character Studio, it will be easier to understand. We are going to do a simple animation that used to be done on paper. This will demonstrate the mechanics of keyframe animation.

The Bouncing Ball

Start by making a sphere in the left side of the Top viewport and choose the Select and Move tool.

Click the Auto Key button in the lower right corner of the interface, just to the left of the selection sets pop-up menu. The outside of the active viewport will turn red. The red border reminds you that any transform you make will be recorded.

The next step is to change the time. Take the time slider bar and move it all the way to frame 100, the end of the slider. With Auto Key Mode on, a key is automatically set at frame 0. Animation is a change in position, rotation, scale, or value over time. So we have to change the time to later than frame 0 when you animate an object.

In the Front viewport, move the sphere to the right. Then change to the Perspective viewport and click the Play button. Your sphere should now move across the viewport. This is the simplest example of keyframe animation. You have one keyframe at frame 0 and one keyframe at frame 100.

To get a better view of your animation you can turn on the path of your sphere. First select your sphere. Then holding down the Alt key and right-clicking to get the quad menu, you can select the Show Trajectories Toggle in the lower right quad. A red line will appear through your sphere, with a small box at each end. The boxes represent the keys, and the white dots represent the frames in between.

The word "key" gets used with a lot of different meanings, but for us one is really important. A keyframe is one that contains user-defined animation values. The values at other frames are derived from these but are defined by the program. Every frame does not have a key; one keyframe per frame is called brute-force animation. Motion capture programs actually generate one keyframe per frame. It is very difficult and unnecessary to create that many keys by hand. Not only that, but it makes for jerky animation.

Figure 5.10

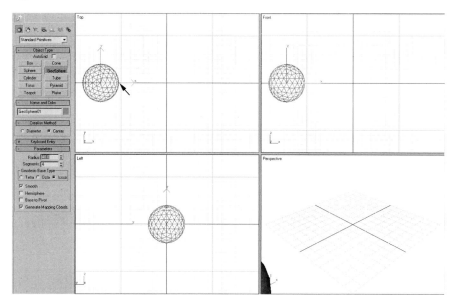

Figure 5.11

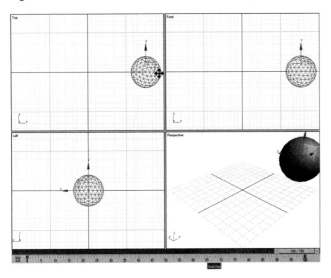

Figure 5.12

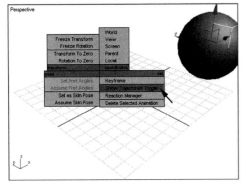

Figure 5.13

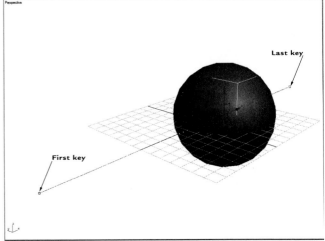

In fact, the best piece of advice I can give you about animation is that less is more. Try and use the fewest keys possible to create your motion.

The faster the action, the closer together the keyframes will be and the more of them you'll have. The non-keyframes are called the in-betweens. In the past when animations were drawn, the senior animator traditionally rendered or drew only the keyframes of the animation. Less-senior artists created the in-betweens. It's much easier for us, because the in-betweens are automatic.

We can add a new key at any time, so let's do it now.

Move the time slider to frame 50, then in the Front viewport move the sphere down. This will change the red line into a curve. Now if you click the Play button, the sphere will move down in a smooth curve and back up to its final position. Each new key you add will change the path of the ball. We do not have to create our keyframes in order, but we can drop one in at any time, and the computer will automatically adjust everything for us. This automatic creation of in-betweens is what gives computer animation its true power. It gives you the power to do the whole job by yourself.

Let's take a look at a couple of ways to edit your animation. The first way is to just edit the position of your object in the viewport with the Auto Key Mode button active. You have to be careful when

Figure 5.14

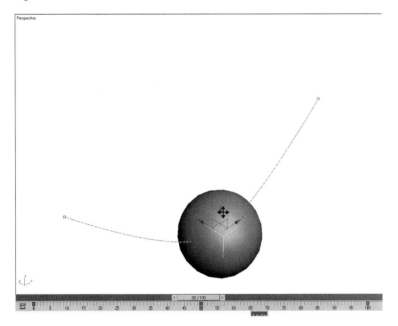

editing in this fashion; you don't want to add additional, unnecessary keys by editing a transform that doesn't have one.

There is a button to help us move from key to key, skipping the frames in between. It's the Key Mode Toggle button, in the timeline toolbar, next to the frame number. Once active, the arrows on either side of the time slider bar and the ones on either side of the Play button will advance time from key to key of the selected object rather than frame to frame.

This makes it easy to adjust existing keys without adding new keys accidentally. This approach does not edit the in-between values. To do that we need to get a little deeper into the animation tools in 3ds Max.

Each of the keys has unique XYZ values associated with it. You can adjust your animation by adjusting these values numerically.

Right-click the little red rectangle above the number 100 in the track bar.

From the pop-up menu, select the first option, X Position. The key info will pop up in a little floating window. In this window you can adjust the value and change the position of the key.

While it's possible to edit your animation this way, it's not easy. Instead, we'll try editing the curves. In the Main toolbar, click the Curve Editor button. The Curve Editor window shows your key values graphed over time. Time is across the bottom, and the values are up and down on the left side. If you don't see anything, make sure you have your sphere selected. The Curve Editor should automatically show the information about the selected object first. Another thing you should notice is the RGB color code used for the curve display. On the left side of the Curve Editor window is the navigation area. If you select only Z Position, only the blue curve should be visible.

Let's play around with our sphere and change it to a bouncing ball. Instead of adding more keys, we'll adjust the shape of the in-between values. In fact, all we have to change is the middle key.

Scroll the graph if necessary to see the middle key.

Figure 5.15

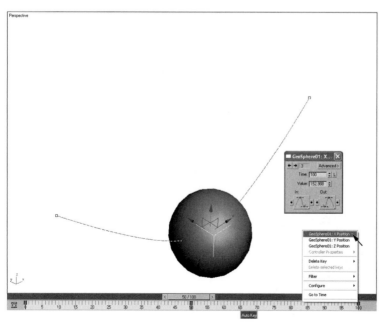

Right-click on it, and the key info pop-up should appear. Take a closer look at the key in the graph area. There are two black lines coming out of it with little black squares at the ends. They are called handles, and they can adjust the curve into and out of the selected key.

Using the left mouse button, click and drag one of them around and see how it affects the curve. You can even click the Play button and adjust the handles while it's playing back. Notice that when you move one handle, the other one moves also, but we want to move them separately.

To adjust the handles independently, you have to open the advanced options by clicking on the Advanced button in the key info dialog box.

In the Advanced area that appears, deactivate the small padlock button between the In and Out values. Now you can move the handles individually. If you pull both of them straight up toward the 0 line, you will get a more pinched curve. Remember that you can click the Play button and adjust the handles while it's playing back. Keep adjusting the handles until you have a solid bounce.

Figure 5.16

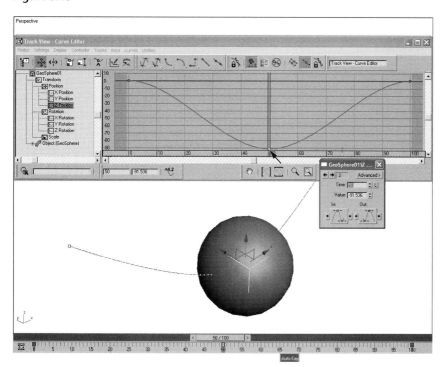

Figure 5.17

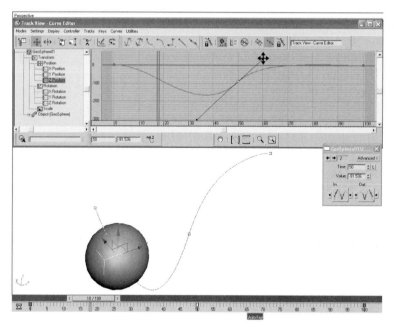

This in essence is keyframe animation. By using the minimum number of keys and editing the in-between transitions to create the animation, we let the computer do as much of the work as possible while maintaining control. When the Biped system creates an animation, or you load a pre-made biped file, the keys are made for you. Then you can edit them directly, in a similar fashion to the bouncing ball example. That's it for this example, so let's get back to the biped.

Biped Animation

The big draw of the Biped system is not only that it makes skeleton creation easy, but it also helps make character animation easier. There are three ways to animate a biped. We'll go over them quickly now and then look at them more deeply later.

The first way to animate with Biped is in Footstep mode. Footstep mode is a powerful form of automatic animation, where much of the work is automated. Basically, to create an animation you can lay out footprints, kind of like a "learn to dance" chart. Character Studio automatically animates the biped skeleton based on how you laid out the footprints.

The second method is hand-animating the bones in Character Studio's Freeform mode. This is animation where no footsteps are used, and all the animation has to be done by hand.

Figure 5.18

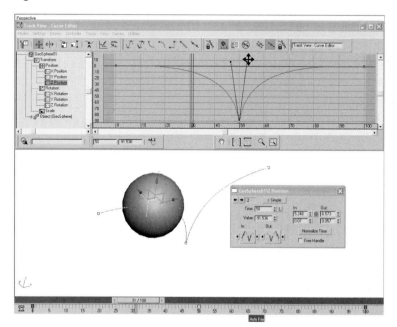

Of course, Biped is set up to make this kind of animation as easy as possible.

You can use both of these methods together by creating a freeform area between two footsteps. You are effectively adding a freeform animation in the middle of a footstep animation. You can also use them together by creating footsteps and converting the animation from footsteps to freeform and back again. This is very common production workflow for Character Studio.

The third method is to use imported motion capture data. That data can be converted into Character Studio's Freeform mode. From there it can be converted into Footstep mode. Once the motion capture data has been converted to Freeform or Footstep mode, it can be saved and loaded into any shaped biped. This allows us to mix and match animations from all three methods. That makes for some strange combinations of action and model. There is a sumo baby model on the DVD that is rigged with Character Studio in the CS Characters folder. You can load any kind of animation into it and make him play basketball or do some ballet moves. The possibilities are endless, as I am sure you can imagine.

Pre-Made Animations

Let's try to add some animation to our test biped. The first thing we have to do is to get out of the Figure mode; no animation can be done in Figure mode. Deactivating the Figure Mode button will take you automatically to Freeform mode. Let's skip over Freeform mode for a bit and play around with Footstep mode.

Click the button with two feet on it, next to the Figure Mode button. Now that you're in Footstep mode, notice that the palette area has changed and that a couple of new rollouts are available. Right under the Footstep Mode button are the Load File and Save File buttons.

Click on the Load File button and navigate to the included DVD and look for the Character Studio Motions folder. There are a couple of folders with biped files in them. The Animation Test BIPs and the More Bips folders have some fun ones to play with.

Open any file. The biped may jump to a new location.

Don't worry if you get the Biped Obsolete File pop-up window. Most of these files have been around since the beginning of Character Studio. It's okay to check the "Do not show this again" option.

Click the Play button in the lower right corner of the user interface, just to the left of the viewport control tools, and enjoy the show.

Load up a couple of different files. Notice that when you load a new file, it replaces the old one. You might also notice that some are in Freeform mode and that others are in Footstep mode. Most of them are cleaned-up motion capture, though some are done by hand. Usually the ones with smoother animation were done by hand.

There is a way to link and blend multiple animations, but for now just know that it's possible. The other thing to notice is that most of the files are short action sequences, with no lead in or lead out, just action. So if you want to create a longer animation sequence out of these pieces, you need to create animation leading in and out of the action.

Let's start creating a new animation by creating some footprints. It's probably a good idea to delete your test biped and make another because Character Studio doesn't allow you to create footsteps for a biped to which freeform animation has already been created or loaded.

Footstep Mode

After creating a new biped, change to the Motion panel. Click the Footstep Mode button. In the Footstep Creation rollout, there are a couple of buttons for different footstep-generation techniques. The most intuitive is the second button; it allows you to place footsteps one at a time. The next one over is Create Multiple Footsteps, for creating a range of animation all at once. Click this and up will pop one of the most complex windows in the whole program. We are just going to use it in its simplest mode, to create a bunch of default footsteps.

In the Number of Footsteps area, type in 30 or more, then click OK. Now you can see in your viewport a bunch of alternating footprints, but the biped is not walking yet.

Figure 5.19

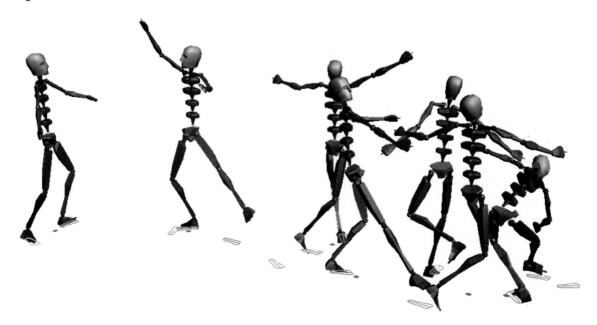

Figure 5.20

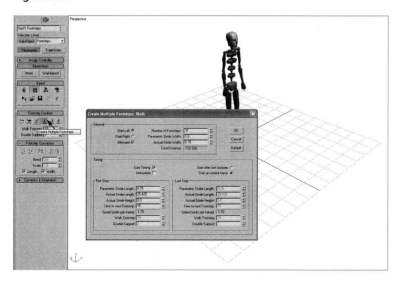

In the next rollout, Footstep Operations, click on the first button. This will create the animation for all new footsteps. If you add more footsteps, you can use this button again to generate new animation that will be added on to the end of the original.

If you click the Play button in the lower right area of the interface, your biped should start walking.

Now you're an animator—NOT! The animation that Character Studio creates is just a rough outline; it takes a human touch to turn it into believable character animation. So let's have a little fun with our biped.

If you de-selected your footprints use the window select tool to select them all. Try changing the Bend value in the Footstep Operations rollout by clicking and dragging on the spinner. You should see the selected footsteps start to bend and eventually go all the way around. You can even do this while the biped is walking, and you can see the change in animation as it plays. Click the Play button again to stop the biped walking. Try selecting a few footprints and moving them around. If you want it to walk up and down, move the footprints on the Z-axis. Wherever you place the footsteps, the biped will follow them. This does not always result in realistic motion. Once you have played a bit, try saving the file using the Save File button in the palette area.

Motion Flow Mode

Another feature in Character Studio that is important for creating extended cinematic sequences is Motion Flow mode. Again, this mode is not directly applicable to real-time game assets but

Figure 5.21

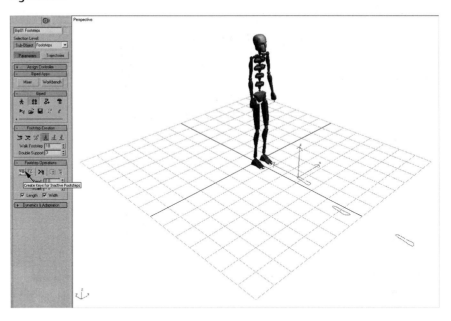

Figure 5.22

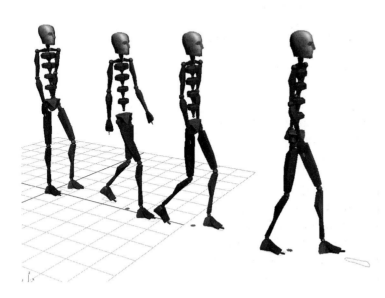

is necessary for longer animated sequences.

Motion Flow mode allows you to combine short animated sequences together and control the transitions between them. This is one of the easier parts of the program to have fun and play with, so let's take a little time for that.

Click the Motion Flow Mode button and notice the new palette and roll-ups. The controls in this window might not be immediately intuitive. That's because it uses a visual scripting workflow.

To start, we need to open the scripting window. In the Motion Flow roll-up, click on the fourth button over, Show Graph. In the window that pops up we have to create a virtual clip object for each animation we want to merge.

Figure 5.23

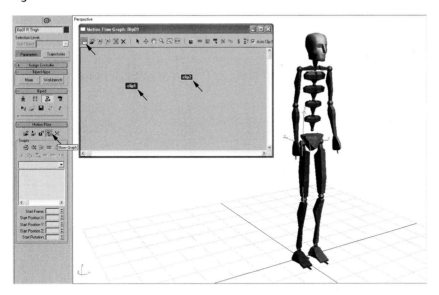

Click the Create Clip button, the first button in the top left corner of the Motion Flow Graph window.

Click two times in the window, and create two clip holders.

Right-click to cancel clip creation.

Right-click again on one of the virtual clips, and up will pop a dialog box.

Click the Browse button and navigate to the DVD's Character Studio folder.

Select the Woozy biped file. Click OK.

Do the same for the second virtual clip object, except this time select the Banana biped file from the same folder.

In the Scripts area of the Motion Flow roll-out, click on the first button. This is the Define Script button.

In the Motion Flow Graph window, select the Woozy virtual clip, and then select the Banana virtual clip. As soon as you click on the virtual Banana clip, a red arrow will appear between them.

Now close the Motion Flow Graph window. Zoom out so that you can see all the footprints and click the Play button. You should see your biped stagger a little bit then slip and fall. Cool and easy, huh?

From here you can save the current animation by clicking the Save File button in the Biped rollout. After you finish the tutorial section of this chapter, you can load the action into your rigged pirate.

Figure 5.24

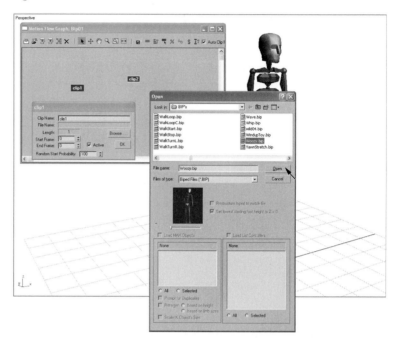

You can use the Motion Flow Graph window to string together as many animations as you want, the same way we created the first script. Now, let's go a little deeper and adjust the transitions between the Woozy and the Banana animation sequences.

In the Motion Flow rollout, select the Woozy animation in the script window. A second row of buttons in the Scripts area will become active.

Click on the last one on the right, called Edit Transition. The dialog box that appears is complex, but don't worry, we are going to keep it fairly simple.

In the upper right corner of the pop-up window is the Go To Start Frame button, which has a small downward-pointing arrow. Click on it, then zoom in on your biped.

You should see a red wire biped and a yellow wire biped. These represent the two clips whose transition you are editing, yellow for the source clip and red for the destination clip. If you don't see the wire biped, click the Play button in the lower left corner of the transition editing window, which should activate them. Together they can help you fine-tune the transition.

Most of the adjustment you will do to the transitions will be fine-tuning the feet. More specifically you will be making

Figure 5.25

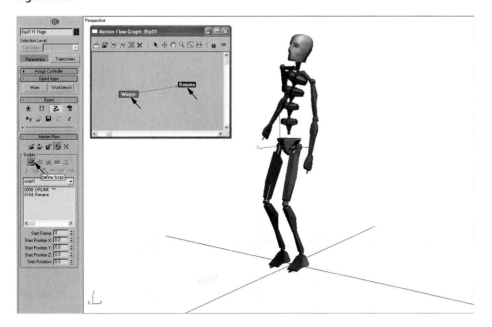

adjustments to eliminate sliding feet, which make the character look like it is ice-skating. This can easily occur when you merge animations where the foot movements are very different, such as a walking action and a standing one.

Even though the end of the Woozy animation is similar to the start of the Banana animation, they still need a little tweaking to get the transition to look good. The problem is that the left foot slides forward in the middle of the transition. Check it out by scrubbing the time slider back and forth, from about frame 145 to frame 165. You can see that the yellow and red left footprints are quite far apart. The easy way to adjust this particular transition is to reduce the start frame of the source clip to 144. The start frame value actually adjusts the transition's starting frame for that clip. This allows a greater flexibility for editing the transition. Now motion flow begins, blending the source clip at a new frame. If you use the spinner's down arrow, you can watch the footprints get closer together as you reduce the start frame incrementally.

Now that your transition has been edited, it's time to save your biped file with a new name. That's all we are going to do in Motion Flow mode, but it is also how you can script the animations for multiple bipeds used in a crowd simulation.

Figure 5.26

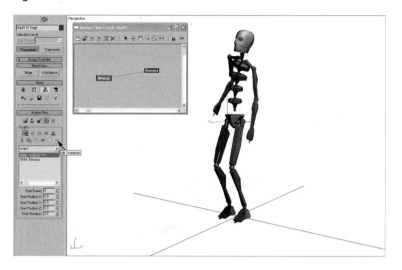

Figure 5.27

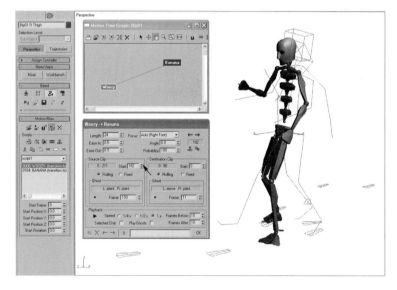

FK/IK and the Biped

Let's start with a new project by choosing File>Reset.

Create a new biped and change to the Motion panel.

We are going to explore another feature that makes Biped a powerful animation system. It's a feature called Inverse Kinematics, or IK for short. IK is an automated method that helps make hand and foot animation easier. IK is not unique to Biped, but it is an inherent part of the Biped system, so you don't need to set it up. To see IK in action, select the hand of the biped and move it on the X–Y axis. You will notice that the elbow bends automatically as you move the hand around. This may seem like a no-brainer because that's how your own arm works. If you take hold of one of your hands and move it around with the other, your elbow will bend automatically. This is IK, or in more simple English "reversed motion," but IK is a little

Figure 5.28

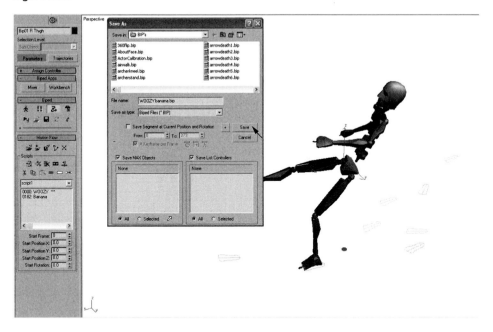

more than that. It's a complex program that lets the child (hand) control the parent (arm). However, it takes a human touch to bring the animation up to the level where we can truly simulate what comes so easy to nature. That brings us to FK.

Before IK, everything was done with FK, or Forward Kinematics. In the FK method, only rotation is used to set the position of the joints. So to move the hand, you have to rotate the shoulder bone, then the biceps bone, then the forearm bone, and that will determine the position of the hand. In order for the Bipeds IK system to work, the FK system has to be set up first. Biped has both controls built in, and you can move seamlessly between them. It takes more time to do that than to just move the hand where you want it. IK lets you move the hand and lets Biped solve the elbow's position and the shoulder rotation automatically.

An IK system is also set up for the knee so that if you lift one of the feet and move it around, the knee will bend automatically.

Another handy feature is that the feet can be forced to stay put, while the body is moved around. This can help you keep them believably planted on the ground to give the character weight, one of the harder things about manual of FK animation. All this IK stuff sounds great, but it does have its limitations, so for the most part I usually end up using both IK and FK to get the animation just right. For example, sometimes the elbow solution that IK generates is not

Figure 5.29

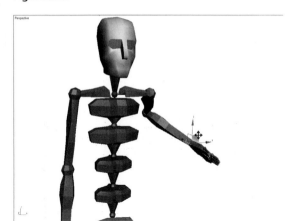

Figure 5.30

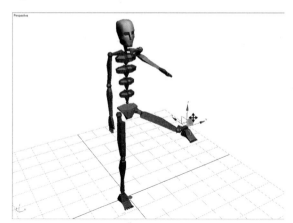

to my liking, so I have to edit it. Using both systems is necessary to create good animation. To get a deeper understanding of IK and FK systems, let's build both.

A Simple Arm Rig

We'll start by building a Forward Kinematic arm rig.

Open a new project and create three boxes in the Top viewport, like Figure 5.31. They will represent the three bones of an arm rig.

Select the long bone and change the name to "Bicep_bone."

Select the next smallest one and change the name to "Forearm_bone."

You guessed it, select the smallest one and change the name to "Hand_bone."

The next step is to move the pivot point of each bone from the default to the spot they should rotate on.

Start with the bicep bone. This bone's pivot is at the shoulder. Change to the Hierarchy panel and click the Affect Pivot Point Only button.

Click the Center to Object button. Choose the Select and Move tool and move the pivot point to the left side of the bicep bone. This is where the shoulder joint will pivot.

Let's do the same for the forearm bone.

Select it and click the Center to Object button. Then move the pivot point to where the elbow should be.

Select the hand and move the pivot point to the wrist area. Make sure you turn off the Affect Pivot Only button.

Figure 5.31

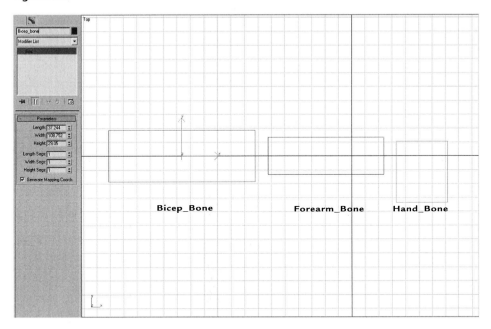

Figure 5.32

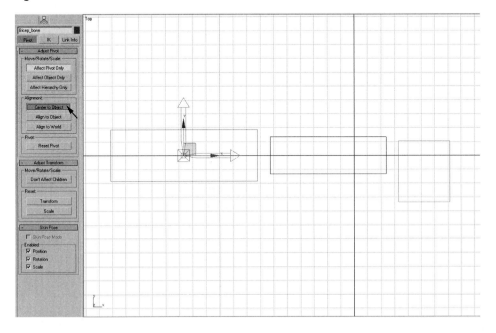

Figure 5.33

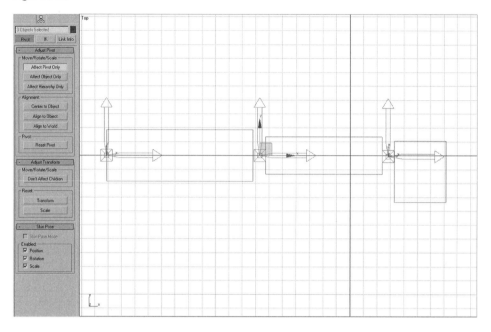

The bones are still not linked. We need to set up a hierarchy of bones, so that when we rotate the bicep bone, the hand will move. We need to link one bone to the other, from the hand to the shoulder.

Start by selecting the hand bone, then just to the right of the Redo button, click the Select and Link button.

Click and drag from the hand bone to the forearm bone. Now the hand is the child of the forearm; if you rotate the forearm bone, the hand will follow.

If you rotated it, then undo it. It's better to keep everything square.

Select the forearm. Click and drag from the forearm bone to the bicep bone. This is the final link in our three-bone chain.

We have created a Forward Kinematic rig for the arm. This is the first kind of rig I learned how to animate with. It takes more time to animate with this rig, but the techniques are closer to those of traditional hand-drawn animation. There are tons of books out there from the masters of the art form on how to do that.

Let's take a run at a simple hand-waving animation using the rig we just made. If you want, there is a finished rig file on the DVD in the Chapter 5 assets folder.

Figure 5.34

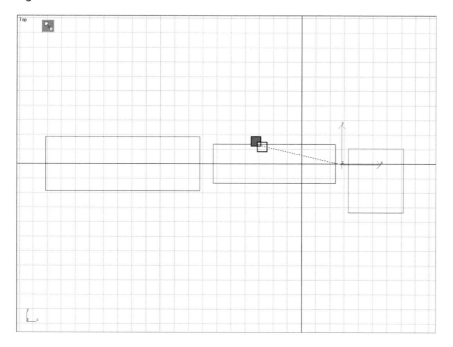

FK Animation

For FK animation, the bones have to be rotated on the local coordinates of the object. The first thing to think about is on what axis the elbow will bend. You want the axis of the elbow bone itself, not the world axis. Change to the Select and Rotate tool, and in the Reference Coordinate System drop-down menu select Local. Now the pivot point will rotate along with the object.

Select the forearm bone, and the rotational transform tool should appear at the elbow. Rotate on the Z-axis. This is the only axis that the elbow will ever rotate on. Let's try positioning the arm.

Rotate the bicep bone down on the Y-axis. This puts the elbow at the side of the body.

Now rotate the forearm up on the Z-axis to move the elbow in front of the body.

Rotate the hand on the X-axis so that the thumb is pointing at the body.

Then rotate on the Y-axis to bring the palm up flat.

To do a simple hand wave, we just rotate on the Z-axis back and forth. Let's give it a shot.

Figure 5.35

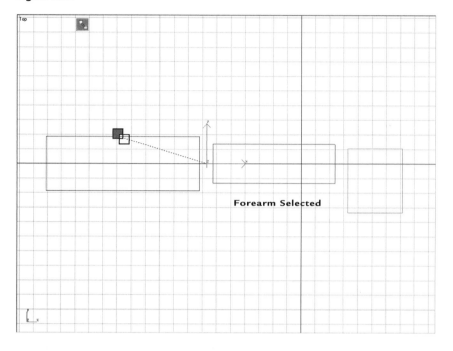

Forearm Selected

Figure 5.36

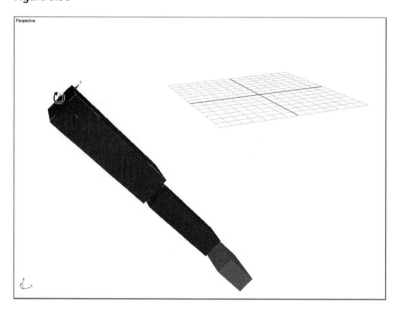

Figure 5.37

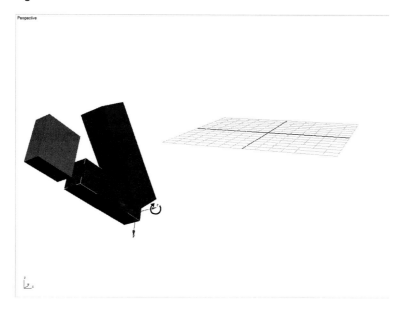

Figure 5.38

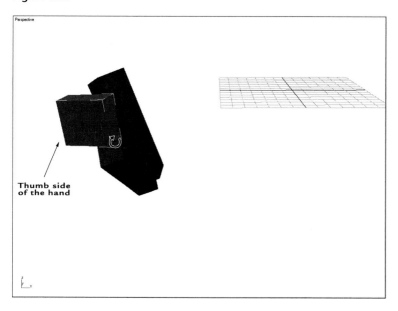

Thumb side
of the hand

Click the Auto Key button to turn it on, and using the time slider, advance to frame 15.

Rotate the hand bone to one side on the Z-axis.

Advance to frame 30 and rotate it back the other way.

At frame 45, rotate it back to the original position.

You can keep going if you want to, but this is as far as we need to go for now. If you want to practice, you should try several different waves, gradually increasing the complexity of the motion. Try portraying the character with the wave. For example, a simple wave

Figure 5.39

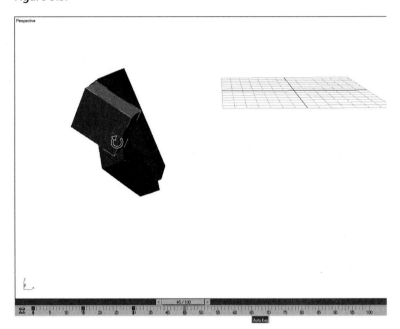

might be the Pope waving from the back of his car, using just the hand. At the other end of the spectrum is something like an enthusiastic mother waving to embarrass her teenage son. That is about as hard a wave as I can think of. Again, if you want more details and examples, check out some cartoon animation books.

IK Animation

Okay, let's change this rig and use the IK system to solve the elbow. We need to make sure there are no animation keys on the object before we add an IK solver. Start by selecting all the bones in the window.

In the timeline, select all the keys by using a rectangular selection marquee.

It's a little bit tricky, but if you start by clicking just to the right of frame 100 and drag to the left, you should be able to pull out a selection window. Drag it all the way past frame 0, then let go;

all the keys should turn white. The safest way to delete them is to right-click in the key area and from the pop-up menu, select "Delete selected keys." All the keys should be gone, and we can use the IK system.

The IK system comes with solvers. Now is a good time for a short word on the different IK solvers. They can be found in the Animation menu.

The first solver in the list is the HI (History-Independent) Solver. This is the latest and greatest IK solver. I am sure you're asking what "history independent" means. It means that the current key's value is not dependent or based on the previous one.

The second IK solver is the HD (History Dependent) Solver. The problem with the HD Solver was that small errors in the values would pile up, causing strange animations to occur spontaneously. So basically after setting X number of keys, the rig would become unusable. If you want to set up your character using IK rigs, *do not* use the HD Solver.

The next is the IK Limb Solver (it works best with two-joint selections). It's based on the HI Solver, and it is designed to solve arms and legs. The IK Limb Solver is okay, but I never used it much. It solves the elbow a little strangely for my taste. For legs, it's fine.

The last one is the Spline IK Solver. This one was created to make it easy to animate tails.

Figure 5.40

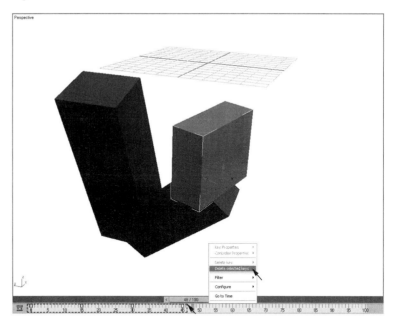

Figure 5.41

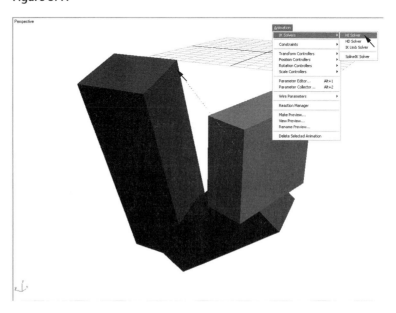

Figure 5.42

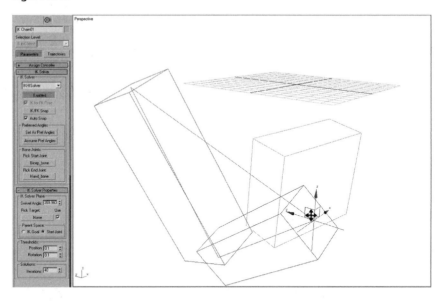

Figure 5.43

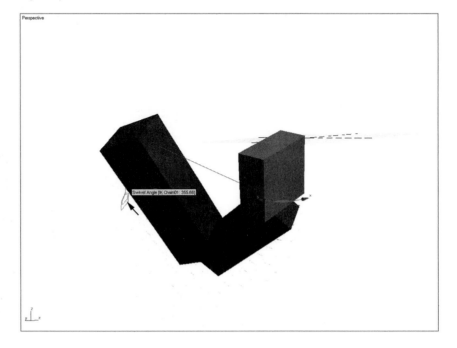

Because flexible appendages like tails need to have more than three bones, they were laborious to animate. All the other IK solvers bend the bone in one direction only. You can have as many as you like per character, so for a tail we used to make a bunch of solvers down the tail. It's not that you can't use them, but it is hard to control that many. The Spline IK Solver allows you to control any number of links using a spline with a minimum of three vertexes. This allows easy animation of a long tail with lots of bones.

Select a hand and choose Animation>IK Solvers. From the next opened panel, select the HI Solver.

We started with the hand because it is effectively creating the wrist's pivot point. In order to control the elbow, we have to start with the link after it, which is the hand. Now we need the other end. Select the bicep bone, and that's it; you've defined an IK chain. You should now see a line going from the wrist to the shoulder. At the pivot point of the wrist, you should see a big 3D plus symbol. This is the target for the IK chain. Move it, and you move the chain.

Change to the Select and Move tool and move the target around. If you Click the Select and Manipulate button, just to the left of the Snaps Toggle. A green flag will appear at the shoulder pivot. You can use this swivel control to change the rotation of the shoulder and therefore the rest of the arm. To animate the hand, we use FK and rotate the hand bone using the local coordinate system. The arm lives.

You have done it. Well, not quite all of it. As you move it about, you'll probably notice that it acts differently than the biped's arm in the IK system. The problem is that the IK chain you created has no limits set. You can add limits to your chain and customize the IK in other ways, but it's a little out of the scope of this book. For our purposes, we will use the predefined IK built into Biped.

If you want to get deeper into the subject of IK, there are plenty of good tutorials in 3ds Max about this subject.

Figure 5.44

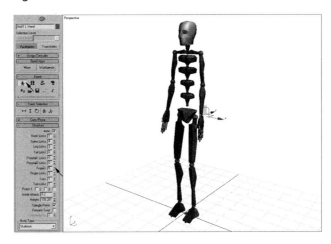

Freeform Mode

Freeform mode is the default mode when you open Character Studio. When the biped is in Freeform mode, the feet are not controlled by footsteps. To animate the biped in Freeform mode, you can use both IK and

Figure 5.45

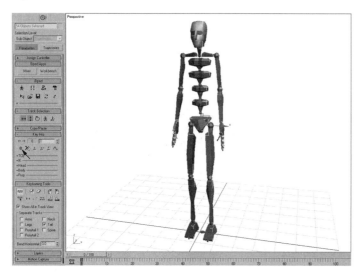

FK. I suggest you start animating with IK and refine the animation using FK. So let's make a biped wave using both systems.

Let's start with a new project by choosing File>Reset.

Create a new biped and go to the Motion panel.

The first thing to do is to activate Figure mode. Then open the Structure roll-up and change the Fingers value to 5.

Click the Figure Mode button to exit out of Figure mode; no animation can be made in Figure mode.

We're ready to animate the biped. Here is where the biped does not act the same as other objects. If we were to change the time, click the Auto Key button, and move the hand, no 0 key would be created. So we are going to avoid the quirk.

Select all the biped parts, and in the Motion panel, open the Key Info rollout. Click on the red Create Key button. This will make a key for all the biped parts at frame 0, or wherever your time slider bar is.

Change to frame 10 and click the Auto Key button. Move the hand up and forward on the Y–Z axes. This will set a position key.

Figure 5.46

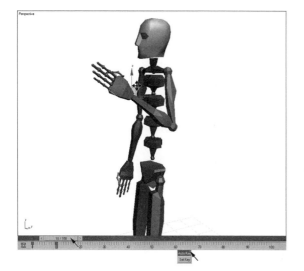

Figure 5.47

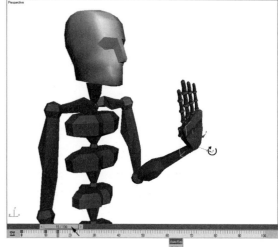

Figure 5.48

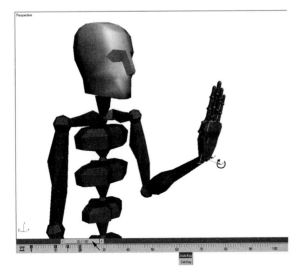

Figure 5.49

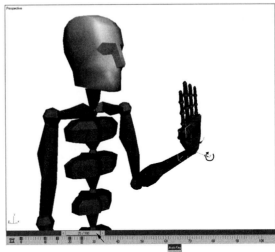

Choose the Select and Rotate tool, advance to frame 15, and rotate the hand on the Y-axis to screen left.

Advance to frame 20 and rotate on the Y-axis to the right, and so on.

This is a simple animation that employs both the Position values from the IK system and the Rotational values from the FK system to create animation. In the same way, the Box arm animation was generated.

Biped Footsteps

We have looked at creating and moving footsteps but not how to edit them. Let's do that now, starting with a new project and a new biped.

In the Motion panel, click the Footstep Mode button.

In the Footstep Creation rollout click Create Multiple Footsteps.

In the Create Multiple Footsteps pop-up window, change the Number of Footsteps value to 15 and click OK. In the Footstep Operations rollout, click the Create Keys for Inactive Footsteps button.

Now click the Play button and watch your biped walk along. It's easy enough to move the footsteps

Figure 5.50

Figure 5.51

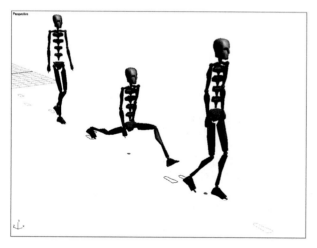

around or up and down as we saw earlier, but we also want to adjust the timing and transitions. For example, if we wanted our biped to jump, we could move the footprints in to the correct position, but that would not get us a jump, because the timing is still wrong. It will look funny, but let's do it anyway.

Select a footprint somewhere in the middle and move it back on the Y-axis until its next to the previous one.

Move the next footstep forward on the Y-axis until it's next to the following one. This will give us a pair of footsteps side by side, then a gap, and then another pair side by side.

Click the Play button and see how strange the animation looks.

Even though we've arranged the footsteps for a jump, the biped is still kind of walking through them. What we want to see is a jump in the space between the pairs.

In the Main toolbar, there is a button on the right side called Curve Editor. Once you click it, the Track View window will pop up, but there's nothing displayed. There are motion tracks that we can edit here, but because we have the Footstep sub-object selected, that's what is automatically displayed. Because the biped "footsteps" cannot be graphed with a curve, they create blocks of keys. So we have to change the Track View from Curve Editor mode to Dope Sheet mode or Key Editor mode.

Figure 5.52

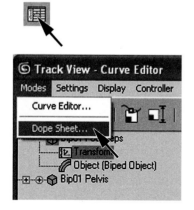

At the top left corner of the Track View, choose Modes>Dope Sheet. Now all you should see is a black bar across the top of the window.

All you have to do to see the footstep keys is click in the left panel on the plus symbol next to "Bip01 Footsteps," and then you should be able to see them all.

The footsteps don't look like the keys we have worked with before. They have a unique interface, the series of boxes you see in the timeline. You might ask, Why do they have boxes? It's to allow you to manipulate all the keys relating to each step as a single unit. You can also edit the keys individually by selecting them inside the box.

Let's start by selecting in the viewport one of the footsteps that we moved. In the Track View window, one of the footstep blocks will be selected. Inside of that block are two white keys. When both white keys are selected, you can move the whole footstep forward or back in the timeline. You can also select and adjust each key separately,

Figure 5.53

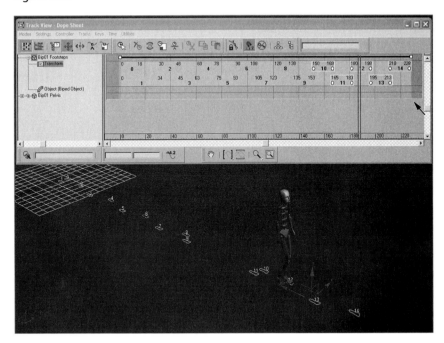

in order to change the duration of the footstep. The duration of the footstep is the time between the two keys in the block.

Each key is color-coded to match the biped: blue for left, and green for right. Most of them, except for the first two, have a duration of 18 frames. They overlap each other by three frames. If you look in the Motion panel, in the Footstep Creation rollout, you will notice that the Walk Footstep value is at 18 frames. This value sets the duration of automatically generated footsteps. If you want to change this value, you need to change it in the Create Multiple Footsteps window. There is plenty more you can do in the Create Multiple Footsteps window, but it's out of our scope. Look at the 3ds Max help files and tutorials for more details on this one.

In the viewport, select all the footsteps after the gap we just created.

In the Track View window, move the selected footsteps forward in time about 100 frames.

Click the Play button in the main interface window, and check what happens to your biped. Wow, that biped can jump! You might need to make a little bit more time visible in the timeline to see all our footsteps.

Right-click on the Play button.

Figure 5.54

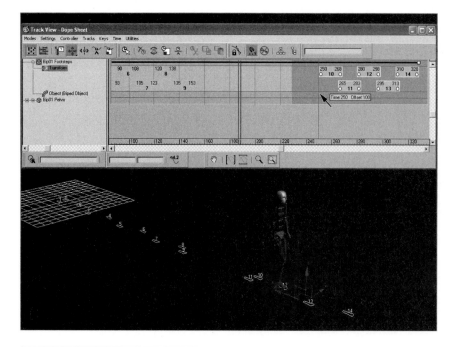

Figure 5.55

From the Time Configuration pop-up menu, change the End Time value until it's past the last footstep, somewhere around frame 330. Click OK.

There are parameters that you can adjust to change how high the biped will jump, but it's better if you just change the time between footsteps to Freeform mode. That's right, we are going to mix Footstep and Freeform modes.

Right-click in the blank space between the groups of footsteps in the timeline, and the Footstep Mode dialog box will appear.

Select the radio button for "Edit Free Form (no physics)." A yellow rectangle will appear in the gap.

Left-click in the rectangle to deactivate the biped physics. It will turn solid yellow, indicating that it is now a freeform sequence.

Return to the Edit Footsteps mode by clicking on that radio button before closing the window.

Now all you have to do is turn on the Auto Key button, and now you can keyframe and animate by hand in the freeform area without having the biped physics impeding your animation.

Figure 5.56 **Figure 5.57**

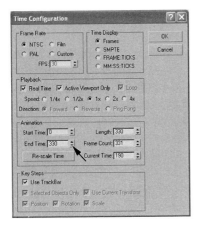

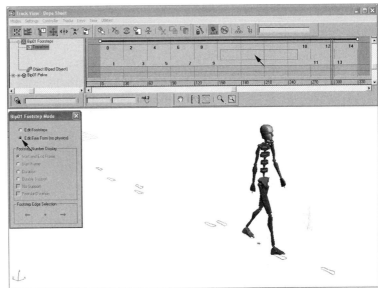

Figure 5.58

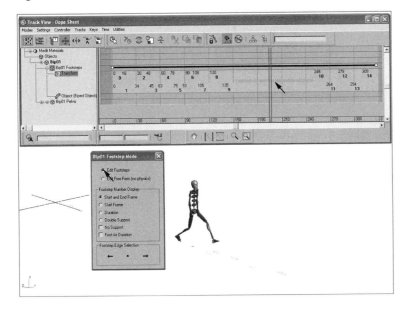

One Small Fix Before Rigging, for Models Used in UT2004

This adjustment is specifically for models being exported for use in the Unreal game engine. No such adjustment is needed for models being used for cinematic animations. Exporting to other game engines will have similar sorts of problems and others specific to each.

One of the quirkier problems in the process of exporting an Unreal character is the wrist pose. When I first saw my character displayed in the game, I was shocked. It looked like he had no wrists! Not just thin wrists, but none. I soon learned that the problem is how Unreal Tournament poses your character in-game. It assumes the character has a big gun in hand. The wrist joint twists around underneath to hold the weapon. If the model remains posed as is, when we see it in game, the wrist will twist into a single point. This will not affect game play but it looks strange and is unprofessional. The solution is to rotate the hands of the model up about 45 degrees. Better to fix it now, instead of having to come all the way back to this point after we have completely finished the project. This also shows how you can go and fix parts of the model without losing all the work you did on your UVs. Open the last version of your character from Chapter 3.

Start by selecting the body mesh and collapsing any modifiers on the body. Don't worry about collapsing the Unwrap UVW modifier. This will "bake" the mapping coordinates down to the Face level and you won't actually lose any of your work. If you want to, you can always add a new Unwrap UVW modifier and edit it any time. It's important do this before we apply the modifier that will connect the mesh and bones.

Open the Material Editor and select a blank material sample.

Apply the material to the body. If you get a pop-up asking you to replace the material, just rename the material to anything and click OK.

Select the head and hide it.

Change to the Front viewport. Right-click on the viewport label. Check the Smooth + Highlights option.

If the Edged Faces option is not activated, right-click again on the viewport label and select it.

With the body is selected.

Figure 5.59

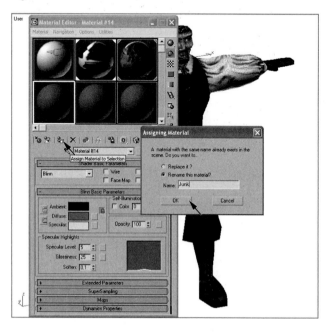

Figure 5.60

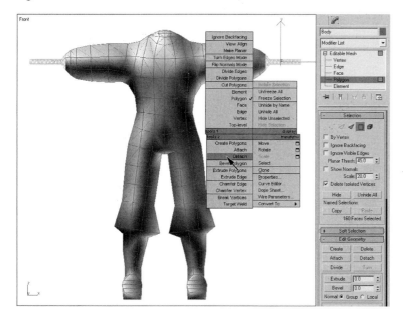

Figure 5.61

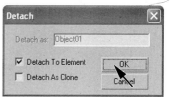

Change to the Polygon sub-object level and select the hands.

Right-click anywhere in the viewport window, and from the lower left quad menu, select Detach.

From the pop-up, select the Detach To Element option. That way the hands will stay part of the body, but we can move them independently.

Rotate your view, and then rotate your model's hands –45 degrees on the X-axis.

Move it back on the Y-axis until it's centered back on the wrist.

Activate Snaps Toggle and change to the Vertex sub-object level.

Zoom in on one of the wrists, and in the Edit Geometry rollout, activate the Target Weld option.

Click and drag the vertexes from the open end of the hand to the closest vertex on the open wrist of the body. Go all the way around the wrist make sure you get the bottom ones.

Adjust the other wrist the same way.

That's it for the wrist fix. Don't worry about the UVW coordinates of the hand; everything will be in the same place. One of the good things about baking the UVW coordinates down to the Face level is that they follow the face so you don't have to edit UV's for the hand again, they shouldn't change.

One more little fix before we get into the rigging. The pivot point of the mesh is not in the center of the mesh. While it's not

Figure 5.62

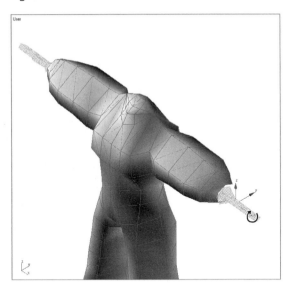

Figure 5.63

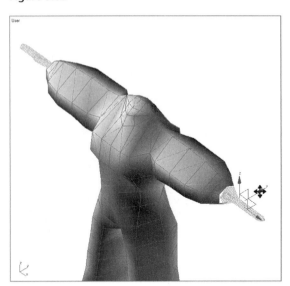

critical to do this, it's better to be safe than sorry. This could save you some headaches later on.

Change to the Hierarchy tab. Activate the Pivot button if it isn't already activated, click the first button, Affect Pivot Only.

Click on the Center to Object button, and the pivot point will snap to the center of the object.

That was relatively painless. Now let's get back to the tutorial and rig our model.

The Body Rig

Now that the mesh is ready to go, we need to attach it to the skeleton. This process is often called skinning.

Remember that there is already a correctly proportioned skeleton included in the Jack-Start project file. All you need to do is unhide it. If you accidentally delete the biped included in the Jack-Start project, you can always choose File>Merge to import it again.

From the Named Selection Sets pull-down menu, select the set called "Bip." Click the Yes button if there is a pop-up window.

The biped should fit your model very closely. If it does not, then you might have to adjust some of the biped's bones. Use the method shown at the beginning of the chapter to scale the bones while in Figure mode.

Figure 5.64

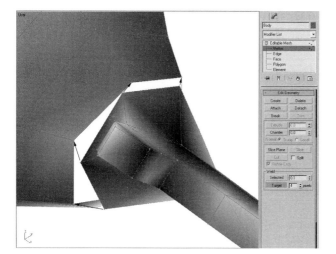

Figure 5.65

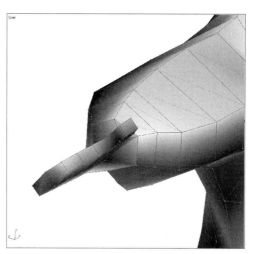

Figure 5.66

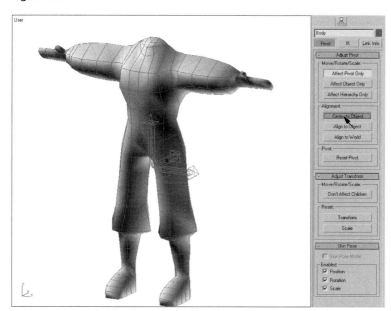

Select the body mesh in the viewport.

From the modifier list, add the Physique modifier.

Make sure that you apply the Physique modifier only to the body mesh. It is possible to apply it to one of the biped parts accidentally, and this will cause problems later on down the line.

The Physique modifier is the part of Character Studio that actually assigns the vertices of your mesh to the bones of the biped. It does a little more than just that; there are several body kinematics that can be automated with it. I have described them in detail at the end of this chapter. If you remember in the previous section called Fitting In, I described how the Physique modifier works without actually naming it. So here is a quick review of the subject.

The size of the bone defines a volume, and the vertices in and around that volume will be controlled by that bone. In the Physique modifier, each bone is represented by a link, and it's this link that holds the vertex assignment. The volume defined by the bone is in the shape of a football and is called an envelope. Physique envelopes are flexible enough to work for the many different areas and bones of the body, making manual vertex assignment a thing of the past, but we will learn that, too.

In the Physique rollout, click the Attach to Node button.

Press H, and up will pop the Pick Object window.

Select the Bip01 object and click the Pick button.

In the Physique Initialization window that pops up, change the Vertex–Link Assignment from Deformable to Rigid.

You might be wondering what the difference is between the deformable and rigid link assignments. Let's start with the rigid link type, because that is the only type that is usable for real-time games at this point. First of all, the vertex link assignment type doesn't actually change anything about your mesh's vertices. It does change the way the information about the relationship of the bones to the mesh is generated and stored. The rigid type of assignment generates information on a per-vertex basis that game editors can understand.

The deformable vertex assignment is a more dynamic method of vertex assignment, but it's not transferable to real-time game editors. I don't think it ever will be.

From the Blending Between Links pull-down menu, select 3 Links. This option reduces how many links or bones can have influence on any one vertex.

At this time, most games can use only vertices that have influence on them by three or fewer links. This "blending" is the closest thing games have to deformable vertices. Unfortunately, it's not even close to the flexibility we have with Character Studio's deformable vertices. The blending amount is determined by a percentage value. The influences acting on each vertex total 100 percent, and they're distributed equally between the links the vertex is assigned to.

For example, with the knee area vertices, you can have a vertex with 50 percent influence from the thigh link and 50 percent influence from the shin link. It will never be 70/30 or any other

Figure 5.67

Figure 5.68

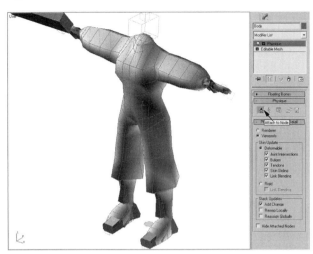

fraction. When you add in a third link it splits the influence three ways, 33.333 percent for each link. This can cause some vertices to not deform as much as they should, or to deform as they would if they were only influenced by two links.

For example, I had a problem with the deformation in the shoulder area of my model. As it turned out, when I was working on the hand vertices assignments I had accidentally selected some of the shoulder vertices and assigned them to the hand. I figured it out only when I moved the hand way up over the head and noticed that a few vertices in the shoulder moved. So after fixing this incorrect assignment, the problems in both areas cleared up.

Now click Initialize. This will start the vertex assignment process; it may take a few seconds.

Here's where the fun begins. Open the Physique modifier and change to the Vertex sub-object level.

We have to make sure that Physique made the right vertex assignments. That means selecting and checking the vertices assignments, link by link. The link structure is exactly the same as the bone structure. For every bone, Physique creates a corresponding link, and that link stores the vertex assignment information for that bone. The links are shown as lines inside the bones.

Figure 5.69

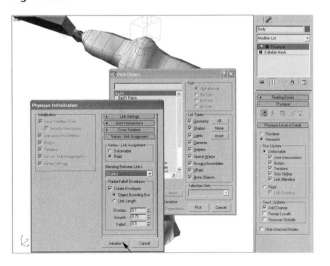

Change your viewport rendering to Wireframe by right-clicking on the viewport label. You can now see the links as yellow lines that run inside the bones.

However, the Wireframe view is not the best one for the next step, so change back to the Smooth + Highlights viewport rendering option. Change to the Vertex sub-object level of the Physique modifier and Activated the Select by Link button.

It's easy to find the links by just moving your cursor over the body until you see it change to the Pick cursor.

Select one of the leg links and look for the vertexes that change color. The vertices of the leg should turn green.

The green vertices are rigidly assigned. If you see any red vertices, you have a problem. Red vertices are assigned to a deformable link. If you see any, you have to remove the Physique modifier and reapply it. When you do the initialization, make sure you set the Vertex Link Assignment to Rigid.

The next thing to look for is any blue vertices. If you see any, that means those vertices are not assigned to any link. This is a critical step in the process; there can be no blue vertices when you export, or your model will not deform properly. Any unassigned (blue) vertex will not animate along with the vertices next to it. So in-game, you would get a spike sticking out of your character that doesn't move—not good.

Figure 5.70

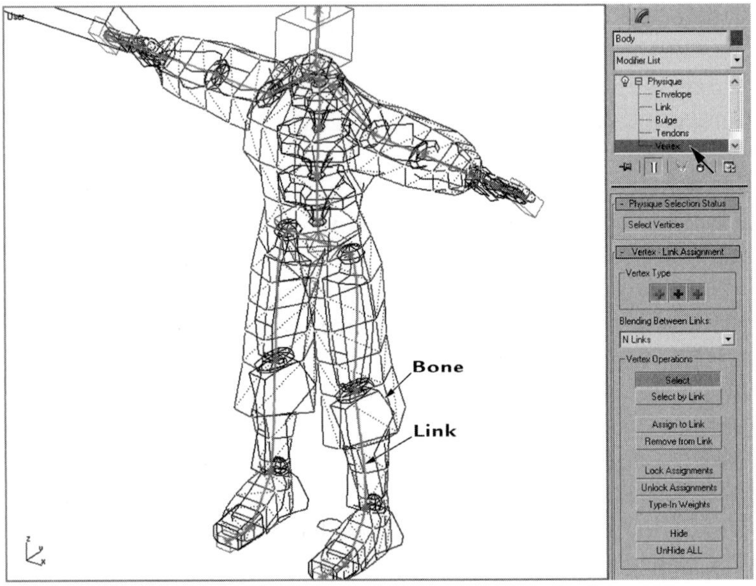

Figure 5.71

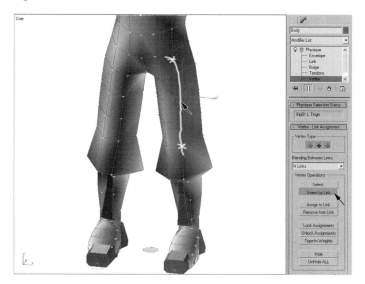

Using the Select by Link button in the Vertex–Link Assignment rollout, select any one link, and all unassigned vertices should show up as blue. Look over your whole model and make sure there are none. Remember to rotate your model to make sure no blue vertices are hiding behind the green ones. The places to look for blue vertices are in the hands and feet or any vertex that is far away from the body. If you do find blue vertices, what follows describes how you fix them.

One little hint: Try changing your viewport to the Wireframe rendering by pressing F3; it's sometimes easier to find the blue vertices.

Click the Select button in the Vertex Operations area of the Vertex–Link Assignment rollout.

In the Vertex Type area, make sure only the blue vertex button is activated so that you select only the blue vertices. You don't want to mess with any green ones yet. Select the blue vertices that should belong to a specific bone.

To assign the selected blue vertices, first click the Assign to Link tool and make sure that only the green vertex button is depressed.

Select the link that should control that vertex. This manually assigns the selected vertexes to that link.

Did your selected vertex turn green? The Assign to Link button is connected to the three Vertex Type buttons which define what kind of vertex the unassigned ones will change into when you select the link. If yours has turned red after you selected the link, undo

Figure 5.72

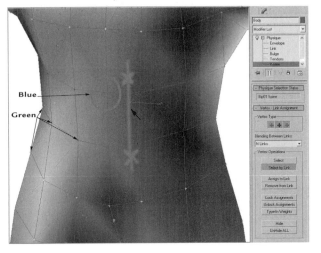

Figure 5.73

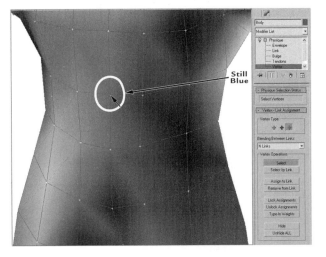

it and make sure that only the green vertex button is activated. Reselect the link, and it should turn green this time.

Remember that the game engine will not be able to understand red vertices, and your model may not work in-game. Green means go.

Now we can select other links and check their vertex assignments. The shin links are sure to be a problem, so let's look at one of them. Select either of the shin links, and you will see that one vertex on the opposite leg will turn green. This is a cross-link, so when the left leg moves up, that one vertex on the right leg will move with it. This is not good. To fix it we have to remove that vertex from the incorrect link and, if necessary, reassign it to the correct link.

Click the Select button in the Vertex Operations area and select the cross-linked vertex of the opposite leg only.

Click the Remove from Link button and select the original leg link to remove it from having any influence over that vertex.

It may not be obvious that anything has occurred.

Click the Select by Link button and select the same link again. Now the vertex on the opposite leg will not show up green. That's what we want.

Repeat the process for the other shin link. More likely than not, the cross-linked vertex will already have influence from both its leg links, so you don't have to do anything. If not, it would turn blue. If it does, then you can always reassign it using the Assign to Link button.

Another problem area is the model's hands. On the left hand, some of the thumb vertices may not get appropriately assigned to the fingers link, but if they are green, then it's okay. You can fix this if you want to, but it is not critical for export to the Unreal engine. However, if we were creating this model for a new game that supported individual fingers, it would be important that all vertices be correctly assigned.

Figure 5.74

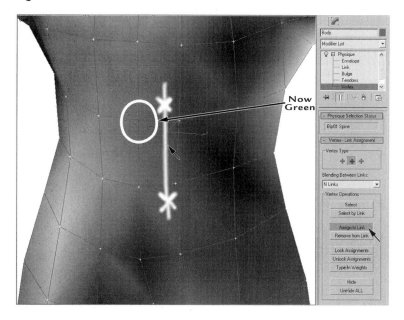

Figure 5.75

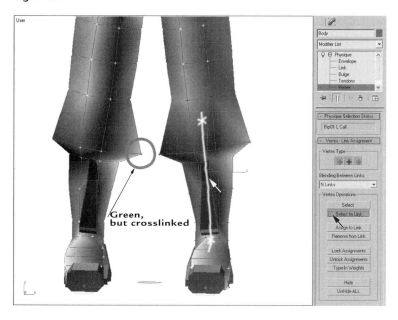

Figure 5.76

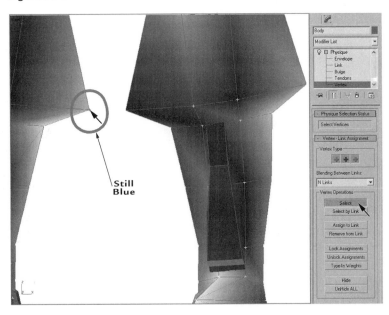

Still
Blue

Figure 5.77

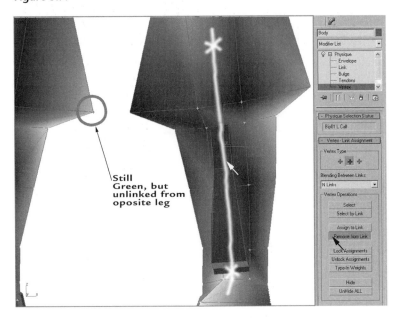

Still
Green, but
unlinked from
oposite leg

Now, because the bones of the hand are covering some of our vertices, let's display them as wireframe boxes.

Select the left hand and finger bones, then right-click and select Properties.

In the Object Properties dialog box, in the Display Properties area, check Display as Box and click OK.

Select the body mesh and change to the Vertex sub-object level. You should now be able to see that more of the thumb vertices are crosslinked. Let's fix them now in the same way we did the shin links.

Select all the crosslinked vertices.

Click the Remove from Link button and remove the vertices from the finger link. If any of them turn blue, select them and assign them to the hand link. Remember, when you assign any vertex to a link, make sure you have the green Vertex Type button active.

Always go back and double-check the vertex assignment after modification by using the Select by Link button.

The model's right hand is a little different. This is the hand that also defines the gun position. The green box that is linked to the hand is a link for the gun. However, Physique did not know this, and it assigned some of the hand vertices to this link. This is not a good thing. The only thing we want the green box to control is the gun. We have to unassign any vertex assigned to the green box's link.

Figure 5.78

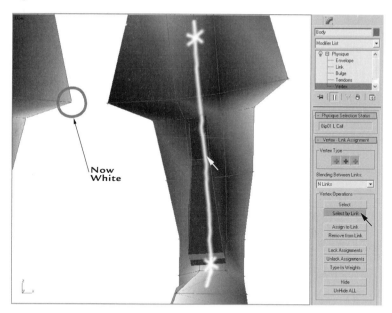

Figure 5.79

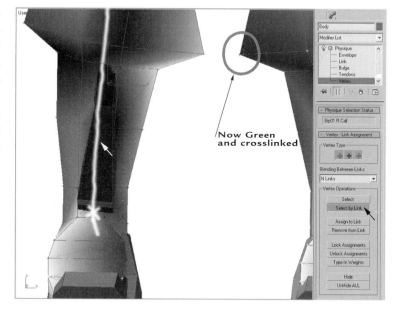

Figure 5.80

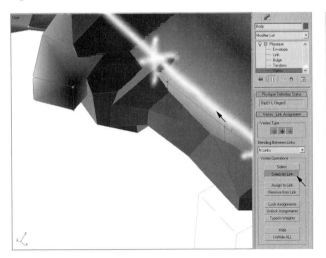

Figure 5.81

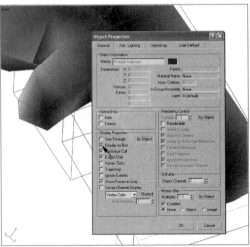

Figure 5.82

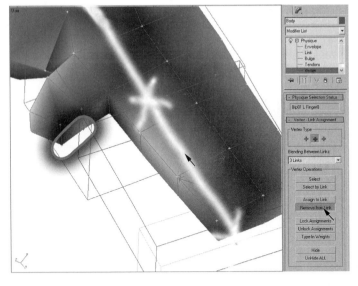

Note: The green box has a specific name so that the Unreal Editor knows that it is the weapon link. It is called "Bone_Weapon." This may not be the same for other games. If you are going to use this model for a different game, check to see how the weapon link is defined.

Select the hand and finger bones, then right-click and select Properties.

Check the Display as Box option.

Select the mesh and change to the Vertex sub-object level. Now you should be able to see a small link somewhere between the thumb and the green box.

Select it after activating the Select by Link button. All the vertices that turn green need to be removed from the Bone_Weapon link.

Activate the Remove from Link button, make sure that the green vertex button is depressed, and select the weapon link.

There is still a little more work to do on the model's right hand. The cross-linked vertex of the hand needs to be fixed, but that should be easy for you by now. Just follow the same process we used on the left hand.

Before we go on to the next step let's double-check the vertex assignment.

Activate the Select by Link button and double-check all three links of the hand to make sure the correct vertices are assigned. Most important, check that no vertices are influenced by the Bone_Weapon link.

The last links to fix are the neck links. For this model, the head and body are completely separate objects, so they will have to be rigged separately, and each will get their own Physique modifier. They will, however, share the same biped. This can cause some confusion when it comes to the rigging, but for the body it's relatively simple. We want no vertices of the body to be influenced by the neck links. Think about it—when your character's head moves around, you don't want the neck or shoulders of your body to move around with it. So we have to remove all vertices of the body from the head and neck links.

Now if your character has a long neck like some of the default female players in Unreal, the rig would be a little bit different. Think about it a little—the bottom vertices of the head mesh's neck area should be assigned to the spine. That way it will follow the body and not the head. The will create a twist between the bottom row of vertices and the top of the neck area's vertices.

Figure 5.83

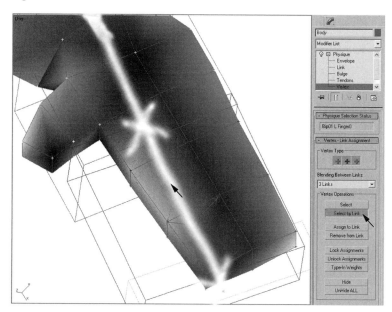

Figure 5.84

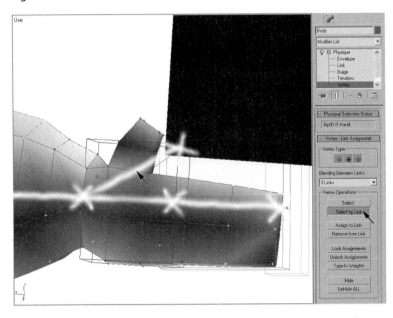

The rest of the head vertices still need to be removed from the body's influence and vice versa in order for the neck and body to have a stable connection.

Select the head link and remove any selected vertices from it. Do the same for the neck link.

Close the Physique modifier and save your file with a new name.

This is all we have to do for the body rig. Now on to the head.

The Head Rig

Rigging the head is very much the same as rigging the body.

Start by unhiding the head mesh. It's not necessary to apply the gray material to the head, as I have, because there is only one link and all the vertices will be controlled by it. As far as I can tell, in the Unreal engine, only the head link does anything.

I will use the gray material for display purposes.

There's one more little fix before we get into the rigging. The pivot point of the head is not in the center of the mesh. As with the body, it is better to be safe than sorry. Adjust the head's pivot the same way you did the body's pivot.

Right-click in the modifier stack and collapse it down to the Editable Mesh.

Figure 5.85

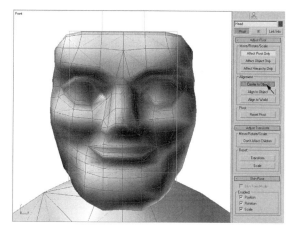

Figure 5.86

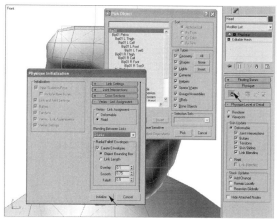

Figure 5.87

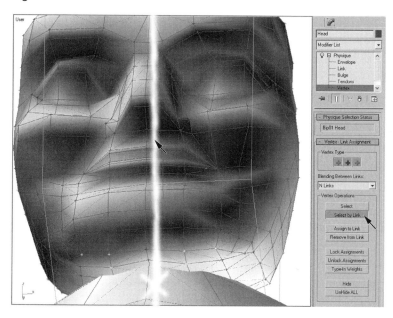

From the modifier list, select and add a new Physique modifier.
Click the Attach to Node button in the Physique rollout.

Press H. In the Pick Object dialog box, select the Bip01 object
and click the Pick button.

From the Physique Initialization pop-up, change the Vertex–
Link Assignment from Deformable to Rigid.

Change the Blending Between Links pull-down menu to 3 Links
and click Initialize.

Figure 5.88

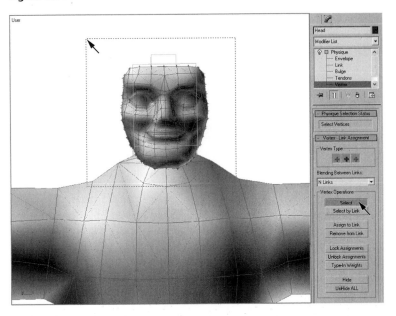

Open the Physique modifier and change to the Vertex subobject.

Activate the Select by Link button and select the head link.

It may look like all the vertices are correctly assigned, however, if you rotate your view, you might see that not all of the head vertices are assigned to the head link. We are going to fix the problem in a different way than we have done before.

Zoom out and choose the Select tool.

Use a rectangular selection marquee to select all the head vertices.

Click the Remove from Link button.

Use a rectangular selection marquee to select all the links of the upper body. All the head vertices will turn blue.

Activate the Assign to Link button and select the head link. Now all the head vertices should be green.

Remember to check the Vertex Type buttons if you have any problems selecting vertices or if your head vertices turn red.

That finishes off the rig for the whole character. Now we have to test it and see if it works. We want to make sure we didn't miss any vertices.

Save your file and add the "@export" postfix to the name. We will come back to this file, because this is the actual file we will

Figure 5.89

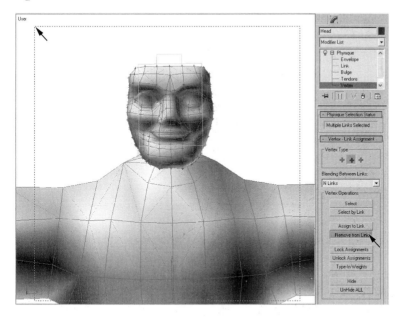

Figure 5.90

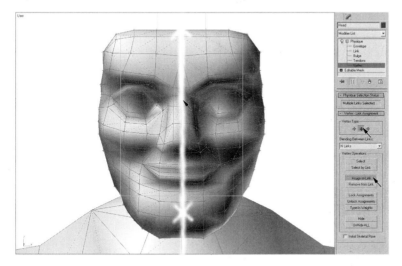

export. Once you add animation to the biped, it should not be used for export. This is more of a precaution than a bug; I have occasionally had problems exporting animated models. So it's best if you export the model and actions from separate 3ds Max projects.

Testing...Testing

The next step is to test our rig by adding animation to the biped. We'll use some extreme action to see how well we've skinned our model. There are a couple of biped files that move the biped to extreme positions. Any problem in the rig will show up as the character goes through these moves. Once you see the problem areas, you can edit them. Editing is easy because you can fix the problem with the character in the extreme pose—the animated position. When the problems are fixed, you can save the Physique vertex information to a file. Then you can load that file into a new biped that has never been animated. This way we get the good rig info onto a virgin biped that can be exported properly.

This next step can get a little confusing, and a good way to keep things straight is to open a non-animated version of your project in a new instance of 3ds Max. You can do this by simply loading 3ds Max again. Unlike other Windows programs, you can have as many separate instances of 3ds Max open as your system will support. That way you have the same file open in both instances. You can play with one and load the result into the other unanimated one. If you never save the animated one, you will never have a problem later.

Open the second instance of 3ds Max and load the last version of the character that you saved.

In one of the 3ds Max instances, select a biped part, and in the Motion panel, click Open File.

Navigate to the DVD. From the Character Studio Motions folder, open AthleteStretch.bip.

Click Play, and watch the pirate stretch out.

Don't worry if your model does not bend perfectly. Some amount of joint distortion is a problem inherent in a low-poly model. There are just not enough divisions in the mesh to make a complex or extreme bend, so you have to do the best with what you have.

In order to really analyze the rig, we have to view it a little slower, by dragging the time slider bar. Also we need to hide the biped bones so we can see the mesh properly.

From the Named Selection Sets pull-down menu, select the Bip set.

Right-click in the viewport, and from the upper right quad menu, select Hide Selection. Remember that to add a new animation, you have to select a biped bone, so you will eventually need to unhide the biped bones.

We are using this animation to see if any of the leg vertices move when the upper body and arms move. They should not. If they do, you will have to reassign them the way we did before, by selecting the mesh, and adjusting the vertex assignment in the Physique modifier. It's not a problem; you can still select the links even though the bones are hidden. As you may remember, Physique replaces the biped bones with its own link system.

Other animations that can be used for analyzing the rig are Exercise.bip and Ballet.bip. The Exercise animation has some deep knee bends that are great for analyzing the knees. It is also good for testing how the crotch area deforms.

Scrub the time slider to frame 43 and take a look at his behind. Scrub back and forth now, watching how the deformation occurs. You can see that when the feet are pointed out, the vertexes in the butt area bunch up a little. We could fix this by changing which links have influence over them, but no one will ever notice, so let's skip it.

The Ballet animation has even more complex leg and arm movement. I usually use it last, to check out the changes I have made with the previous ones. Once you get any gross errors fixed, load a bunch of different biped files, and watch the mesh deform from different angles.

The worst-case scenario is that you have to go back and add more segments at one joint or another in order to get the deformation you need from your character.

If you have made any changes to the vertex assignment, save the Physique data to a file.

Close the Physique modifier by clicking on the word Physique until it turns gray.

In the Physique rollout, click Save File and save a .phy file.

Switch to the other 3ds Max instance open with the unanimated version of your project and select the pirate mesh. From the Physique rollout, click on the Load File button and select your newly made .phy file.

Just trust that it worked, and save your project with a new name.

You are now ready to export your model for use in the Unreal Editor.

Advanced Vertex Animation

Physique's Bulge

There are a number of tools in Physique that are used only in rigging high-resolution characters. It is beyond our scope to get into these step by step, but you should know that they are there and how they work.

In high-polygon models, controlling the crease at a joint can be a real challenge. Physique includes some tools that are designed to let you tweak the skin deformation based on the rotation of joints. The Bulge tool and the Skin morph are ways to add extra deformation to your model on top of the straight bone animation. These tools are not limited to joints but are very useful there.

The Bulge feature will allow you to create parametric mesh deformations based on the animated angle of bones. Basically, it simulates the effect of muscles flexing and relaxing. For example, when you flex your arm the bicep muscle bulges, and the triceps muscle relaxes. The Bulge is an automated animation controlled by the angle between two links. In the case of the bicep, as the angle at the elbow gets smaller, the bicep gets bigger. You only have to set it up once, and from then on the deformation will occur automatically when those bones rotate. Bulge is based on parameters that affect the mesh regardless of resolution. You can copy the bulge information from a high-resolution character to a low-res one, and it will recreate the bulges as best as possible with the geometry available.

Skin Morph

The Skin Morph modifier was introduced in 3ds Max 7 and can replace or can be used in addition to the Bulge editor. It is a vertex-based morph that is controlled by the angle between two bones. The big difference between the Skin Morph and Bulges is that Skin Morph works directly on the vertices of the model. Unlike a Bulge, you can't copy a Skin Morph between models of different resolution or topology. Like Bulge, Skin Morph is driven by adjacent bones' angles in the same basic fashion. The angles of the bones are linked to a specific morph shape; you change the angle and the morph percentage. The strength of this modifier is that you can position the vertices of your model to be exactly the way you want, instead of having to tweak some parameter to get it right.

Morpher

One more note on morphing animation. So far I have been talking about ways to animate the body of your character. The next logical question is how do I animate the face. This is a job for the Morpher modifier! It is beyond the scope of this book, so I will not go into it, other than to tell you it exists. Luckily for you, there are some good tutorials about how to use the Morpher modifier included in 3ds Max's help files.

Skin Wrap

One of the features introduced in 3ds Max 7 is called Skin Wrap. It allows you to copy the skinning of a character to another character of similar shape. The exciting part is that you can rig a low-poly model and use Skin Wrap to apply that rig to a high-poly version of the same model. If you think that rigging our simple model is hard, try one with a million polygons and tens of thousands of vertices. The Skin Wrap modifier helps simplify the process a lot. It can even be used to copy the rigging between similarly shaped characters. So if you have 10 different army guys that are all about the same size, all you have to do is rig one. Then to the other nine you just apply the Skin Wrap modifier and define the reference model.

Conclusion

Character Studio is a powerful tool for character animation. With all tools, the creative process is controlled by the user of the tool, not the tool itself. Because the process of character animation is an artistic endeavor, the tool that facilitates the process is the one you should use. Character Studio is not a bad choice. For all its quirks, the benefits and flexibility of Character Studio far outweigh them.

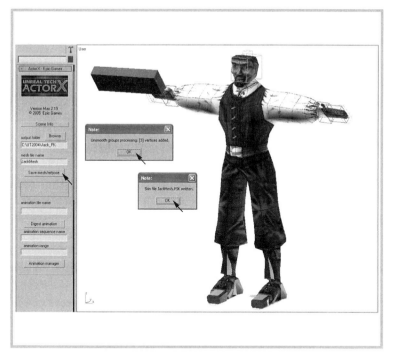

6

Exportation

Export is the final step before we see our character in-game. It is a three-part process. First we have to export our model and vertex assignment from 3ds Max into a format that the Unreal Editor can understand. Second, we have to import and compile the data in the Unreal Editor and then export it one more time. This will create files that the game engine can understand. Third, we have to edit a couple of data files in the game's install folders and move our files into the right folders. Then all we have to do is start the game, and we should find our character in the player's roster. How cool is that? Let's get started.

ActorX

3ds Max does not have a way to export our data into the format that the Unreal Editor can understand, so we have to add a small program to 3ds Max. This program is called ActorX. It's a plug-in that runs inside 3ds Max. Navigate to the included DVD and look in the "ActorX" folder for the version of ActorX for the version of 3ds Max that you're using. In that folder is a small file called ActorX.dlu. Right-click on it and select Copy. Navigate to the 3ds Max install folder. Right-click on the "stdplugs" folder and paste ActorX.dlu into the folder. Restart 3ds Max. Go to the Utilities panel and click on the More button at the top of the Utilities rollout. In the Utilities dialog box, you should see ActorX listed. Select it and click OK. In the Utilities panel, you should now see a new roll-up called ActorX–Epic Games. Now the program is running. We can get started exporting our data.

Well, before we actually do that, we have to do a little work on our project file. It's important that you have only what's absolutely necessary to make a clean export. That is your head and body mesh, the Bone_weapon object, and the biped. Any extra objects will cause problems in the Unreal editor, and your character may not show up in the game. This can be a frustrating problem and hard to diagnose, so let's do it right the first time. Start by opening the project you saved before we tested the model and that has never had animation on the biped, ever. I can't stress that enough.

Right-click in the viewport, and from the upper right quad menu, select Unhide All. Select everything that is not your character's head, body mesh, or any part of the biped system, and delete them. One of the easiest ways to do this kind of operation is to use the Select Objects dialog box. First, select your meshes and all of the biped parts including the Bone_weapon object. Then press H. In the Select Objects dialog box, click Invert. Now all the other objects are selected; delete them. This is a good time to save your projects with a new name.

Now that we have a clean project, let's get started. Go back to the Utilities panel. The ActorX plug-in should still be running.

The first button in the ActorX rollout is the Scene Info button. Click it. Look at the "scene info" dialog box. There should be only

---

Figure 6.01

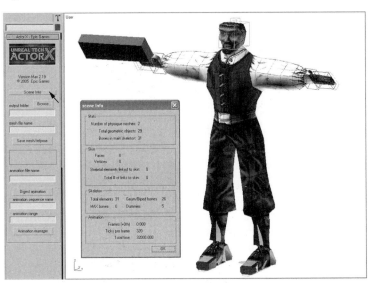

two physique meshes, and the total number of geometric objects should be 29. These are the only numbers that truly matter. If there are any other numbers, then you have extra objects in your scene. Make sure you find the extra objects and delete them. Once you get the right numbers, you're ready to export your data.

The other thing we should double-check before we go on is that the meshes have the correct map in their assigned materials. So open up the Material Editor, navigate to the Diffuse map channel of both, and check the name of the bitmap in the slot. It should be the TGA version of your final body and head maps. If they are not, then change them now, so that when we import the meshes into the Unreal Editor, the materials will be automatically assigned. It works most of the time, but not always. Close the Material Editor. This is a good time to save your project with a new name, like "Jack@export."

The next thing to do is select a folder for output, so back in the ActorX rollout, click the Browse button. In the dialog box, navigate to the UT2004 folder. Make yourself a new folder with a suffix of "PK," for example, "Jack_PK." Click twice on the Use Path button. In this case the suffix is arbitrary, but from now on, it's important to keep an eye on your file names.

In the mesh file name area, type in the name of your character with the suffix of "Mesh," for example, "JackMesh."

Note: It is *vital* to give different names to the exports of the different parts of this process. The different packages of data must have unique names, for example, "Jackmesh," not "Jack," otherwise the game will not be able to figure out what's what.

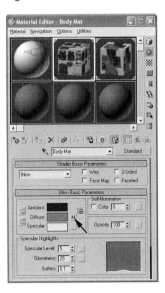

Figure 6.02

Figure 6.03

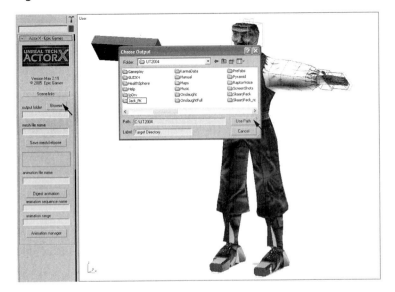

Figure 6.04

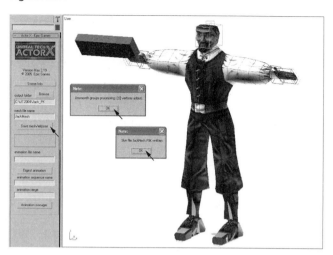

Finally, click the "Save mesh/refpose" button and click OK in the two or three dialog boxes that follow. This will make two files for you; the important one is the file with the PSK extension. In this file is stored the vertex information about your mesh that the Unreal Editor can understand. The pose is how your mesh is positioned at the time of export. The refpose is vertex assignment categorized by bone and translated in a format that the bones system in the Unreal Editor can understand. The refposes of your biped and the game engine's bones system have to match fairly closely, otherwise your model will not animate properly or will not animate at all. This is why I included a biped where the joints are in close proximity to the bones used in the game system.

This is also why it's so important that you export the biped project that was never animated. If there is even a little bit of difference in the values of the mesh and the biped, the whole thing will not work.

That's all we have to do with the ActorX plug-in if we are going to use the default animations for our character. If you're going to make something other than an "average Joe" character, then the animations will need to be altered as well. A really unusual character might require a completely different set of animations. You would have to compile the new animation sequences in the ActorX plug-in and export them into a file format that can be imported into the Unreal Editor. This process is fairly well-documented at the Unreal Developers Network site at http://udn.epicgames.com/Main/WebHome. There you can find tons of tutorials and the latest ActorX plug-in. If you're interested in finding out how to use the Unreal Editor to create your own game, all the information is in here. Not all of the newer features can be accessed by the public, but there are more than enough to keep anyone busy for a couple of years.

We still have one more thing to add to our character's folder in the UT2004 install folder. Well, actually three things: the face map, the body map, and the portrait image. Make sure that you copy and paste only the TGA version of your images. Again, the Unreal Editor can use only files in the TGA or BMP format as maps. Now that we have all the assets we need gathered into one place, let's open up the Unreal Editor and put it all together.

Importing

From the Start button in Microsoft Windows, navigate to the All Programs area and then to the Unreal Tournament 2004 folder. Inside of that should be a shortcut to the UT2004 Editor. Select it, and the Unreal Editor 3.0 should open.

In the Unreal Editor, there should be a floating window open. This is where we are going to be working. The major part of the interface is where maps are created and edited. The floater is where everything else is compiled for use in the game.

There is a row of tabs across the top of the window. We are going to use only the first tab, Textures, and the fourth tab, Animations. The other tabs are for noncharacter types of objects and options.

Because the pop-up starts in the Textures tab, let's begin there. From the Files>Import. Navigate to your character's folder in the UT2004 install folder. Select the three TGA files of your head, body, and portrait, and click Open.

The Import Texture dialog box needs a little editing before we confirm. First change text in the Package area to your character's name plus the suffix of "_Pack." Then clear the Group area; there is no need to add sub-groups to this package. Click OK All.

Figure 6.05

Figure 6.06

Figure 6.07

Figure 6.08

Figure 6.09

Figure 6.11

Figure 6.10

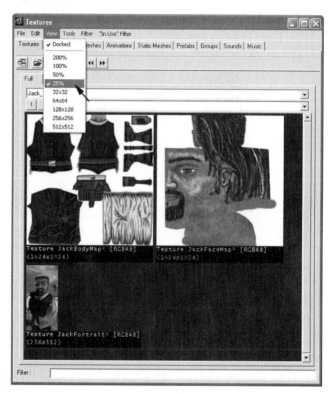

Now you should see all three images in the lower window. If they are big, you might have to scroll down to see them all. To make the Textures tab's thumbnails smaller, click on the View menu and select the 50% option. This seems easy enough, but there have been some problems in class with importing images. Sometimes the images are not exported from Photoshop correctly, and even though it looks like they were importing, they do not show up in the window. The most likely problem was with the size of the image. For images to be used by the Unreal Editor, they must be 1024x1024, 72ppi, 24-bit, and TGAs or BMPs.

Remember that you have the choice to use BMP if you want to. If for some reason you can't get the TGA format image to work for you, just try saving the image in the BMP format. One or the other should work.

Go back to the File menu and save the package in the UT2004/ Textures folder, using a different name this time. Add the suffix of "_Tex_Pack" to your character's name and confirm to save.

Note: It is *most* important that there never be any spaces in the file names for export. Not all programs understand spaces, and

Figure 6.12

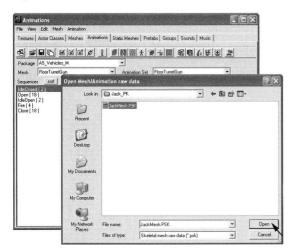

Figure 6.13

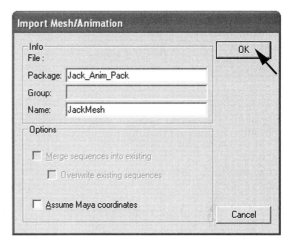

UT2004 is one of them. It's better to never have spaces in any of your names just to be safe.

Now your maps can be found and used in-game. Let's import the mesh and put the two together.

Click on the Animations tab and choose File>Mesh Import. Again, navigate to your character's folder in the UT2004 install folder and select the PSK file. Click Open.

Change the package name to that of your character's name plus "_Anim_Pack" and confirm.

You should now see your model in the viewport but with some strange map on it. Not to worry; we will fix that in a minute.

In order to get the correct scale, position, and orientation, we are going to cheat a little and copy the setting from one of the default players and paste it into ours.

Figure 6.14

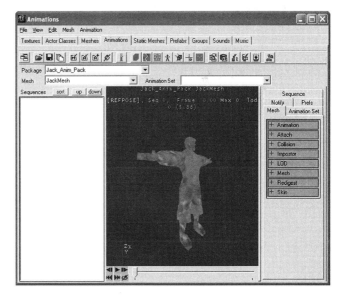

From the Package menu, select the Thunderchrash package. You should see a small dude appear. This is the Jakob M character. From the Mesh menu at the top of the window select the Copy Mesh Properties option. It may look like it hasn't done anything, but it has put the information into a clipboard, so we can paste it into

Figure 6.15

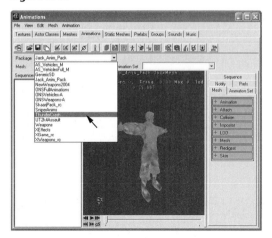

Figure 6.16

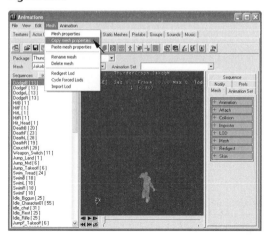

Figure 6.17

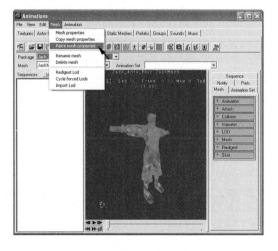

our character in a moment. However, we are not quite done robbing the Jakob character. There is one more bit of information we need from it. Unfortunately, the Unreal Editor can sometimes crash at this point.

So let's go back to our character's package and from the same menu select Paste Mesh Properties. Your model should get smaller and change orientation.

Now, go back to the Thundercrash package and copy the animation file's path name before we go back to our character. Over on the right hand side of the interface there is another set of tabs. The Mesh tab should be activated. Underneath that, the Animation roll-up should be open. If it's not, then click on the plus symbol to open it up. Just to the right of the words Default Animation is the name of the path for the default animation file for a human biped. Select it and copy it by pressing Ctrl-C. Now we have all the information we need from the Jakob character.

Just to let you know, what we copied is not some magic words, it's actually a path name. The text is "MeshAnimation'HumanMaleA. BipedMaleA'." For more details on how to create your own mesh animation file, see Chapter 7.

Now change back to your character's package. Then in the Mesh tab, open the Animation roll-up. In the Default Animation, area it should say None. Select the word None, then press Ctrl-V to paste the animation file name, replacing "None." Click on the Use button. If it doesn't seem to work, just close the roll-up, and it should stay put.

Figure 6.18

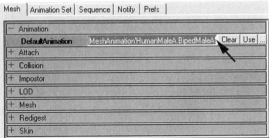

Figure 6.19

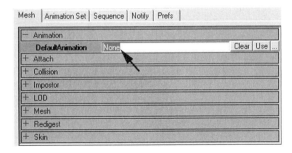

Figure 6.20

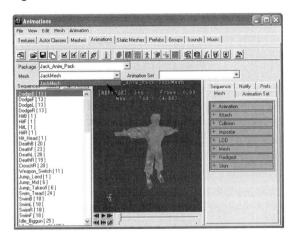

Figure 6.21

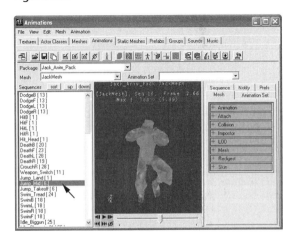

Over on the left side of the window in the big blank area should be a list of all the animations, so where are they? It's a little buggy, but right above it is the Mesh drop-down menu. Click on it once, then click on the only option available, and magically the animations should appear in the window! Let's give them a test drive. Select any animation in the list. At the bottom of the floater, click the Play button. Down and to the right is a Loop button. Activate it. Now you can see the animation repeated. All you have to do is select a new one and watch it go. Some of the funnier ones are at the bottom of the list. Check out AssSmack.

Now is a good time to save your animation package file. Choose File>Save and change the name to your character's name plus the suffix of "_Anim_Pack" in the UT2004/Animations folder.

Figure 6.22

The last thing to do is to add the textures to the model, making it a complete package. The last roll-up in the Animations tab is Skin. Open it, and you will see two map channels, #0 and #1. Most of the time, the #0 channel is the head and the #1 channel is the body. This is one of the quirky parts of the Unreal Editor; sometimes they get switched. So if it doesn't work right the first way, you may have to switch them. Select the Textures tab and then select the Face map "Thumbnail" image. Around the outside of the thumbnail image, a dark green highlight should appear, indicating it is selected. Back in the Animations tab, select the number 0. The path to your texture should automatically be inserted. Then click on the Use button. If the map appears on the body instead of the head, then select the number 1 and click the Use button, and hopefully the map appears on your head this time.

Figure 6.23

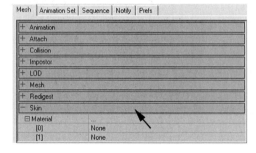

Figure 6.24

If you had more than two objects, you would have more than two map channels. In that case, you might have to just test to see what's what.

Go back to the Textures tab and select the body map. In the Animations tab, select the number 1 and click on the Use button. The body map should appear on the body.

The last thing to do is to save and replace the Animation package from the File menu.

Now, we're not done with the Unreal Editor just yet, so don't close it. Just minimize it for a little while.

Figure 6.25

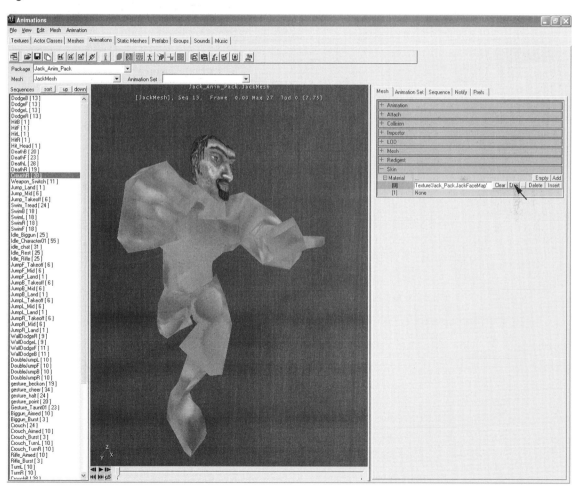

Figure 6.26

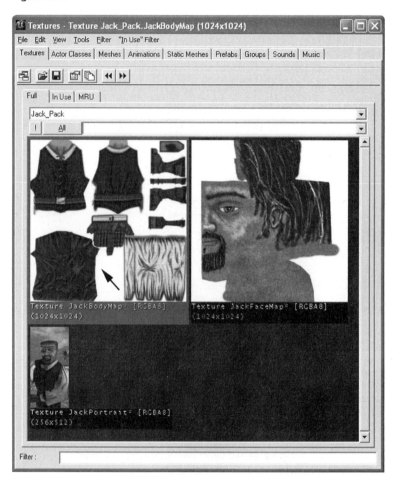

Ugh, Text Work

Now we're ready to tell the game engine to add our character into the game. This is actually one of the trickier parts of this process, because it involves text. Yuck. You have to pay close attention to the names of things, and spelling counts. Let's get started.

Basically there are two files we will work on. One file we need to edit, the contents of the other will be inserted into another file. You can start by navigating to the included DVD and open the "Jack the P\UTsystemFolder" folder. That will have the two files ready for the Jack character. Let's take the first one, Jack.upl. The UPL extension tells UT that this is a character. If the contents of the file are complete, a new character will automatically be added to the game.

Figure 6.27

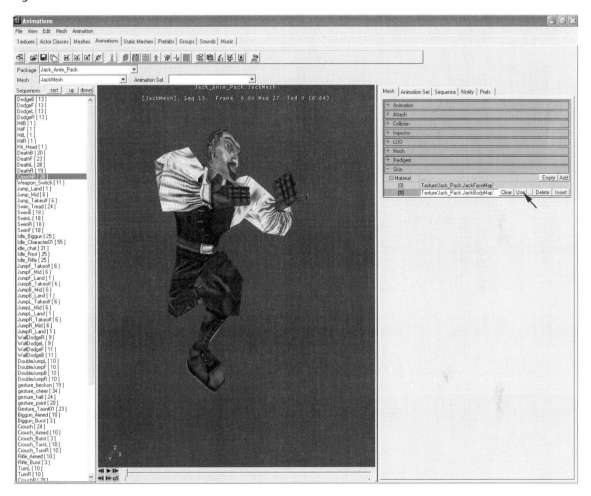

Double-click on the Jack.upl file, and Windows will tell you it doesn't know what program to open the file with. Click on the radio button for the "Select the program from a list" option and confirm. In the Open With window, scroll all the way down to the bottom of the list and select the NotePad program and confirm.

Now that the file is open in NotePad, you can see that it's just text. It defines the paths for all the different aspects of your character. Now I will go thru and tell you exactly where to get the correct information so you can create your own.

The first section is where the character's stats that will show up in-game are set—Player=(DefaultName="One-Eye Jack",Race="Unknown"……. The name and the

Figure 6.28

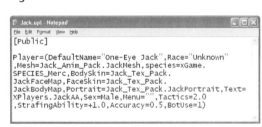

Figure 6.29

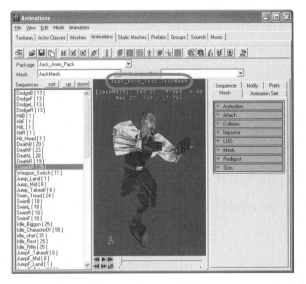

Figure 6.30

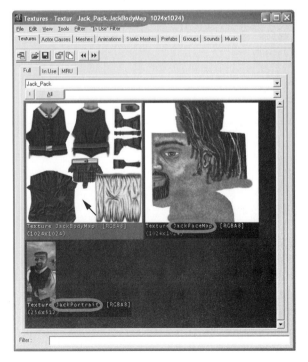

race value show up in the players' bio. In my research, I have found references to different races having different stats, but in practical terms they all seem the same to me in-game. The only rule is that you can change only what's inside the quotes.

The next section is where the game is going to look for your model in the animation pack file—Mesh=Jack_Anim_Pack.JackMesh,……. To find the exact path, take a look back in the Unreal Editor. Select the Animation tab. At the very top of the window where your model is, you will see a path inside the animation pack. Copy it exactly with no spaces. In Notepad, replace the existing path after the "Mesh=", with no spaces.

The next section, species=xGame.SPECIES_ Merc,……. is not critical and need not be edited. If you want to change the taunts or voice style of your character, you should take a look at the file XGame.int in the UT2004/Systems folder for other default settings. It is possible to create your own audio taunts for your character, but it is a little out of the scope of this book.

The next section is where the game is going to look for your model's body map in the texture pack file BodySkin=Jack_Tex_Pack.JackBodyMap,……. If your #0 map channel was not your head, then you may have to put your face map path in here instead of the body map path. To find the correct path name in the Unreal Editor, change to the Textures tab and select the body map thumbnail image. At the top of the floater you should see the correct body map path. It should say something like Textures–Texture Jack_Tex_Pack.JackBody-Map (1024x1024), but all you need is the middle part. That is between the word "Texture" and "(1024x1024)," which is the actual path.

The next section is where the game is going to look for your model's head map, in the texture pack file FaceSkin=Jack_Tex_Pack.JackFaceMap, To get the right path, just select the head map in the Textures tab and look where you found the body map path. Remember, you should never have any spaces anywhere in the whole text file.

Figure 6.31

Figure 6.32

Now we'll define where the game is going to look for the portrait image. That will show up in the player roster area—Portrait=Jack_Tex_Pack.JackPortrait,...... Just select the portrait image in the Textures tab and again look at the top of the floater for the exact path name.

The next section is a little more complicated—Text=XPlayers. JackAA. It may look simple, but it's not. The "Text" is what appears in your character's bio, but where's the text? It's actually in a file called Xplayers.int. I have included an edited one in the same folder as the Jack.upl file. The original one is in the UT2004/Systems folder. Open up the Xplayers.int that I gave you in NotePad, and you will see the line starts with "JackAA=." This is the tag that is referred to in the Text section of the UPL file. If you select all the text in this file and paste it into your UT2004/Systems folders Xplayer.int file, whatever you put inside the quotes will show up in the game's players' bio area. This, of course, does not change the way the character will work in-game, but it makes it complete.

The last few sections have to do with some of the aspects of your character's in-game play—Sex=Male,Menu="",Tactics=2.0,StrafingAbility=+1.0,Accuracy=0.5,BotUse=1)....... You can guess what the first three mean; the last one is the BotUse value, which isn't as easy to guess. It is an off/on toggle. If you want to allow your char-

Figure 6.33

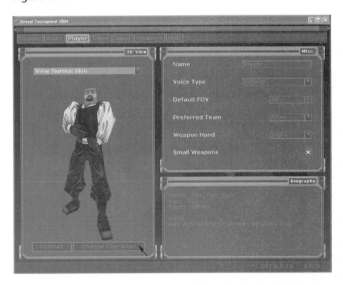

Figure 6.34

acter to be used as a bot, that is, played by the game engine not by the player, set the value to one. If not, then set the value to zero. Leave it at one for now.

That's all, folks! Now just move the Jack.upl file to the UT2004/Systems, and you're good to go.

Close the Unreal Editor, start UT2004, and from the main menu select the Setting option.

Change to the Players tab. At the bottom of the Players window, click on the Change Character button. Select your character's portrait, and you should now see your character in the window.

If either your character's portrait or model does not show up where it should, then you most likely did not get the correct path in the UPL file. If you go back and double-check it and try again, it should work. Again, if the first fix doesn't work, just keep trying. Sometimes it takes several tries, and then all of a sudden it works like magic.

The second time around usually works, because you pay much closer attention to the little details. One of the more frequent mistakes is having other objects in the 3ds Max project at the time of export. Another strange mistake that happened a couple of times to my students was that they accidentally applied the Physique modifier to a part of the Biped system. You could tell because at export time when they clicked on the Scene Info button, it came up with three or more Physique objects when there should only have been two, the body and head.

Click the Back button in the lower right corner to get back to the main menu and click on the Instant Action option. Choose the

Figure 6.35

Figure 6.36

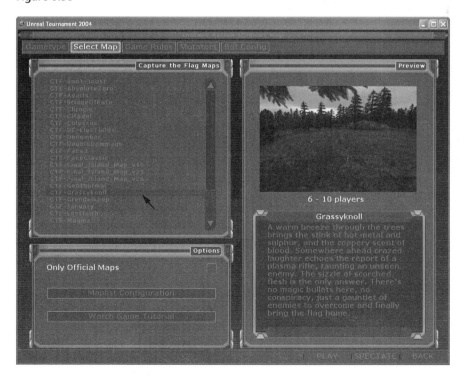

Figure 6.37

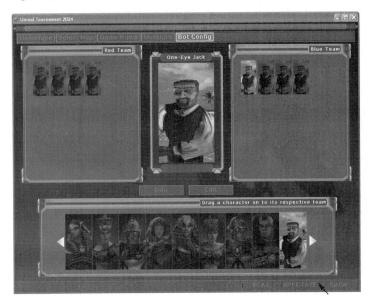

Capture the Flag game style and select a map like the Grassyknoll so you can easily see your character.

Change to the Bot Config tab and at the bottom find your character's portrait. Drag your character's portrait a bunch of times into both teams. That way you can watch and fight your own character.

Click on the Spectate button in the lower right corner and click the left mouse button until you find one of your characters, and watch him run about!

That's it; we're finished. Congratulations! You have done something that only a handful of people on the planet have ever done. Now that you have the basic understanding of all the process involved you can make your own, or expand your existing character, or even get a job! Good luck!

Figure 6.38

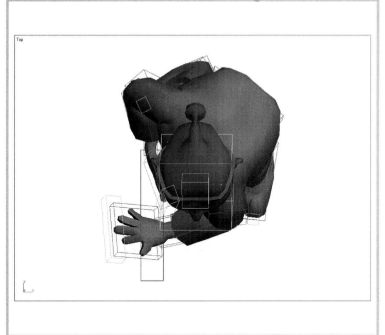

Animation

7

In this chapter we are going to take a look at how to change the default character animations to fit a custom-shaped model. Not all your characters are going to have the same proportions as humans. So in order to make a functional character that is not the same size or shape as the standard characters, the animation cycles will have to be changed.

The animation cycles not only animate the player but also set the scale of the bones and position of the gun. Of course, I found this out by making some spectacularly funny mistakes. For example, I had run backward animation, where the weapon got accidentally relocated to an inappropriate place. When I ran backward in the game, the gun would jump down, and then back up when I ran forward. Quite humorous, but I don't think an employer would like it. Like most of the aspects of game production, the devil is in the details. All the animations that you see your character do in-game are individual animations.

There are at least 30 animations, at a minimum, needed to make any character functional in the standard games. There are as many as 90 animations total programmed into the game, and others can be added. This way, complete Unreal MODs can have completely different animations mapped to their characters. There is one example that can be easily downloaded and viewed in the

Unreal Editor. It's the Raptor (Deinonychus) player. It is a uniquely shaped biped with a tail and hands too small to carry a weapon. The animation for this character has to be completely different from the defaults. I am going to use a much less extreme example.

Let's get started on making our custom animation pack. First check out the files I have provided on the DVD. Look for the Chapter 7 assets/BLE Max files folder. That stands for Bad Luck Elf. This is a character I made a few years ago that was not meant for import into Unreal, but I adapted it so that it could work in Unreal. In that folder are all the files you should need to make this tutorial work. I have also provided files for the standard character animations that can be modified for any character in the UT Game BIPS folder.

The Bad Luck Elf

To start, open the BLE-Start.max file. This file has the character all rigged up with just a basic material setup on it. It could be exported at this point and be played in-game, but several small problems would appear in-game. The first problem would be that because the legs are so short, they would get stretched out to the normal size if we used the standard human animation sequences.

The second problem would be the position of the arms. Because the body is fat, the arms need to be higher up so that they don't go inside the body. There is no technical problem with self-collision, it just looks bad.

Go to the Utilities panel and activate the ActorX plug-in. Click the Browse button and create a new folder called BLE_Export, then click the Use Path button.

Figure 7.01

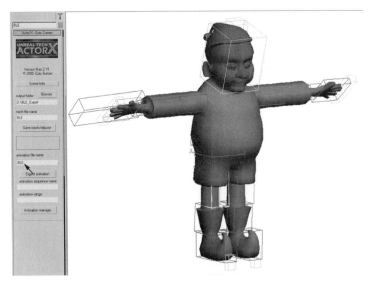

Add BLE in the mesh file name area and activate the "Save mesh/refpose" button. Then click OK in the dialog boxes that follow. You will have a BLE.PSK file in the folder you made. Now we are going to create the animation pack.

There are some memory issues with the Unreal Editor, so I am showing you a less automatic but more stable approach.

First type in the animation file name area "BLE_Anim." Make sure you use the underscore. Remember the golden rule—no spaces.

Now change to the Motion panel, then select the biped head bone. You should now see the Character Studio plug-in rollouts. First make sure that the Figure Mode button is not activated. Then click on the Open File button in the Biped roll-up.

Navigate to the DVD, to the Chapter 7 assets/UT Game BIPS folder. You will see a bunch of BIP files already named what the game needs them to be. In order to get it all correct, select the first animation file Biggun_Aimed.bip, then highlight and copy the name.

You may get a dialog box asking to change the frame rate. Select the MAP FRAMES radio button and confirm.

Now the character should be posed. If you click the Play button, you will notice that the total animation is only 10 frames. That's the first thing we need to fix. In order for the automated animation digestion to work, only the frames with animation should be displayed. So for this animation we need only frames 0-10 to be visible.

Figure 7.02

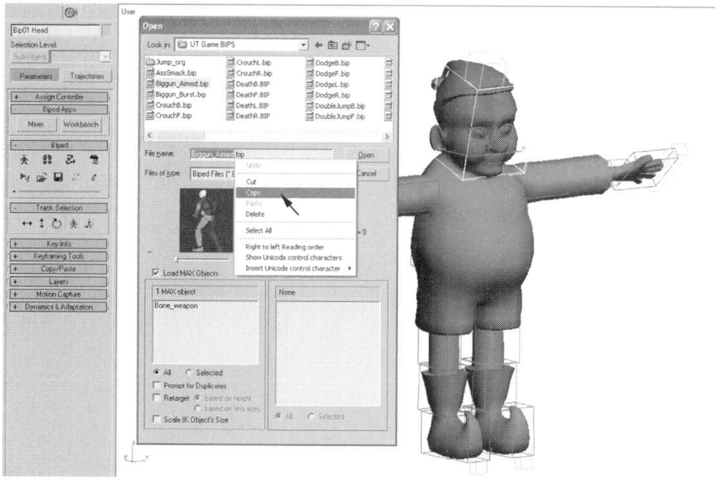

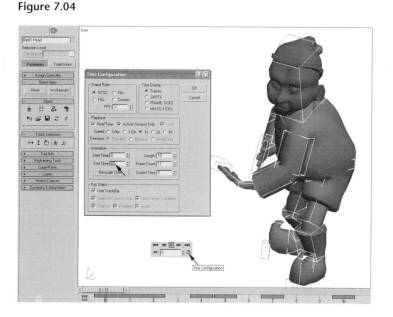

Figure 7.03

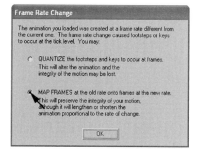

Figure 7.04

To set the number of visible frames, right-click on the Play button and in the Time Configuration pop-up, change the End Time to 10 and confirm. Now when you click the Play button you can see the cycle.

One of the inherently tricky parts of creating animation cycles for real-time games is that they lack blending between them. In other words, during game play the animations jump from one to the next with no overlap. If there is a significant difference in the two, it will create a pop in the animation. So it's important that we keep some consistency in the starting and ending poses of most animations.

If you change to the top viewport, you can see that the Weapon_Bone is pointing directly down. This orientation needs to be maintained in the animations that have to do with weapon firing. Those are Biggun_Aimed, Biggun_Burst, Rifle_Aimed, Rifle_Burst, and Weapon_Switch.

Figure 7.05

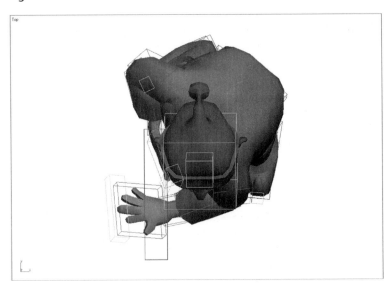

This goes for the movement animations also. The Run, Walk, and Jump animations need more specific gun orientation to avoid contradictory animations for the weapon.

In the other animations, it's less important, but to keep the transition between animations as seamless as possible, try to keep in mind the beginning and ending position of the weapon when you first load the animation file.

Another important thing to take note of is the position of the feet. They can be moved a little bit, say two to three units and maybe two to five degrees of rotation, but that's it. Otherwise the feet may jump oddly when the next animation sequence starts.

Keeping all those things in mind, you can click the Auto Key button and adjust the biped's bones until the pose at frame 0 is correct.

Then, using the Named Selection Sets pull-down menu, select all the biped bones. You can now see where the next key is. In most cases there will be only a couple of frames that have no animation keys.

Now move the time slider to the next keyframe and adjust the biped bones until the position is correct. Keep repeating the process until the end of time, or at least the end of the timeline.

Now for the final critical step, save the file with the same name as the biped file you loaded. Remember—there can be no spaces in the file name. That's why I asked you to copy the file name of the biped animation in the beginning. It's best if you make a new folder and put all the new animated 3ds Max files in it. That way, when it comes time to batch-process all the animations, all you have to do is pick the folder and ActorX does all the work.

Here's where the fun begins. In order to make a complete animation package, all the animations need to be edited and saved as 3ds Max files. That is, all 78 biped animations have to be loaded, edited, and saved as new 3ds Max files before they can be compiled by the ActorX plug-in. Take your time; I'll wait. Just kidding—I have made max files for BLE so that you can test out the process we are going to do next.

Figure 7.06

Figure 7.07

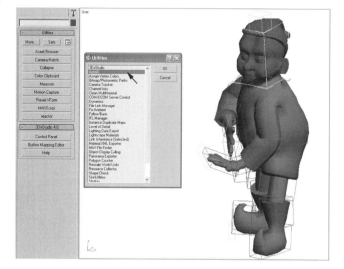

Figure 7.08

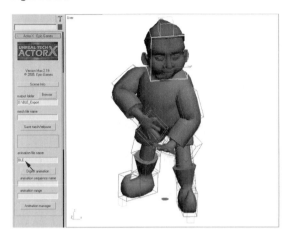

Figure 7.09

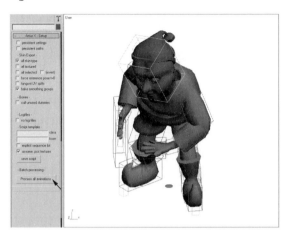

Figure 7.10

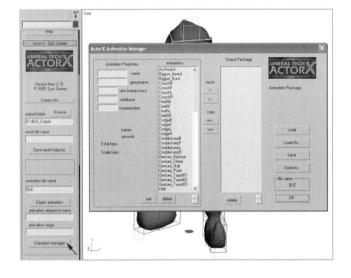

ActorX

We have already used the ActorX plug-in for the exporting of the model and vertex assignment. Now we are going to use it to compile a sequence of animations into a single file that can be use in the Unreal Editor.

Let's start up the ActorX plug-in from the Utilities panel by clicking the More button and selecting the word "ActorX."

The first thing to do is to set the output folder by clicking the Browse button. Create a folder to keep all your exported files.

You can also set the animation file name by just typing it in the area as shown in Figure 7.08.

Then at the bottom of the ActorX–Setup roll-up is the button to activate the batch processing of the 3ds Max files I created especially for the BLE character. Click on the "Process all animations" button, navigate to the DVD in the BLE folder, open the BLE_ANIM_MAX folder, and click the Use Path button.

As soon as you do, ActorX will start loading the 3ds Max files one by one and digesting the animation of each.

Figure 7.11

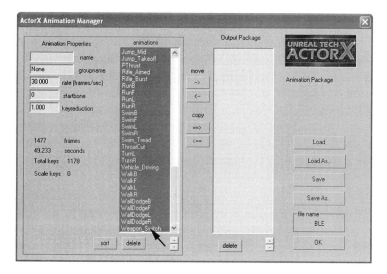

Figure 7.12

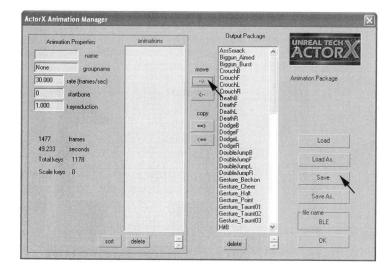

Figure 7.13

Go back up to the first roll-up and click on the "Animation manager" button. Then select all the animations in the left column and click on the right arrow button under the word "Move." Now all the animations should be in the Output Package column. Click the Save button. This will create a file called BLE.PSA in the output folder. We are now done with 3ds Max, and there is no need to save the current file.

Unreal Editor

We have already used the Unreal Editor to put a character into the game, but this time we are going to use our custom animation file instead of the default one.

Open the BLE texture file. In the textures tab, open the BLE_TX from the folder Chapter 7 assets/BLE-Exports. It's not anything complex, but we need something to cover the model.

Then change to the Animations tab so that you can import the mesh data. The BLE mesh data is in the same folder as the texture file was, and it's called BLE_Mesh.PSK. Remember to change the package name to BLE_AM before you click OK. You should now have a model in the editor window.

Figure 7.14

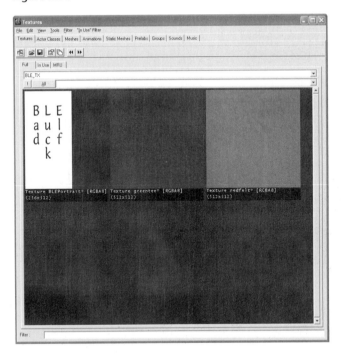

Figure 7.15

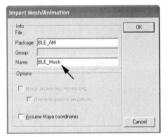

Figure 7.16

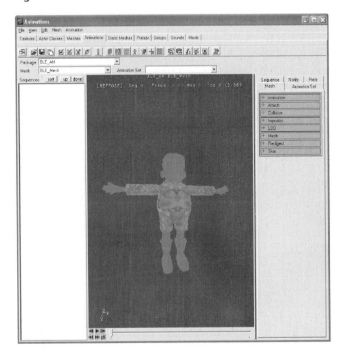

We still have to copy the mesh settings from the ThunderCrash package. So from the Package menu select the ThunderCrash package. Then from the Mesh menu select the Copy Mesh Properties. Go back to the BLE package, and from the Mesh menu select Past Mesh Properties.

When we went through this procedure with the other character, I didn't explain exactly what all the properties are that get pasted. This time I want you to take a little deeper look into how a character can function in-game.

Open the Attach rollout. You should see 12 numbers underneath Sockets. Click on the plus symbol next to them, and you can see the raw data behind the skeleton. These links, or sockets, help define where the weapons show up and what hand the flag will be in for CTF games. It also defines the ragdoll simulation parameters and where your body parts are so that they can be blown off when you die. Now I don't want you to change anything here, I just want you to look.

Figure 7.17

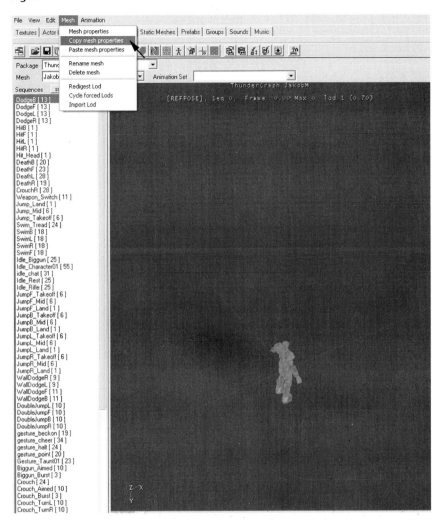

Figure 7.18

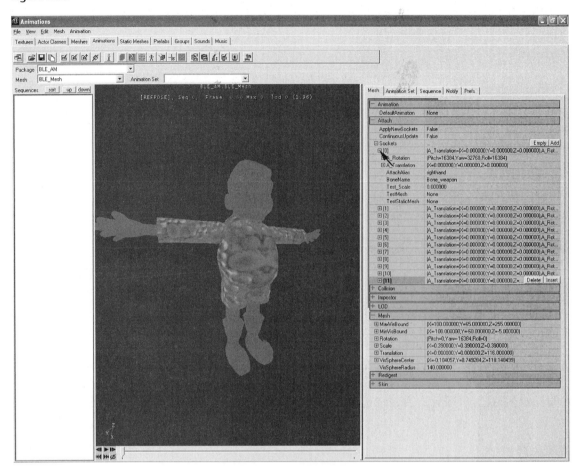

Let's take a look at Mesh rollout's contents. Here is the data about the position, rotation, and scale of the character. If you have the time, you can play around with the values and test their effects on the character, but for now I just want you to know where they are. One quick note about how rotational values are used in the Unreal Editor and game. Take a look at the value of the Meshes Yaw rotation. It should be 16384. I am sure you're asking yourself, What in the heck does that value mean? As I understand it, the rotational angle to Unreal units goes like this:

0 Degrees = 0
90 Degrees = 8192
180 Degrees = 16384
270 Degrees = 32768

Figure 7.19

These values are generated by a very complex mathematical equation that converts X, Y, and Z rotational values into a global surface value. I have read some papers on the subject, and it seems like when it comes to programming the rotational controls of objects, it's easer to use the quaternion value system than the XYZ style. Now let's add our custom animation pack.

From the File menu, select Animation Import. Navigate the folder you created to put BLE.PSA file in and select it. In the Import pop-up window, change the name to BLE_Anim and confirm. Now you should be able to see the animations in the Sequences area.

Figure 7.20

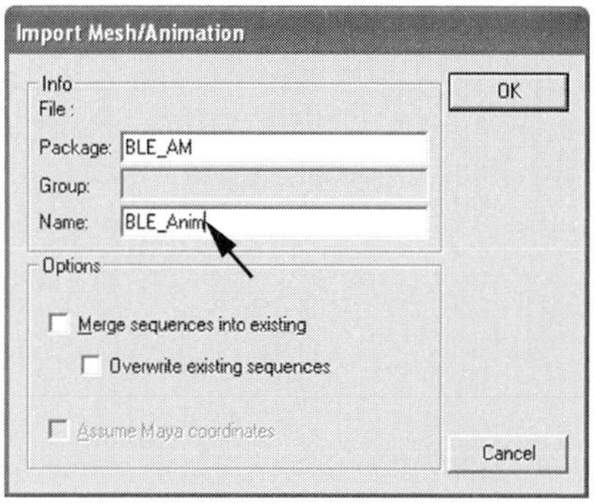

Figure 7.21

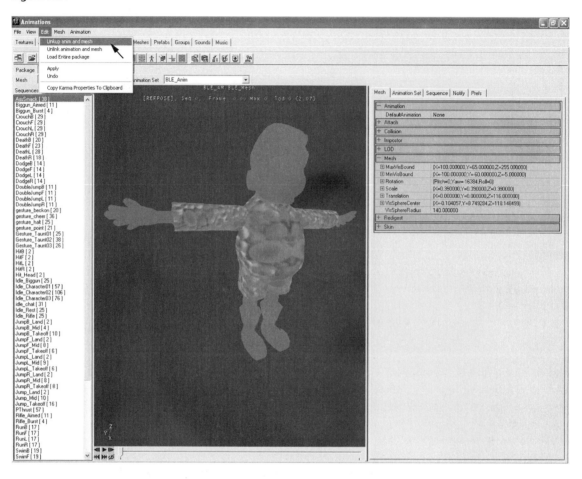

Figure 7.22

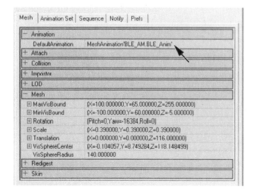

Almost done. The last step is to link the animation to the model. First open the Animation roll-up so you can see what is happening. Then under the Edit menu, select the "Linkup anim and mesh" option. It doesn't look like anything has happened, but it did. To refresh the changes, click on the Mesh menu and select BLE_Mesh. In the Animation roll-up it should say MeshAnimation'BLE-AM.BLE_Anim.' Now you should be able to select an animation and click the Play button to watch him go.

The only thing left to do is to add the materials and save the completed character as just the one file BLE_AM.ukx. That's it. I have included the UPL file, so if you put it and the BLE texture file in their appropriate folder you can play him.

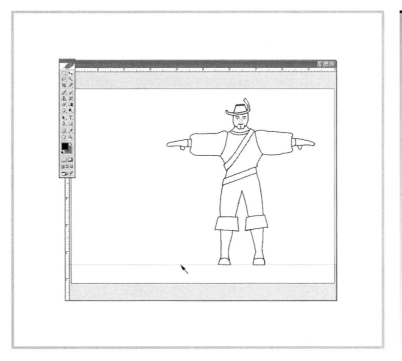

Appendix A

Setup to Build Characters

In this appendix I will show you how I set up the Jack-Start file and how you can use my setup for any character or model. It all starts with the model sheet. A model sheet or sheets usually contain an artist's rendering of a character or object. It can also take the form of photographs, useful if you have a specific model you want to duplicate, famous or not. You can always use photographs as reference images. When designers are working on a character, they usually pose the character with several different costumes. If you want to see some examples, try a search for "model sheet" and you should be able to find out tons of different model sheets. Another place to look is at www.anime-model-sheets.com. May I also suggest you take a look at the *How to Draw Books*…advertised there. They can give you lots of details about how to draw people. Things like male, female, and child body proportions and how they affect the viewer. I even found a bunch of models sheets for sale on eBay. The one thing they all have in common is the way they are created; they are hand-drawn, posed model sketches. While this makes a good reference for animators, directors, and modelers, it's not exactly what we need for 2D reference images.

Figure A.01

Figure A.02

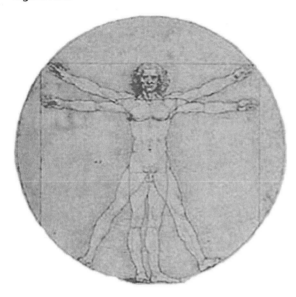

If you have access to the artist who created the model sheet you could ask him or her to give you a sketch of the character in the classical DaVinci pose.

Unfortunately, most of us will be making our own model sheets. I have started by using tracing paper. I copied the body parts into a composite character in the DaVinci pose. Then I scanned it in and cleaned it up using Photoshop.

Remember, you have to make only one good half, because you can always delete the bad half and mirror the good one. Or you can just fake it, starting with the head size and working down. Using general body proportion parameters, it's not too hard to sketch a workable front view of a body. You can find the body proportions of men, women, and children online.

The tricky part of the process can be creating the side view. This is where Photoshop can come in handy. I like to start by turning on the Rulers option first. Then under the Image menu I selected Canvas Size. Here I added more to the left side of the image. With the Move tool selected, I clicked and dragged from the ruler area at the top. A blue line should appear, which I dragged to the

Figure A.03

Figure A.04

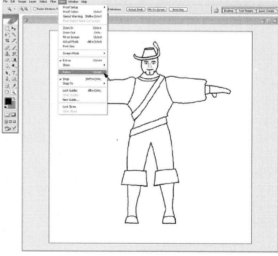

bottom of the boot. I repeated the process for all the major parts: knees, fingers, chin, eyes, and the top of the head. Then from the left ruler I pulled out a vertical ruler to create a centerline for the side view. I started with the boots and worked my way up the body using the brush tool. Once I'm happy with my sketch, it's time to save my file as a JPG and set it up in my 3ds Max project.

Figure A.05

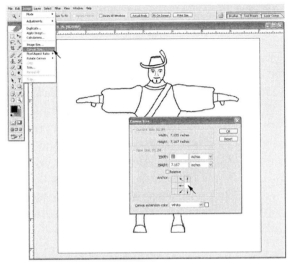

Figure A.06

Figure A.07

Figure A.08

The Max Setup

Now that I have the front and side view at the same scale, I need to set them up so that I can use them as reference images in 3ds Max.

I started with a new 3ds Max project and created a plane in the front viewport about the size of the model sheet I made.

I added the model sheet image to a material in the Diffuse color channel and applied it to the plane. You can also increase the Self illumination so it will be clearly visible no matter what your viewport lighting is.

In the Modify panel, I added a UVW Map modifier to the plane. In order to get the correct aspect ratio into my UVW Map modifier's gizmo, I clicked the Bitmap Fit button in the Alignment area. Then navigate to your model sheets folder and select the bitmap.

I changed the size of the plane so that only the front part of the image is showing, not with the scale tool, but in the plane's length and width values. That way the mapping coordinates stay the same size. I moved the gizmo a little on the X axis to center the image. The last step is to zero out the X, Y, and Z axes by right-clicking on spinners at the bottom of the interface. This way the plane is in the dead center of the world.

We need another plane for the side view, so I created one in the left viewport about the same size as the first. Then I applied the same material as the first to it.

Figure A.09

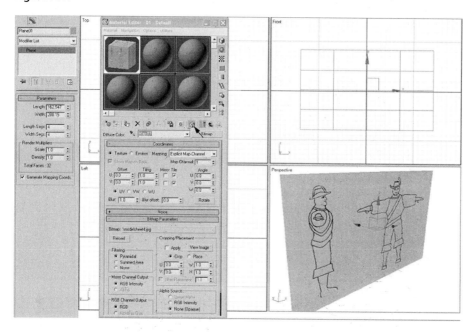

Figure A.10

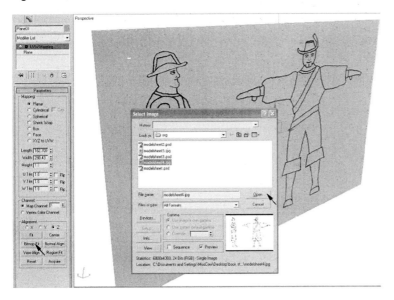

Figure A.11

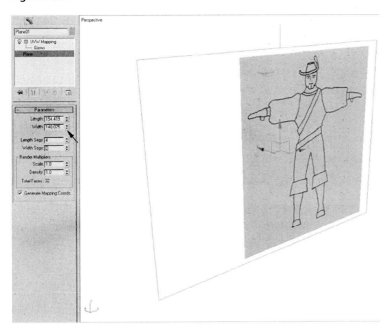

Figure A.12

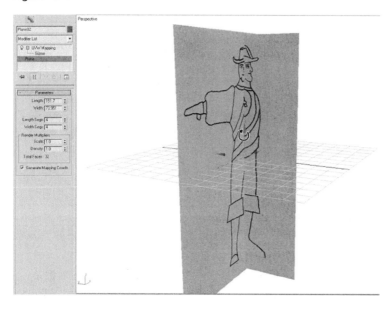

A little shortcut is to copy the UVW Mapping modifier from the first plane and paste it onto the second. Then all I had to do is center the plane and adjust the mapping coordinates by manipulating the UVW mapping gizmo so that only the side view will show. I adjusted the plane's size so that it showed just the side image. I then I had to center the side image on the front plane as close to the centerline ruler as I could.

Up to this point, the setup can be used for any model. If you want to use it for creating a character for Unreal, one more small step needs to be done, and it has to do with where the model is positioned in the world space. The solution is easy. All I did was to move the two planes up so that the center of the world is between the feet of the characters image. This will place my model in the correct place for use in Unreal. The last thing to do is freeze the planes and start modeling.

If you want to use the same biped that we used in the Jack the Pirate project, all you have to do is merge it from the DVD's Jack-Start.max file.

Figure A.13

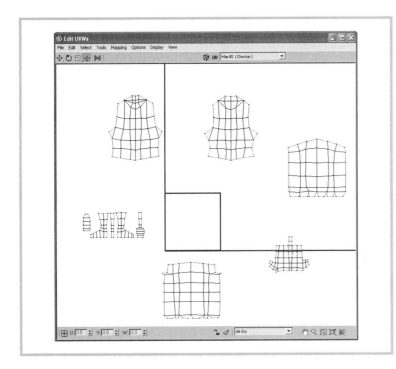

The unwrapping of a character is one of the hardest parts of the entire process. The best thing I can say is that the more you do it, the easier it will be to do next time. In fact, you will start to think of how you will make your model so that you can unwrap it easier. For someone doing this for the first time, it can be quite a challenge just getting used to using the tools involved with the process, not to mention thinking ahead as to how to make the layout easy to paint and how to pack the UVs as efficiently as possible into the blue square.

The optimal shape for any UV patch is square. This makes the scale of image constant throughout the UV patch. This will make it easier for someone to paint a map in Photoshop.

So what I am going to do is tell you how to use an image with all the UV of Jack the Pirate laid out for you to complete your mapping. This will give you a big jump ahead in the process, but it's not perfect. Your model may be a little

Figure B.01

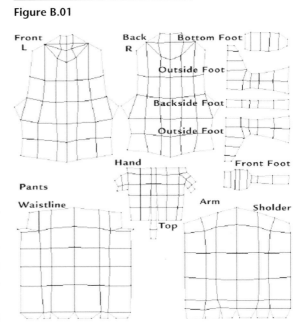

Figure B.02

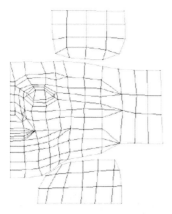

Figure B.03

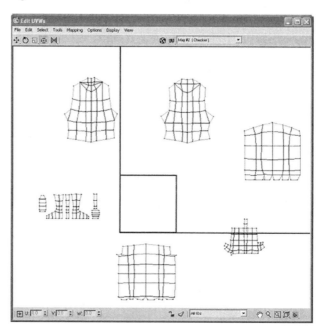

Figure B.04

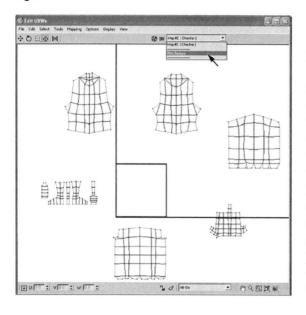

bit different than mine, so you can use mine for the overall placement of the UV patches. You will have to use the checkers to check the placement of the internal vertexes. Another good way to check your mapping is to use my final map, and if everything looks good your mapping is complete.

Open your project at the point where all your modeling has been completed and unwrapping is only half-done, as shown in Figure B.03. Select the body and in the Edit UVWs modify panel, click on the Edit button. At any point in the unwrap process, you can change the map that will be displayed in the Edit UVWs window. So let's do it now. In the top right corner is a drop down menu; click on it. Select the Pick Texture option. The Material/Map Browser will open. In it, select Bitmap. Then navigate to the DVD's folder Jack the P/Jack UVs and open the JackBodymap_w_UVs image. Make sure that the Show Map in Viewport button is active.

Some of the other options I like to change in order to make this process easier are under the Options button in the lower right corner of the Edit UVWs window. In the Bitmap Options area, change the Width and Height to 1024x1024. I also unchecked the Tile Bitmap box and changed the Brightness value to 1.0. This makes the map appear only in the center tiling area and brightens up the map display. Now I can select the patches of UVs and move them to the right place.

Figure B.05

Figure B.06

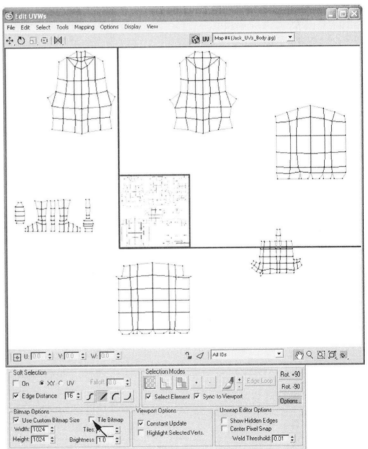

Figure B.07

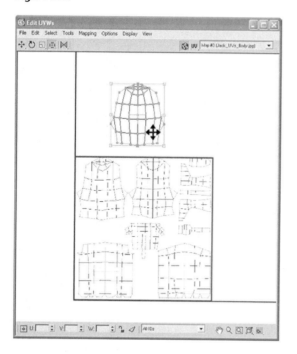

Figure B.08

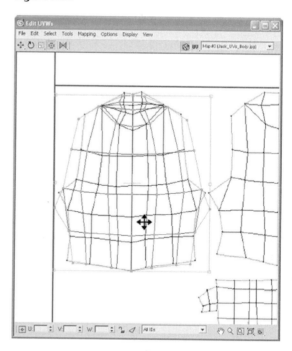

Figure B.09

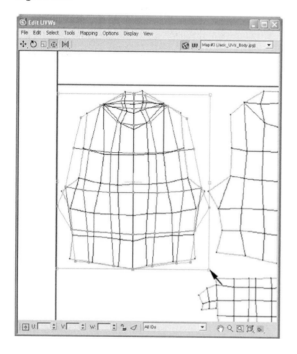

Start with the chest patch first. Select it in the Edit UVWs window and scale the chest patch uniformly using the Freeform mode and Ctrl key, and move it close to the blue square. Then move it so that the centerline vertices are in line with the image's centerline vertices. Make sure the Select Element box is unchecked. So that you can select individual vertexes.

Then you can start with the outside vertices and move them so that they match the image. Then you can start moving the next row of inside vertices. Remember, you only have to do the right side of the front and back. You might need to change the tiling so that the squares are smaller. Then continue the process you started in Chapter 3.

Figure B.10

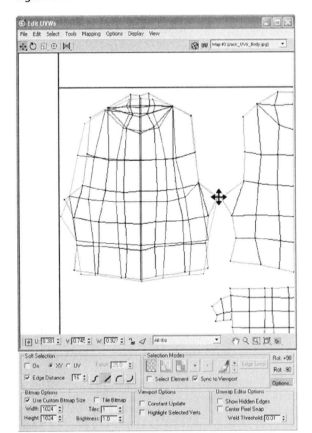

Figure B.11

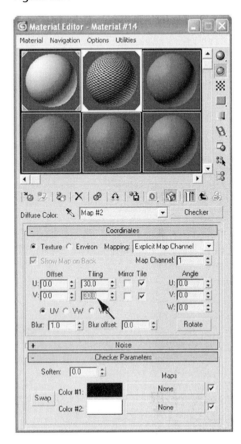

Figure B.12

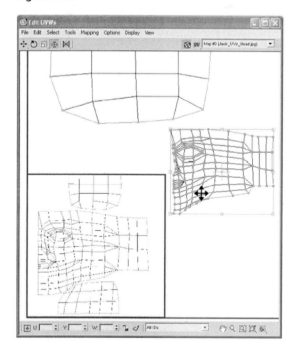

Figure B.13

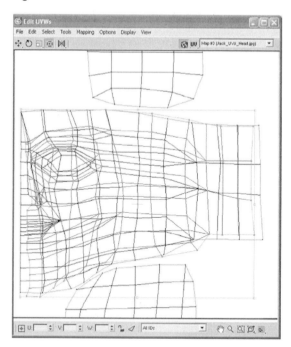

For the head unwrap, the process starts much the same. The only change is to add the JackHeadMap_w_UVs map to the Edit UVWs window. Then move the face UVs so that they are centered on the eye as best you can. Then you can start working the vertices along the centerline of the face following the tutorial in Chapter 3.

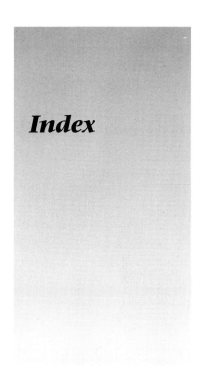

Index